Visions, Revelations
and the Church

VISIONS, REVELATIONS

AND THE CHURCH

By Laurent Volken

TRANSLATED BY EDWARD GALLAGHER

P. J. Kenedy & Sons · New York

VISIONS, REVELATIONS AND THE CHURCH
is a translation of *Les Révélations dans l'Église*
by Laurent Volken, originally published by
Éditions Salvator, Mulhouse, France, 1961

Nihil obstat: JAMES F. RIGNEY, S.T.D.
             Censor Librorum
Imprimatur: ✠ FRANCIS CARDINAL SPELLMAN
             Archbishop of New York
New York, September 25, 1963

Library of Congress Catalogue Card Number: 63–18883
Copyright © by P. J. Kenedy & Sons, New York
PRINTED IN THE UNITED STATES OF AMERICA

CONTENTS

Foreword

THIS BOOK proposes to supply a theological interpretation of particular revelations and of the role they play in the Church. It considers the principal facts of these revelations and shows the link which gives meaning to them as a whole. Basically, it amounts to an attempt at a theology of revelations.

The work has been written to fill a gap. There are innumerable publications on this or that revelation; few, however, concern themselves in a theological way with the actual problem of revelations, and even these dwell upon certain aspects only, without considering the problem in its entirety.

The historical facts to which reference is made in this study are mentioned only in so far as they serve to arrive at a theological interpretation. The aims of such an interpretation are to clear away the confusion which prevails on this subject among many Christians—even educated Christians—and to place in perspective two attitudes toward revelations which, although very widespread, are equally inadmissible: one is an unthinking enthusiasm for them, the other their deliberate rejection.

I wish to express my gratitude to Reverend J. Imhof, M.S., and to my other colleagues who have helped me especially by taking the trouble to revise my text. I also thank Reverend J.-H. Nicolas, O.P., who willingly read my manuscript and made some valuable suggestions.

L. V.

Abbreviations

A.A.S.	=	Acta Apostolicae Sedis (Rome).
C.S.E.L.	=	Corpus scriptorum ecclesiasticorum latinorum (Vienne).
D.T.C.	=	Dictionnaire de Théologie catholique (Paris).
Denz.	=	Enchiridion Symbolorum, H. Denzinger (Friburgi, 1957).
P.L.	=	Migne, Patrologiae cursus completus. Series prima latina.
P.G.	=	Migne, Patrologiae cursus completus. Series graeca.
Sum. Theol.	=	Sancti Thomae Summa theologica.
In Sent	=	Sancti Thomae Aquinatis commentum in . . . librum sententiarum magistri Petri Lombardi.

CHAPTER I

Introduction

1   REVELATION AND REVELATIONS

IN OUR DAY, more than in the past, Christians have
come to realize that the Church owes her existence to a completely gratuitous condescension from God, who deigned to
reveal Himself to men. While rationalism, positivism, and
other systems which deny transcendence have taken over vast
tracts of modern thought, Christian thinking on Revelation
has deepened as never before. It was, in fact, only at the First
Vatican Council, in the dogmatic constitution on the Faith,
which was the first and most important doctrinal expression
of that Council, that the Church laid down a body of doctrine
on Revelation.

Within the domain of dogmatic theology a preliminary
treatise on Revelation has begun to develop. Books upon books
will soon be written upon this problem, and in the end an apologetic based upon the justification of Revelation will be established as a branch of theology.

We note that a similar situation exists among Protestants.
For the past thirty years or so a great many of them have been

making a vigorous effort to understand better what Revelation
is. Has not the theology most in evidence among them since
1925 been called "theology of the Word" or "theology of Revelation" (*Theologie des Wortes, Offenbarungstheologie*)? [1]

The gratuitousness and transcendence of Revelation have
become one of the great themes of religious thought in our
time. Today we are in a position to appreciate the importance
of the doctrine which the Church officially promulgated in
1870 at the Vatican Council: "It has pleased God in His wisdom and His generosity to reveal Himself in a supernatural
way; the Apostle, in fact, said: 'God, who at sundry times and
in divers manners, spoke in times past to the fathers by the
prophets, last of all, in these days hath spoken to us by his
Son'" (Session III, chap. II).

Should it be assumed from this text that the Son of God
told us everything and that Revelation came to an end with
His Ascension into heaven? Not at all, since Christ left us His
formal promise of the coming of the Holy Spirit who would
make further revelations: "I have yet many things to say to
you but you cannot bear them now. But when he, the Spirit
of Truth, is come, he will teach you all truth . . . what things
soever he shall hear, he shall speak; and the things that are
to come, he shall show you" (John 16: 12–13). Further still,
He manifested Himself to St. Paul after His Ascension: "But,
as it is written: That eye hath not seen, nor ear heard, neither
hath it entered into the heart of man, what things God hath
prepared for them that love him. . . . But to us God hath
revealed them by his Spirit" (1 Cor. 2: 9–10).

But even these two texts are susceptible of varying interpretations. Would the Spirit of God who, according to the promise of Jesus Christ, was to tell all and to announce the things
which were to come, reveal Himself solely to those who heard
that promise or to others also, whether in the time of the
Apostles or after that time? And if St. Paul speaks of things
which "ear hath not heard," and which the Spirit reveals to
us, does this pronoun in the first person plural refer to the

Apostles or does it apply to all Christians? Finally, does this mysterious wisdom comprise all common Revelation or does it also include particular communications destined for the use and the sanctification of certain people only?

Whatever be the interpretation given to these texts, it is nevertheless true that the Church, during the course of her history, has accepted revelations or manifestations coming from the world beyond.

Thus St. Ignatius of Antioch affirms in his letter to the Philadelphians: "He for whom I am in bondage is my witness that I have not learned this from the mouth of man, but it is the Spirit who communicated it to me, saying to me: Do nothing without the bishop; keep your bodies as shrines of God." [2]

St. Augustine, who was not afraid to relegate certain revelations to the domain of the psychic, accepted others as true communications from above. In the sermon *De Urbis excidio* he gives a detailed account of a revelation—of which he himself had no shadow of doubt—received by a pious soldier.

Throughout the course of the centuries we shall come across responsible writers who vouch for this or that particular revelation. Many of these revelations were indeed to be universally recognized. Thus it is with the apparitions of Lourdes and of Fatima, which are in the public category and are accepted not only by the faithful but also by the pastors of the Church. So, what Pope Gregory XV proclaimed in the bull of Canonization of St. Teresa in 1622, holds good for all time: "In the following centuries He (God), according to predetermined times, has deigned to visit His people through the agency of His servants; most frequently He has chosen the insignificant and the humble to communicate great things to the Catholic Church. It is in fact to them that, according to His promise, He has revealed the mysteries of the Kingdom of Heaven which remained hidden from the wise and the prudent. . . ." (cf. page 98 and note 77). In this same document the Pope states that St. Teresa had been

favored with numerous visions and revelations of Our Lord
(cf. note 77).

On the other hand, since the evidence of these revelations
rests solely upon the sincerity of the person favored with
them and upon the faith of the person who believes in them,
it would be easy to counterfeit them. That is why false
revelations are to be found beside genuine ones. In the days
of the Old Testament, as in apostolic times, it was necessary
to be on one's guard against "pseudo-prophets." St. John expressly warned his brethren: "Dearly beloved, believe not
every spirit, but try the spirits if they be of God: because
many false prophets are gone into the world" (1 John 4: 1).
And these latter would always be at work. The defenders of
the Church would soon have to struggle against a whole
prophetic movement, that of Montanism, which would seek
to bestow upon the prophets an authority superior to that
of the bishops.

2   REVELATIONS: A PROBLEM OF
THE PRESENT TIME

There have always been these false prophets and occasionally, especially from the Middle Ages on, we witness a
positive epidemic of visionaries. In our own time, for example, innumerable crowds were drawn to Exquioga, in the
Basque country or to Heroldsbach, in Bavaria, where visionaries and revelations so multiplied and vied with each other
that the Congregation of the Holy Office was obliged to intervene and to condemn such manifestations.

But it is not condemnations only which issue from the

Church. Through her ordinary magisterium the Church in our own time has approved many particular revelations. On many others she reserves her judgment even though years pass by. This attitude is, on the whole, in their favor.

Quite significant in regard to the present situation of particular revelations is the article "Siate cristiani, a muovervi più gravi!" ("Christians, be less carried away!") by Cardinal Ottaviani, published in the *Osservatore Romano* of February 2, 1951, before he was made cardinal. First of all he briefly and vigorously emphasizes the fact and the providential role of particular revelations. But this is only the introduction to a grave warning: "It is a curious thing," he writes, "that it is but a short time since the Church had to defend the fact of revelations, and now she has to give a warning against the abuse of them; the craze for the marvelous is such that it is becoming a grave danger to the Christian life; people are running in crowds to places of reputed apparitions and neglecting the sacraments and defying the authority of the Church."

There are indeed people who irresponsibly acclaim every revelation, apparition and vision which is being discussed. They quickly accept them as important facts in history or as a fulfillment of the Gospel text. Eager for signs from heaven, they are convinced that apocalyptic times are at hand. They look upon those who do not believe in these things as rationalists and unbelievers, or as blind men who do not wish to see the signs of the times and whose distracted minds refuse to accept the designs of God.

That there should be excessive reactions against such a situation is very understandable. There are Christians who refuse all credence to revelations. For them all revelations, or practically all, came to an end with the death of the last Apostle. All later manifestations appear to them as no more than illusions and frauds, the machinations of man or of the devil. Those who know something of the power of hallucination or of hysteria, the latent forces of the unconscious, are apt to think in these terms. . . . How many fanatics are there who, through curiosity, through the need to emerge from their spiritual dryness or because of their social isolation, believe that they hear voices from the next world while all the time they are merely talking to themselves!

Nevertheless revelations are a fact, and they are perhaps more actual today than they have ever been since the beginning of the Church. In any event, they are more than ever directly destined for the general public which is at times the witness of them. Why is this? God knows the answer. But it would seem that the following facts have something to do with it.

It has always been observed that at turning points of history, at periods of upheaval, God has shown Himself more visibly in the directing of human events. We are in one of these periods now. For the last hundred years we have been observing a social and religious upheaval of a scope never witnessed before in history. World wars have followed closely upon one another. Their disastrous repercussions have been immense, no less in the religious sphere than in the others. Many people have lost their way even in the most essential affairs of life.

In addition to this, Christians are mixing in a new way with pagans, with unbelievers or with the followers of other religions. A Christian society does not protect them as it did before. They have more need of divine guidance since they are more exposed to danger.

And here is something no less important. Confidence in the laws of thought, the metaphysical mentality, has largely disappeared. An infinite number of doctrines are in circulation and being presented as the truth despite the fact that they contradict one another. Moreover, the positivism of the last century has left its traces upon our mental processes; existentialism, whether atheistic or religious, which has penetrated everywhere in one form or another, has put man and his experience into the center of our philosophical thought;

the technological age, as Pope Pius XII has called our era, links us almost irresistibly to visible things. In short, our day has a particular need of *facts*, we are thirsty for experience, we want to *see*.

This attitude is a fact which is explicable also on grounds other than those we have just mentioned. There is sometimes a question of temperament or even a mysticism which seems to us to be disturbing. For example: "Concentrate all your prayer," wrote Ernest Hello to Léon Bloy, "and that of your friends, upon this necessity for actual facts. For these are the water, the blood and the fire which give testimony upon earth. Facts! Facts! Facts! Signs! I would rather have one *now* than a hundred thousand *to come*. Send up all the prayers possible on this problem and, since I can do no more about it, obtain that I SEE *today*." [3]

God adapts Himself to man in order to reach him. That is why He became Man; that is why He changes His methods of acting as the outlook and the situation of men change. It is not surprising, therefore, that in our day perhaps there should properly be more heavenly revelations than at other periods. But for the very reasons which I have just given, we may also expect an extraordinary number of pseudo-revelations.

It is not surprising that a great deal has been written upon particular revelations. It is chiefly historical and apologetic writing, intended to edify the faithful and to protect them against the influence of pseudo-revelations. For the past twenty years, and especially since the last world war, people have begun to be more genuinely interested in revelations and to study them from the standpoint of sound theology. A list of articles which have appeared in specialized reviews would be a long one. Certain authors are content to recall, with respect to revelations, the traditional findings of theology; others feel that this is not sufficient. Actually the thing to do is to study them from within and to show their significance inside the framework of the history of salvation.

We are thus beginning to speak of a "theology of revelations."

3   THE PURPOSE AND PLAN
OF THIS BOOK

But only certain aspects of the problem are dealt with in
these publications, and in none of them is it treated in all its
essential aspects. To make a theological synthesis of the most
important questions concerning revelations is precisely the
aim of this book, for it is by raising it to a strictly theological
plane that one can best serve the Christian and the spiritual
life.

It would be impossible to calculate the amount of harm
which has already been done in the domain of revelations by
those who advance every type of superficial argument with
the intention of serving religion. But piety must be soundly
established upon the bases of faith. The title of this book,
Visions, Revelations and the Church, gives an indication of
its pupose and plan. Revelations are considered not solely
in themselves but also in their finality, that is to say, in so far
as they influence life.

We are dealing with revelations which are commonly
called "private." It is these we wish to designate every time
we use the plural form, "revelations." They are, by definition,
divine manifestations making known hidden realities which
relate to a particular situation of the Church or of one or
more of her members. We say "divine" manifestations in
order to indicate their origin. That is to say, it is God who is
manifesting Himself, whether directly or through intermedi-

aries. Obviously, then, so-called "natural" revelations—those which have no religious character or which are the result of the work of man, such as those of astrology, of necromancy, divination, etc.—do not enter into the scope of our work.

The same holds good for parapsychological phenomena, such things as divinatory dreams, clairvoyance, hallucinations, double visions, the eidetic perceptions of children and primitive people. On the other hand, there are phenomena which do come more directly from God but do not present an object of knowledge sufficiently direct to come within the scope of our study, such as stigmata, levitation, corporal incorruptibility, and other mystical epiphenomena. We are also excluding miracles properly so called, which are revelations of a certain type, for they manifest God's power. But this type of manifestation remains silent and is limited to things and to signs.

From the definition of revelations we also exclude the effects of mystical contemplation as they are habitually described—delights poured into the depths of the soul like a torrent of joy; experience of divine contact wherein the spirit and the senses taste deeply of God; and, in the order of knowledge, illuminations of an extraordinary strength and sweetness which enlighten the understanding.[4] These graces are not presented to man as clearly formulated knowledge, and consequently they are not suitable for transmission as such to other people.

We shall, therefore, consider only revelations expressed in words which can be communicated integrally and without alteration to other people. Undoubtedly the signs which accompany the words are not to be neglected, but the words represent the highest power of expression.

The object of these revelations may be most varied. A revelation may contain prophecies, promises, threats. One may find in it directives which God is making known to the whole world, or to a state, to a province, a family, or to a single specific person.

Along with the term revelation we also use the terms vision, apparition or prophecy and it may be useful to define them more precisely.

Strictly speaking, a *vision* is a visual perception of a reality which in ordinary circumstances cannot be known. Analogically this term is also applied to intellectual perceptions and to all kinds of supernatural knowledge. Thus it is with the visions of St. Paul as, for example, in II Cor. 12: 1–5. These visions contain not only things seen but also the words that accompany them. From ancient times the term vision has had a place so privileged among the sensible perceptions that it may even designate a very vivid non-visual one.

An *apparition* differs little from a vision. Every apparition is a vision, but every vision is not an apparition. The latter is restricted rather to the domain of the senses, so that only exterior or imaginative visions are strictly apparitions. The term vision refers to a perception while that of apparition signifies an object seen.[5]

The visions and the apparitions may be *prophecies* in so far as they are destined to be communicated. Prophecy is not, therefore, a purely personal matter which has reference to the visionary only; it has a communal aim. It is less determined by its object than by the mode of communication. It may be experienced in a dream or in the waking state; it may be expressed in words or in less explicit signs: according to St. Thomas (*Sum. Theol.*, II-II, 174, 3), when the prophet sees someone speaking or showing something to him, we are dealing with the highest degree of prophecy. This is prophecy under the form of apparition: in this form it is always a revelation.[6]

Space does not allow us to dwell upon the distinction between these three modes of revelation. What is important is that the revelations be of divine origin and that they be explicit, that is to say, that they comprise at least words and that they have a communal aim or, in other words, that they be destined not for the visionary alone but for the Church in whole or in part.

We shall limit ourselves to revelations within the Church. So we must define precisely what we mean by the Church and what this embraces. The Church is a community. Therefore, a revelation made within the Church, even if this revelation is called private, will always have a communal meaning by reason of the organic nature of the Mystical Body of Christ.

The meaning we ascribe here to the word "private" should be clearly understood. This meaning depends upon the significance given to the term public. Thus, if we are to designate as public all revelations containing a truth which is or could be officially proposed by the Church to the faithful, all other revelations should be called "private." In our day this term is more or less generally accepted.

Let us note that the Council of Trent did not use it. To designate the same thing it adopted the expression "special revelation." It taught in the decree on Justification (chap. xii) that without special revelation one cannot know whom God has chosen. This expression is used again in the discussions upon this doctrine; but here, what later on would commonly be called private revelations were equally designated by the expression "particular revelations." [7]

If we divide revelations into public and private, we must rank among the latter those revelations which are public to the point of being liturgically sanctioned by the Church, such as those of Lourdes. The meaning generally applied to the word "private" scarcely corresponds with the idea which should be expressed here.

That is why it is better to speak of *particular* or *special* revelations. Particular or special is opposed to universal or general. Those revelations commonly called private are really particular or special because they are not addressed *immediately* to all the faithful. It has been said that revelations may be private in two ways:

1. by the mode of presentation: all revelation which is not officially proposed by the Church to all her members are considered private;

2. by the content: everything which is not found in Scripture or Tradition has a private character.[8]

It would be better to say particular than private, for if the method of presentation and the object do not have universal value this does not mean that all public character is thereby excluded. Particular revelations are found in the Church and approved by her, but they are not in themselves addressed to the universal Church, that is to say, to all the temporal dimensions of the Church.

It is very important not to forget that "private" revelations are distinguished from the Revelation of the Faith not only through their mode of presentation and their object, but more profoundly through their aim: that is to say, the welfare of the Church in a particular situation whether in her own history or in the history of one or several of her members. We shall expand upon this important point when the question of the meaning of revelations arises in the third section of this book.

To avoid all confusion we shall keep to the following terminology: *Particular* will mean for us all revelations which do not aim at setting up a basic dogma of Christian faith or law and which, in principle, are not addressed to all the faithful with obligation to believe in them. We shall call *private* only those revelations whose sole aim is the welfare of one person or of a restricted number of persons. When the question arises of revelations which are particular but not private in the sense we are giving to this latter term, we shall use the expression *social revelation*. Although the word "social" has through usage received a particular and universally accepted meaning, it nevertheless still retains its etymological and general significance which indicates relationship with society in the widest sense of this word.

"Social" revelations, such as those of Lourdes, while they depend upon particular revelations, exclude no one from the scope of their message: they may be addressed to all the members of a society whether it be a nation or the Church herself.[9]

Particular revelations are not the foundation upon which the Church rests, but they do exist and act within the Church. It is the Church which approves them and it is in her that revelations find their aim, for they form part of the charisms which are bestowed for the edification of the Church. Undoubtedly they do not possess the importance of the sacraments, but they are normal means willed by God to direct and strengthen the life of the Church.

Here then is the plan of our study. In the first part, through the testimony of the Scriptures, the Fathers, the theologians, the saints and the magisterium of the Church, we shall establish the existence of revelations. The second part treats of the discernment of revelations. Charlatanism, the prodigious resources of human nature, the permanent influence of demoniacal powers, make verification difficult. That is why it is necessary to have recourse to the criteria of discernment employed by the Church. Finally, once the existence of the revelations and their verification have been established, a third section must be devoted to determining their meaning and their fruit.

Such a division, while following the logic of the subject under discussion, also follows the advice of St. Paul to the Thessalonians (5: 19–21). The first part of this book, which aims at the acceptance of the fact of revelations, is no more than a commentary upon his precept: *Extinguish not the Spirit. Despise not prophecies.* The second part, which deals with the discernment of revelations, is an explanation of the continuation of our text: *but prove all things!* The third part corresponds entirely with the final Pauline advice: *hold fast that which is good.* This deals with the finality and the fruit

of these divine communications. Thus our study is presented
as a theological interpretation of the scriptural data in regard to particular revelations which, moreover, have often
been advanced by the Fathers and by theologians.

PART ONE

THE FACT OF REVELATIONS

AT FIRST SIGHT it might seem useless to open an inquiry into the fact of revelations as these have existed at all times in the Church and played a well-known role down the centuries of her existence. But as false revelations abound beside the true, and as it is often difficult to discern the one from the other, there are people who refuse to give any credence to revelations, rejecting them entirely or at least ignoring them deliberately. In face of this negative, if not hostile, attitude, it is important once and for all to tackle the question of principle in this matter and, above all, to fathom the feeling of the Church with respect to it, an indispensable condition for fruitful theological consideration.

We shall not attempt to report all the various theological pronouncements regarding revelations. It will be enough for us to confine ourselves to some testimonies which will allow us to form a judgment upon the facts and upon the value which it is fitting to attribute to them.

We shall seek these testimonies:

1. In the primitive Church.
2. In the patristic era.
3. In the later course of the history of the Church.

CHAPTER II

Revelations in the Primitive Church

1   THE CHURCH AT THE TIME
OF THE APOSTLES

GOD IN HIS sovereignty reveals Himself when and to whom He wishes. Ever since Creation He has communicated with mankind. In the history of Israel He spoke to His People in various ways, first of all through the Prophets and later through His Son (Heb. 1: 1). Then God manifested Himself through the Apostles to the Church.

It is this manifestation to the Church which before all else interests us in this study. By the Church one may understand, in a wide sense, the "people of God" of the Old Alliance. Thus it has been rightly said: the Israel of God, the Church, is not 1,900 but 3,400 years old. The Church can also be called the "Kingdom of God," as preached by Christ. The Church then is the union in Christ of all spiritual beings over whom God reigns according to the designs of His providence. It is the Church in all her possible dimensions: in her journey upon earth and in her glory in heaven.

But here we are considering the Church in a strict sense,

as a special form of the Kingdom of God. And we are considering this kingdom in its current and historic state. We shall not consider its future and eternal state which is another aspect of the same reality. In other words, we shall be dealing with the Apostolic and Catholic Church, with the Church of exile and of the cross, not that of the kingdom and the glory.

She is the apostolic Church. The "Kingdom of God" contains her, precedes her and prolongs her. When Christ said to the Pharisees: "The Kingdom of God is within you" (Luke 17: 21), the Church had not yet been established. Our Lord Himself said to Simon, son of Jona: "Thou art Peter; and upon this rock I will build my Church."

It was He, Jesus Christ, who was building the Church, and Peter would be the base of it. But Christ was speaking of the future: "I will build" (Matt. 16: 18). The Church would rest upon Peter who would be its visible head. It was to him that the keys of the kingdom would be given. It was he who would exercise the powers of jurisdiction over the faithful. In other words, Christ, the Head of the Church, had been formed at the Incarnation; His Body, the Church, was formed immediately around the preaching and suffering Christ: "It is upon the tree of the Cross that Christ acquired His Church" (A.A.S., 35 [1943] 206).

But the Church did not begin her life proper until after the Ascension of the Lord—to be precise, at Pentecost. This feast is properly considered to be the day of the birth of the Church, the day of the great manifestation of the Holy Spirit. Now it was just at this moment that Peter with the "Eleven" —therefore with the whole Apostolic College which had just been completed—was presented to the world as the visible government of the Church. Once the Master, who took all the decisions of the nascent Church, had disappeared it was Peter with the other Apostles who took His place. It was in their hands that the newly converted placed their lives:

"Brethren, what shall we do?" It was Peter who determined their needs: penance and baptism (Acts 2: 37–8).

But who were these people who witnessed the first great manifestation of the Church? Here is the answer of Scripture: "Now there were . . . devout men out of every nation under heaven" (Acts 2: 5). The apostolic Church showed herself catholic right from the first instant of her life. The fact was emphasized by a sign, the miracle of tongues.

Certainly Christ conceived His Church as universal. He praised the centurion: I have not found so great faith in Israel! He declared that many would enter into the Kingdom of Heaven who were not of the people of Israel (Matt. 8: 11). He excluded no one from His ministry. To the Samaritan woman He foretold that the hour had come when the true adorers of the Father should honor God not only in certain places but in spirit and in truth.

Nevertheless—and this is surprising—although Christ constantly moved about, He never left Palestine. The Apostles traveled from country to country and the missionaries ranged over whole continents. But Jesus declared plainly: "My errand is only to the lost sheep that are of the house of Israel" (Matt. 15: 24). And during His life on earth He asked His Apostles to restrict their missionary activities as He had done: "Go ye not into the way of the Gentiles, and into the city of the Samaritans enter ye not: But go ye rather to the lost sheep of the house of Israel" (Matt. 10: 5–6).

But after Christ's departure this changed. At the moment of the Ascension, after having openly affirmed His universal power in heaven and on earth, He ordered the Apostles: "Going therefore, teach ye all nations, baptizing them . . ." (Matt. 28: 19). And as a matter of fact, a few days afterward the Apostles baptized three thousand pilgrims "of all nations." The Church, conceived as catholic, effectively became so. Very significant was the miracle of tongues on the day of Pentecost. It shows us that if the people of Yahweh had their sacred language the Church had not. She did not

keep any Gospel in Aramaic. She used chiefly Latin and
Greek, because they ensured the widest communication in
the world of that time.

2   THE CHURCH AND THE HOLY SPIRIT

God revealed Himself to His people through the prophets.
When the time was accomplished He revealed Himself
through His Son. And once the Church was established, He
continued to reveal Himself through the "Spirit of the Son."
We have dwelled upon the apostolicity and the catholicity of
the Church designedly because it is of capital importance for
this work to establish that it was through the Holy Spirit that
the Church effectively became apostolic and catholic. It is to
Him that she owes her life: she is truly invisible and truly
visible; and we may note that it is to the origin of the Church
that there applies that apparently paradoxical law of her
existence mentioned by Father Journet: namely, the more
spiritual she is the more visible she appears. "She is the
Church of the Incarnate Word, the Church of the last period
of mankind. When the final day of history dawns God will
not have to establish a new economy for His Church: He
will simply allow to shine forth in their glory all the powers
of grace which she has nurtured in her bosom since the days
of the Incarnation and of Pentecost. So at the same time that
the Church reaches the supreme degree of incarnation and
visibility, she reaches the supreme degree of spirituality." [10]
When Jesus Christ, the Son of Man, traced on earth the
outline of His Church, her members were not very spiritual.
How many times did He complain of the lack of faith of His
own, of their lack of understanding of suffering. Even after

long intimacy with Christ the Apostles had such little com-
prehension of the adoration of the Father in spirit and in
truth that they asked at the very moment of the Ascension:
"Lord, wilt Thou at this time restore again the kingdom to
Israel?"

After the coming of the Holy Spirit everything changed.
We witness a blossoming of spiritual values at the moment
when the presence of Christ was replaced by men on the one
hand and the invisible Spirit on the other. The government
of the Church became at once more visible and more invisible. For the Apostles were only men—and they were
many in number: the Holy Spirit remains the Invisible in
the highest sense even though He is always present in the
orders which He gives to the Church. The mysterious saying
of Christ: "It is expedient to you that I go" (John 16: 7) reveals the divine plan to us: Jesus had to disappear so that
His Spirit might continue His work invisibly from the moment when the Apostles took charge of the Church, which
by this very fact commenced its life as the Mystical Body of
Christ.

The action of the Holy Spirit and the exercise of the apostolic power penetrate one another in such a way that Pope
Leo XIII could teach that the Holy Spirit is the Soul of
the Church just as Christ is its Head: what the soul is to the
body, the Holy Spirit is to the Mystical Body which is the
Church.[11]

In fact the Holy Spirit and the Apostles were at work together; it is sufficient to read the history of the primitive
Church to be convinced of this. This unity of action was
solemnly affirmed by Peter and the Apostles. They declared
before the Sanhedrin: ". . . and we are witnesses of these
things and the Holy Spirit" (Acts 5: 32) and they announced
the grave decision of the Council of Jerusalem to all the
faithful in this way: "For it hath seemed good to the Holy
Spirit and to us. . . ." (Acts 15: 28).

According to God's plan, the birth and the whole life of

the Church depended of necessity on both the Holy Spirit
and the Apostles. Erick Peterson goes so far as to say: "There
is a Church on the sole condition that the twelve Apostles,
under the inspiration of the Holy Ghost, took the decision to
go to the Gentiles. . . . If the Eleven had not believed in
the strength of the Holy Spirit, if they had remained with the
Jews and had not admitted the Gentiles, then there would
have been no Church. . . ." [12] The union of the spiritual and
the jurisdictional character is essential to the whole life of
the Church. St. Peter, or his successor, governs the Church,
it is true: but it is ruled equally by the Holy Spirit. In accom-
plishing this work the Spirit heaps charisms upon the
Church. Now, amid these charisms is to be found prophecy,
which is, by definition, one method of communication from
God to men; it presumes a revelation.

It is clear where this line of thought is leading us. The
question of revelations in the Church is founded upon the
charism of prophecy. We must, therefore, consider it. We
are dealing here with facts. We find evidence of them
throughout the whole history of the Church. For the moment
we simply want to draw attention to the importance of the
charism of prophecy on the very day of the Church's birth.

It is an amazing thing that at the precise moment when
the Church, and within the Church the Holy Spirit, were
manifested to the world, the man upon whom Christ chose
to build His Church began his first sermon by insisting upon
the charism of prophecy.

After the strange scene of the Descent of the Holy Spirit,
Peter felt obliged to explain the cause of the extraordinary
phenomenon of the gift of tongues. And he did so in a very
solemn manner. Peter "stood up" with the Eleven (Acts 2:
14). Then, dominating the hubbub of the voices of the other
Apostles, he raised his voice and began his discourse with a
solemn formula: "Ye men of Judea, and all you that dwell
in Jerusalem, be this known to you, and with your ears receive my words. For these are not drunk, as you suppose,

seeing it is but the third hour of the day: But this is that which was spoken of by the prophet Joel: *And it shall come to pass in the last days, (saith the Lord), I will pour out of my Spirit upon all flesh: and your sons and your daughters shall prophesy, and your young men shall see visions, and your old men shall dream dreams. And upon my servants indeed, and upon my handmaids will I pour out in those days of my Spirit, and they shall prophesy. And I will show wonders in the heaven above, and signs on the earth beneath: . . . that whosoever shall call upon the name of the Lord, shall be saved"* (Acts 2: 14–21).

Three things were made known by this text: the pouring out of the Holy Spirit over all without distinction of race, sex or condition through prophecy communicated in different ways; the precursory signs of the parousia: the assurance of salvation to all those who call upon the Lord.

The question of knowing when this time will come is of particular interest to us. Peter said, "in the last days," thus replacing the formula "after that," which we find in Joel. But the two expressions indicate the same epoch. According to modern exegetes, Peter was referring to the Messianic period by the use of the phrase "the last days." According to Jacquier, for instance, for whom the visions mentioned here are revelations "in the fullness of time," what Peter meant was this: "The pouring out of the Holy Spirit has just happened. Therefore the ancient times are completed and the new times, inaugurated by Jesus the Messiah, are beginning. . . . This is the last period of the world, begun with the appearance of the Messiah, which will finish with His glorious return." [13] The whole period was meant, and first of all its beginnings, unless Peter's argument has no meaning. That is why Trinquet, in his notes on the text of the prophet Joel, could write that the Acts of the Apostles put these "last days" in the era of the nascent Church in which took place the outpouring of the Holy Spirit. [14]

For Peter to have been thinking especially of the moment

present to him, when the first manifestations of the Holy Spirit were particularly abundant, is normal. But we do not see how one could restrict the times indicated here to the beginning of the Messianic period. That would be contrary to the obvious meaning of the text, contrary to the common opinion of the exegetes and would not agree with the context which mentions the signs from heaven: the "last days" denotes in the Prophecies the Messianic period, rarely in the New Testament the end of the period, but never exclusively its beginning.

If this is so, if the outpouring of the Holy Spirit upon all flesh extends throughout all the Messianic period, one can foresee important deductions for our study, deductions which the teaching of the Church and certain facts of her history will confirm. We shall therefore consult that history, beginning with the primitive Church. Were there any particular revelations in those days?

3   REVELATIONS AND HOLY SCRIPTURE

In order to pass any judgment upon revelations in the primitive Church it is necessary to investigate the Acts, the Epistles and the Apocalypse. But, it may be said, how can one, in treating of revelations called "private" relate them to Scripture? Does not all that Scripture contains belong to public revelation?

We could reply that it is at least possible to find information in the Bible upon our subject, information, for example, upon questions of principle. We could also find prophecies about revelations which Christians would receive later throughout the whole life of the Church. Does not St. Peter's first discourse reflect something of this kind? And should not the Apocalypse which describes in imagery the future history of the Church contain something of interest to our subject?

The question is even more ticklish if we go in quest of revelations in the inspired books. It would be a mistake to believe that Sacred Scripture and particular revelations are a priori mutually exclusive. Such a supposition could be founded only upon an inaccurate idea of revelations.

According to a rather widespread superficial conception, all revelations of which the authenticity is not infallibly guaranteed by divine Inspiration are particular revelations: these are the non-biblical revelations. Now this conception is inexact. It is true that one thinks generally of post-biblical revelations when one speaks of particular revelations, and that in this case the absence of that universally valid infallible guarantee is a certain sign that the revelations in question are particular. But even in the latter it is necessary for this guarantee to be founded in divine Inspiration and for it to be universally valid, since there can be particular revelations which are infallibly certain, not for the whole world but for those who receive them (cf. *Conc. Trid. de justific.*, can. 16). And the infallible certitude, in this case, would not be due to divine Inspiration which helps the person who relates the revelation, but to an illumination or to another grace which creates the infallible guarantee in the mind of the visionary.

The true idea of particular revelations is not negatively established, as for example by comparison with the Bible; these revelations are positively defined through their object, their aim and their recipient (cf. chap. 1, para. 3, and below, chap. 8, para. 2). Now if these specific elements are particular, then the revelations are particular, even those guaranteed by Inspiration—they remain what they are through definition. The particular revelations which the Bible contains, while possessing their essential characteristics, have in addition the guarantee of Inspiration which assures their authenticity for all Christians. And since this Inspiration, like the Revelation which constitutes the object of Catholic faith, ceased with the death of the last Apostle (cf. Decr. *Lamentabili* [Denz., 2021]), this type of private revelations ceased with it.

If one accepted the conception which we considered earlier to be inexact, there should have been particular revelations which would have been particular during a certain period and then would suddenly have ceased to be so. Scripture relates revelations which must not, as it says, be revealed to anyone at least during a certain time. This was the case with the revelation at Thabor, a revelation destined solely for three of the Apostles. Zachary communicated his only to his wife. All the relations who insisted that the child be called by his father's name were ignorant of it. With regard to the announcement to Mary—an announcement which was a particular revelation, at least in its destination if not in its object—even St. Joseph was not warned of it. Mary kept silent even at the risk of being put away.

Besides, one may say that all revelations in general have kept at least for a certain time, or even for a very long time, their private character. We, who for long centuries have possessed a scriptural canon definitely established and solemnly proposed to all by the Church, have a tendency to forget how the situation presented itself previously. Supported by canonicity we believe in the appearance of the Risen Christ to Mary Magdalen and to the disciples on the road to Emmaus. But the Apostles did not believe them. "And they . . . did not believe. And after that he appeared in another shape to two of them walking, as they were going into the country. And they, going, told it to the rest: neither did they believe them. At length he appeared to the Eleven as they were at table: and he upbraided them with their incredulity and hardness of heart, because they did not believe them who had seen him after he was risen again" (Mark 16: 10–15).

We must not judge the Apostles. In their place would we have escaped our Lord's reproach? They were certainly not in a situation any more favorable to the acceptance of appearances of the Risen One than the Curé Peyramale, when faced by Bernadette Soubirous' recounting her experience at the grotto of Massabielle.

That is not to say that the problem of revelations presented itself in the same way to the Apostles as it does to us. Today, indeed, it depends upon the canon of Scripture. Now this canon has its own story. Soon after the death of the last Apostle certain Fathers of the Church or ecclesiastical writers did not accept the Apocalypse and its revelations as canonical; as against that, others ranked within the Canon of Scriptures the *Shepherd* by Hermas whose writings contain so many visions. They did not ask themselves then if such and such a revelation in the *Shepherd* was private or public but rather if it was apocryphal or not (see below, pp. 44–51).

Today the question with respect to a revelation is whether it is false or "private." It is significant that the term "private revelation" entered the theological vocabulary only after the Council of Trent: it was this council which solemnly fixed the canon of Scriptures. But the reality indicated by the term did exist in all periods of the history of salvation.

We shall give some examples of revelations which are private or particular at least in relationship to their object and their recipient. One day the prophet Elias, discouraged, fled into the desert. Seated under a juniper tree, he cried out: "It is enough for me. Lord, take away my soul. . . ." And he cast himself down and slept. And an angel of the Lord touched him and said to him: "Arise, eat." . . . And he ate and drank; and he fell asleep again. And the angel of the Lord came again the second time and made him eat. Sustained by this nourishment Elias walked "forty days and forty nights" (III Kings 19: 4–9). Does this not relate a private event? The angel seems to have come solely to comfort the exhausted prophet.

One might consider as particular the revelations made to Balaam (Num. 22) and to the wife of Manue (Judg. 13) and so many others too. St. John of the Cross quotes particular revelations of the Bible. In the *Ascent of Mount Carmel* (Book II, chap. XXI, especially 1, 6, 7) he proves that God displayed annoyance when people asked revelations of Him but that nevertheless He did make or permit them. The holy Doctor mentions the case of Saul's causing a sorcerer to call upon the dead Samuel. The latter appeared unwillingly and said to him: "Why have you troubled my rest by calling me?" And Samuel made him a prophetic revelation of a kind that so terrified Saul that he collapsed (1 Kings 28: 5–20). The prophecy of Samuel which was verified very soon afterward is, for all that it forms part of Sacred Scripture, a particular revelation, for its object and its aim concern Saul only, its recipient. It would not even have taken place if he had not insisted—wrongfully too (1 Kings 28: 6–7).

So Cardinal Bona, in his book on revelations, can confidently assert: "It is evident that the particular revelations of which we treat here have existed in all centuries and in all the ages of humanity from our first parents to us, whether according to Sacred Scripture or according to proved historical facts." [15]

4   REVELATIONS TO THE APOSTLES

The examples we have just supplied make it possible for us to reply clearly to the question concerning revelations in the primitive Church. Let us say it immediately: they took place so frequently that they conditioned all its history; acting as levers, they released new actions and gave rise to doctrinal decisions.

St. Peter, who was not a visionary, after having announced the age of the Holy Spirit who would operate through visions and prophecies, must have received them himself. It was through a particular special revelation that he was advised of the way to behave in regard to Cornelius (Acts 10). He also received revelations which concerned his person more than his mission: while he slept in chains in a prison an angel awakened him and said to him: "Arise quickly." And the chains fell off his hands. The angel said then to Peter: "Gird thyself, and put on thy sandals." Peter did so and the angel continued: "Cast thy garment about thee, and follow me." (Acts 12: 7-10). The words of the angel in this apparition were completely insignificant, but the effect of them was enormous. The revelation was perfectly real, as Peter's attitude proved. He mechanically obeyed the angel's orders; he took his garment, which he would probably have forgotten if the angel had said nothing to him. It was only out in the road that he realized the grace of which he had been the object: he was free.

St. Paul, to whom was abundantly revealed the mystery of Christ which he announced under the form of doctrine and precepts, received in addition many "individual revelations" destined primarily for his personal life.[16]

It was through a special revelation that he was converted to Christ. God could very well have chosen some other method. The occasion of his conversion, an event of capital importance for him and for the Church, was a personal encounter with Jesus Christ. The dialogue is significant: "Why persecutest *thou me*?" "Who art *thou*?" "*I* am Jesus." "What wilt *thou* have *me* to do?" "Arise . . . go to Damascus. . . ." Action was demanded here; the command concerns the life of St. Paul himself. Christ did not deal precisely with the details; Ananias would look after that (Acts 22). From this moment Paul often received revelations, by day and by night.

He was so much guided by the revelations which both the Holy Spirit and Christ Himself made to him that he was compelled to relate some of them in order to explain his behavior. He admitted: ". . . the Holy Spirit in every city witnesseth to me, saying: That bonds and afflictions wait for me" (Acts 22: 23). In Jerusalem, during his prayers, he was carried away in ecstasy and he saw Christ who said to him: "Make haste and get thee quickly out of Jerusalem; . . . it is unto the nations I now send thee." Jesus came to encourage him during the night: "Do not fear, but speak," He said to him (Acts 28: 9). Paul himself encouraged the travelers in his boat as the result of a revelation which was typically particular, because directed uniquely to him and to a small number of people. Paul spoke to these despairing people: "An angel of God, whose I am, and whom I serve, stood by me this night, saying: Fear not, Paul, thou must be brought before Caesar; and behold God hath given thee all of them that sail with thee" (Acts 27: 23–24). At Troas, during the night, he had a vision. A Macedonian appeared to him and said: "Pass over into Macedonia, and help us" (Acts 26: 9).

These revelations—we are not citing all of them, and not all were preserved in writing—were given almost exclusively in connection with the missionary activity of Paul. But he also received revelations of a strictly private kind. The Corinthians forced him to make this admission: "If I must glory (it is not expedient indeed), but I will come to the visions and revelations of the Lord. . . ." [17] He related how he was caught up to the third heaven and how he heard ineffable words which it was not granted to man to utter . . . (II Cor. 12: 1–6). Paul would have preferred never to speak of such graces, about which he had maintained secrecy for fourteen years. But since the privilege of ecstasies and revelations gave great prestige in the community of Corinth and since

Paul's own prestige had just been attacked, he decided to speak about these intimate matters while recognizing that it would have been normal to keep them for himself: "I am become foolish: you have compelled me!" (II Cor. 12: 11).

Just like the Apostles Peter and Paul, St. John was favored with revelations. Before describing to us his grandiose visions in the Apocalypse, he communicated to different churches or to their representatives very particular revelations. These related less to doctrine than to the life of an individual or a community. One hears them as the grave advice of a spiritual director. There was question of this or that virtue, this or that negligence, or such and such a person to be dealt with.

John received an order, for example, to write to the church of Thyatira: "These things saith the Son of God, who hath his eyes like to a flame of fire, and his feet like to fine brass. I know thy works, and thy faith, and thy charity, and thy ministry, and thy patience, and thy last works which are more than the first. But I have against thee a few things: because thou sufferest the woman Jezabel, who calleth herself a prophetess, to teach and to seduce my servants, to commit fornication, and to eat of things sacrificed to idols. And I gave her a time that she might do penance, and she will not repent of her fornication. Behold, I will cast her into a bed; and they that commit adultery with her shall be in very great tribulation, except they do penance from their deeds. And I will kill her children with death, and all the churches shall know that I am he that searcheth the reins and hearts, and I will give to every one of you according to your works" (Apoc. 2: 18–23).

5   REVELATIONS TO OTHER MEMBERS OF
       THE PRIMITIVE CHURCH

The revelations were not restricted to the Apostles. Certainly they were by right the beneficiaries of revelations.
Given charge of the universal Revelation, they needed to
possess all the charisms useful for their mission. But in the
primitive Church many other people received revelations, as
the book of the Acts tells us: "Now there were in the Church
which was at Antioch, prophets and doctors, among whom
was Barnabas, and Simon who was called Niger, and Lucius
of Cyrene, and Manahen, who was the foster brother of
Herod the tetrarch, and Saul" (Acts 13: 1).

Among these inspired men one of the most important and
best known was Agabus: "And in these days there came
prophets from Jerusalem to Antioch: And one of them
named Agabus, rising up, signified by the Spirit, that there
should be a great famine over the whole world, which came
to pass under Claudius" (Acts 11: 27–28). Later the presence
of Agabus at Caesarea is mentioned. There he took the
girdle of Paul and bound his hands and feet with it, saying:
"Thus saith the Holy Spirit: The man whose girdle this is,
the Jews shall bind in this manner in Jerusalem, and shall
deliver him into the hands of the Gentiles" (Acts 21: 11).

The reaction of the witnesses who began to weep and to
beg Paul not to go to Jerusalem shows very plainly how seriously they took the prophets. Agabus was a prophet just as
were those of the Old Testament. His predictions came to
pass and his symbolic action accentuated their tragedy. But

the content and the destination of his revelations did not possess a universal character. With their fulfillment they attained their aim and passed into history. But they were particular revelations.

The Christian prophets took their place in the community after the Apostles: "And God indeed hath set some in the Church; first apostles, secondly prophets, thirdly doctors . . ." (1 Cor. 12: 28; cf. Eph. 4: 11).

When St. Paul said to the Ephesians: "You are . . . built upon the foundation of the apostles and prophets" (Eph. 2: 20), he was probably referring to these inspired men. For the Epistles mention prophets and apostles on several occasions, and the context clearly shows that St. Paul was referring to the prophets of the New Testament: "He that descended is the same also that ascended above all the heavens, that he might fill all things. And he himself gave some men as apostles, and some as prophets, others again as evangelists, and others as pastors and teachers, in order to perfect the saints for a work of ministry, for building up the body of Christ" (Eph. 4: 10–12). "The mystery of Christ was not known in other generations to the sons of men, as it is *now* revealed to his holy apostles and prophets in the Spirit" (Eph. 3: 5). The Christ who descended from heaven had therefore called certain men to be prophets; their work would consist in fashioning the Body of Christ.

Doctrinal reasons or respect for a venerable tradition have, it is true, led serious commentators to understand these texts as referring to the prophets of the Old Testament. These latter, however, were incontestably a part of past generations; on the other hand, the Holy Spirit came solely to manifest Himself. Consequently how could the prophets to whom was revealed *now and in the Spirit* the mystery of Christ, unknown to past generations, not be the prophets of the New Testament? And if the texts we have quoted refer to these men, they were undoubtedly the same as those spoken of in Ephesians 11: 20.

In our days exegetes are admitting more and more plainly that according to St. Paul the foundations upon which the household of the faithful arose were the Apostles and the Christian prophets. This is what Father Benoît notes with respect to Ephesians 2: 20: "While other interpreters are thinking here of the prophets of the Old Testament, the reference is probably to those of the New. . . . They constitute, with the Apostles, the generations of the first witnesses who received the revelation of the Divine plan (3: 5) and who preached the Gospel (Luke 11: 14). They are therefore as it were the foundation upon which the Church is built. It will be noted that elsewhere St. Paul attributes this role of foundation to Christ Himself" (1 Cor. 3: 20).[18]

We may surmise from this the importance of the prophets and, consequently, the importance of private revelations in the life of the Christian community. The role of the prophets was, however, subordinated to that of the Apostles for the prophets were controlled by the Church as St. Paul indicates in his first Epistles to the Corinthians.[19]

But, it may perhaps be objected, prophecies and revelations belong therefore to two different domains: strictly speaking, may one pass from the one to the other? Is not Msgr. Cerfaux right? "The prophets should be conceived of as the leaders of the Church." [20] Was not their task to teach the faithful the doctrine of salvation (1 Cor. 14: 31), to exhort them, to console them (1 Cor. 14: 31–33) and to edify the Church (1 Cor. 14: 3–4)? All this is true. But it would be false to see in all these ministerial activities the essential and integral mission of the prophet. To define such a mission is difficult and perhaps we shall not succeed in doing so.

It seems to us, however, that their mission was not principally of a juridical and doctrinal order. Essentially it consisted in "prophesying," that is to say, in communicating that which God revealed for the good of the community, for the edification of the Church. That is the whole meaning of the

word "prophet." In fact, where the Acts mention important
groups of prophets, the Holy Spirit chose some of them for
apostolic work. Thus we see Barnabas and Paul set apart
from the others by order of the Spirit (Acts 13: 1, 2). "In the
list of charisms," writes J. Bonsirven, "the prophets come
after the Apostles: on several occasions in the New Testament these interpreters of God make their appearance, making predictions and reading the secrets of hearts; they do not
seem, except at Antioch (Acts 13: 1–3) to have had any share
in the direction of the communities; whether they traveled or
stayed in the one place, they were the bearers of the divine
word." [21]

Eminent members of the Church, they were distinguished
from the simple faithful by the charism of prophecy which
they had received from the Holy Spirit. To speak in the
Spirit, to reveal secret things, such were the functions of the
prophets in the primitive Church. That gave them great influence over the communities, to such an extent that they
were considered fitted to help the Apostles in the government and to exercise teaching functions. In fact, certain
prophets "ministered to the Lord" and directed communities
(Acts 13: 2). Clearly shown is the fact that the prophets
taught as doctors and through their revelations had sufficient
knowledge of the doctrine of salvation, since the mystery of
Christ was revealed to them as to the Apostles (Eph. 3: 5).

Besides, their charism was not constantly in action, as
St. Paul shows (1 Cor. 14: 30): If among the prophets one has
a revelation, the others are to keep silent! The community
could not allow a grace which was destined for it to be lost.
It is only in thus understanding the position of the prophets
in the primitive Church that one may distinguish them from
other "dignitaries." Except for prophesying, "the others" did
all that the prophets did. The Apostles, it is true, prophesied
also, but if all the Apostles are prophets, not all the prophets
are Apostles. Conversely, in the opinion of Lietzmann, the

prophets are distinguished by the fact that they remained in one area while the Apostles were traveling missionaries.[22] The Apostles were necessarily priests; this was not so with the prophets, among whom were included women (Acts 21: 9). On the other hand, if teaching had been the task proper of the prophets, why would the Lord have raised up doctors and Evangelists? Moreover, women had not the right to teach; now, as we have just mentioned, women were to be found among the prophets, the four daughters of Philip the Evangelist, for example (Acts 21: 8–9).

What St. Peter had declared on the day of Pentecost was accordingly fulfilled in the Church: the Spirit was poured out upon "all flesh." Here, unlike what we find in the matter of the hierarchical functions, there was no restriction: anyone, women as well as men, might receive the inspirations of the Spirit. St. Paul was addressing himself to all the faithful of Corinth when he wrote: "Be zealous for spiritual gifts; but rather that you may prophesy. . . . I would have you all to speak with tongues, but rather to prophesy. . . . Wherefore, brethren, be zealous to prophesy: and forbid not to speak with the language of tongues" (1 Cor. 14: 1–5, 39).

To prophesy did not necessarily mean to reveal; however, to communicate revelations apparently was an act which expressed in the highest sense the prophetic function. The following practice, imposed by St. Paul, proves this: "And let the prophets speak, two or three; and let the rest judge. But if anything be revealed to another sitting, let the first hold his peace" (1 Cor. 14: 29–30).

This is how the work of the prophet may be regarded: Inspired by the Spirit he gave the assembly an exhortation, an interpretation or simply a few words of edification (1 Cor. 14: 3–4). But moments would occur when he had something more precise to say, a true revelation from God; the usual order then dropped into abeyance because the divine word was being transmitted by the prophet.[23]

Such a revelation, a manifestation of secret things, emphasizes the importance of prophecy. "But if all prophesy, and there come in one that believeth not, or an unlearned person, he is convinced by all, he is judged by all: The secrets of his heart are made manifest, and so, falling down on his face, he will adore God, affirming that God is among you indeed" (I Cor. 14: 24–25).

The halo that surrounded the prophets in the first Christian communities is obvious from the above. And it is not surprising that men of evil intent yielded to the temptation to imitate them. So the primitive Church had its share of pseudo-prophets. St. Paul, at the beginning of his first missionary journey, found one of them in Paphos; he was an individual called Barjesus. This man lived in the entourage of the proconsul Sergius Paulus whom he sought to turn away from the Faith.

Later St. John was obliged to state that "many false prophets are gone out into the world" (I John 4: 1). There is nothing surprising about this, for the false assumes the true and is opposed to it. And counterfeits of the true are easiest in the domain of the sign, the world of communication by sensible means. Now, unlike sanctifying grace, it is on this plane that charisms are found, and in particular the charism of prophecy which is the first among them.

Let us conclude this chapter with an important observation which is to be found in the supplement to the *Dictionary of the Bible:* "The language of St. Paul hardly allows us to think that he looked upon charisms on the whole as a privilege of the Apostolic age, and this charismatic organization as something linked to what may be called primitive fervor, a fervor that was destined to fade away. . . . St. Paul and the Acts, in teaching as in fact, bring into striking relief a certain organization of the Church and the Churches which we have called charismatic, and which the Apostle in no way passes on to us as a temporary or superficial phenomenon." [24]

Theologically, it would be useful to compare with these Pauline findings what history teaches us regarding the charism of revelations in the life of the post-apostolic Church. This we shall attempt to do, or at least outline, in the next two chapters.

CHAPTER III

Revelations in the Age of the Fathers

NOTHING IN THE New Testament indicates that the
charisms, and consequently the revelations, were to disappear from the life of the Church after the apostolic age.
Nowhere, on the other hand, is it affirmed that they would
always continue. For that matter, we would not gather from
the Scriptures that the world would last two thousand years,
and undoubtedly quite a lot longer, after the coming of the
Messiah. In fact, St. Paul and the first Christians believed
that the parousia was imminent. But these forecasts did not
come to pass and the Church has known a long history.
Hence it is impossible to evade the question: were not explicit communications of the Spirit, considered by the first
Christians as a normal force in the life of their communities,
a charismatic manifestation reserved for the primitive
Church? In this chapter we shall attempt to determine what
answer the Church of the post-apostolic age gave to this
problem.

Two preliminary remarks must be made in order to set the
limits of our exposition. First, we shall not try to be exhaus-
tive. It will be sufficient for our purpose to draw attention to
several valuable testimonies to show the basis for our conclusions. Second, in referring to revelations contained in

writings which are important but non-canonical, we do not thereby intend to accept the authenticity of such revelations but simply to stress the fact that people believed in them, and the consequences which arose from that fact.

1   THE FIRST TESTIMONIES OF
POST-APOSTOLIC TIMES

The year A.D. 67 is usually considered to be the date of the deaths of St. Peter and St. Paul. Our research into the first testimonies of the post-apostolic era will start at the time when the disciples of the Apostles began to govern the Church, and extend through the first half of the second century, to the period in which the *Shepherd* of Hermas was being disseminated.

It will readily be understood why we are not thinking of St. John. Before his exceptionally late death the other Apostles were being succeeded by their disciples in communities of first importance such as Rome. The Apocalypse already seems to reflect the situation of the post-apostolic Church. And it is not impossible that the *Didache*, for example, may have been written before the Apocalypse. The chronological order, in any event, is only of relative importance since we are concerned with describing a living reality at a given moment in its development.

But while the *Didache* may have been composed in its entirety between the years A.D. 70 and 100, as we believe, or in the first half of the second century, it is certain that it does not belong to the apostolic age. It clearly distinguishes between the missionary hierarchy and the local hierarchy. The latter, composed of bishops and deacons, seems quite plainly inferior to the other, which took upon itself the three functions mentioned all together in the apostolic writings. The *Didache*, in fact, felt the need to request the faithful to respect the members of the local hierarchy: "They also fulfill the ministry of prophets and doctors." (*Did.* 15: 1–2). The Apostles were not named because their ministry was superior to the others.

The prophets, therefore, came immediately after the Apostles, a rank already assigned to them by St. Paul. The *Didache* is more interested in them than in all the others. Adolf von Harnack believes that, according to the *Didache,* they took first place in the Christian community.[25] Nothing is less sure, for if the *Didache* gives them the first place this is not because of their importance but because of the nature of the function they performed. The regulations with respect to them had to be more detailed because their charismatic activity gave them a liberty which was not easily controlled. They were, in fact, granted much latitude; but some discipline had to be preserved.

The mission proper of the prophets was to speak under divine inspiration. Here is a significant regulation: "You shall not test nor criticize any prophet who speaks in the Spirit, for every sin shall be forgiven, but that shall not be forgiven" (*Did.* II: 7). " 'To speak in the Spirit' is," according to Hemmer, "to speak under God's influence a language intelligible to men, a language which edifies them, exhorts them, consoles them, if necessary reveals mysteries to them. The pouring out of the Spirit may cast the prophet into an ecstasy, transport him with enthusiasm, urge him irresistibly to communicate revelations." [26]

The gift of speaking in the Spirit was sufficient to invest Christians with exceptional credit. Normally they moved about from community to community. But they were not obliged to do so, and they could linger in one community or even live in it, as distinct from the Apostles who could not

remain in one place longer than two days (*Did.* 13: 1; cf. II:
5). In the latter event the faithful had to maintain them, a
favor not accorded to everyone (*Did.* 12: 3). Even when a
prophet worked "with an eye to the earthly ministry"—an
obscure expression undoubtedly signifying some action
which would normally have lent itself to criticism—they must
let him be: God would judge. It was to the prophets that the
faithful generally gave their offerings and these inspired
men could celebrate the Eucharist as it suited them (*Did.*
10: 7). They were called "high priests" of the Christian communities (*Did.* 13: 3).

How could such an advantageous and creditable position
have failed to attract intriguers? The *Didache* puts Christians on their guard against these. Here were the rules which
it laid down for the discernment of true and false prophets:
From the fact that someone spoke in the Spirit—or that he
seemed to do so—it did not follow that he must be an
authentic prophet. Every prophet was false:

1. Whose way of life was not that of the Lord's.
2. Who profited from his position to eat according to his
choice.
3. Who asked for money for his personal use.
4. Who taught without practicing what he preached.
5. Who professed some doctrine other than that of the
Church (11: 2–8).

These regulations imply the presence of a fairly considerable number of prophets in the communities and the existence of frequent revelations.

The *Didache* reflects the position in one community. Here
is a personal testimony of great interest. St. Ignatius of
Antioch, who died around the year A.D. 110, wrote to the
Philadelphians: "For, even though some were willing enough
to lead my human spirit into error, yet the Spirit is not led
into error, since He proceeds from God. Indeed, He knows
where He comes from and whither He goes (John 3: 8) and

lays bare what is secret. I cried out, while in your midst, and said in a ringing voice—God's voice: 'Give heed to the bishop and to the presbytery and to the deacons.' Some, however, suspected I was saying this because I had previous knowledge of the division caused by some; but He for whose sake I am in chains is my witness, that I had not learned it from any human source. No, it was the Spirit who kept preaching in these words: 'Apart from the bishop do nothing. . . .' " [27] He was unquestionably, as the quotation from St. John proves, referring to the Holy Spirit. It was this Spirit who "reveals secrets." Here is a remarkable thing: St. Ignatius, "this man of government, this theorist on episcopal authority, is a mystic . . . living under the motion of the Spirit and endowed with the gift of prophecy" (Camelot). At the time of his intervention in the difficulties of the Church at Philadelphia it was the Spirit who cried in his plea: "Submit to the bishop." Thus the strongest affirmation that any man had made in favor of episcopal authority since the days of the Apostles came from a revelation of the Holy Spirit.

Here, too, is what is attested in the *Passion of St. Polycarp:* "When Polycarp entered the stadium, a voice from heaven was heard: 'Courage, Polycarp, and be a man.' No one saw him who spoke, but those of our people who were present heard the voice." Three days before being arrested, Polycarp had received a revelation, and the chronicler who related how the old man prepared himself for martyrdom made this observation: "*It was necessary that the vision which had been shown him should be accomplished.*" During his prayer, seeing his pillow on fire, he had said prophetically to those who were with him: "It needs must be that I shall be burned alive." And the author adds that the glorious martyr Polycarp was "in our days a master, both apostolic and prophetic, the Catholic bishop of Smyrna; every word which came from his mouth has been or will be accomplished." [28]

Like the *Martyrdom of Polycarp*, the dialogue of St. Justin with the Jew Trypho expresses the thought of the Church at this period. The great apologist tries to prove to Trypho the existence of the reign of a thousand years. He quotes Isaias to him, but also the Apocalypse of St. John; the Jewish prophet and the Christian prophet both speak of this reign of a thousand years "according to a revelation which they had received." And he seizes this opportunity to insist upon the fact that prophecy does not belong exclusively to the Jews: "Among us, too," he says, "the prophetic gifts are now to be found. This fact should help you to understand that what happened heretofore among your people is now happening among ours. Just as with you, side by side with the holy prophets there existed the false ones, so with us, beside the true there are the false prophets and false doctors." [29]

These early testimonies, the most remarkable of which we have quoted, prove plainly that prophecies, and as a consequence, private revelations, continued to be an element of prime importance in the life of the Church during the post-apostolic period up to the middle of the second century.

2   "THE SHEPHERD" OF HERMAS

At the period we now approach, approximately under the pontificate of Pius I (A.D. 140–150), Hermas, a pious merchant, wrote a curious book, *The Shepherd*. It is divided into three parts—visions, precepts, and parables—but the last two are scarcely more than an explanation of the visions. Here, by way of example, is how Hermas described his fourth vision:

"Twenty days after the preceding vision, my brethren, I

had another, a figure of approaching tribulation. I was walking along the road to my property situated somewhat over a mile from the main road. It is an easy road to travel. While walking thus alone, I prayed the Lord to accomplish the revelations and visions which He had communicated to me through His holy Church, to give me strength to lead to penance those of His servants who had fallen, and to exalt thereby His own sublime and glorious name. Had He not judged me worthy to contemplate His marvels? While I was thus giving glory and thanks to the Lord, I heard as it were a voice which said to me: 'Have no doubts, Hermas!' "

He then perceived a cloud of dust, then an enormous beast, "a kind of sea monster from whose mouth belched forth fiery locusts." Hermas prayed to the Lord and passed close to the beast without its harming him. But a new vision came to arrest his passage:

"I had just passed the beast and had advanced some thirty feet when I saw coming towards me a virgin dressed as (a bride) coming from the nuptial chamber, wholly clothed in white, shod in white shoes, her head covered as far as the forehead by a miter which acted as her headdress; she had white hair. Following my previous visions I recognized her as the Church, and the sight of her overwhelmed me with joy. She greeted me with these words: 'Greetings, O man!' and I returned her salutation: 'Oh, lady, I greet you.' 'Have you encountered nothing?' she asked then. 'Lady,' I replied, 'I have encountered a monstrous beast, large enough to destroy a whole people; but thanks to the power of the Lord and to His great mercy, I escaped it.' 'If you were fortunate enough to escape it,' she told me, 'it is because you cast your care upon God and opened your heart to the Lord in the belief that there are no other means of salvation for you but His great and glorious name. . . . Go then, and recount the marvels of the Lord to His elect, and tell them that this beast is the figure of the great tribulation which is at hand. Prepare yourselves in advance and return to the Lord with all your hearts through penitence; then you will be able to escape this tribulation on condition that you make your hearts pure and spotless and that all the days of your lives you remain blameless in the service of the Lord. Cast your cares upon the Lord and He Himself will deliver you. Believe in the Lord, men of wavering faith! Believe that He can do all: whether turning His anger away from you, or sending His chastisements upon you if you persist in your doubts. Woe to them who hear these words without profiting by them! It would be better for them if they had never been born!' " [30].

The numerous revelations listed by the *Shepherd* won for it the reputation of apocalypse or revelation; so it took its place by the side of the Apocalypse of St. John, of that of St. Peter and of the *Ascension of Isaias*.[31]

We are not called upon to judge the truth of these revelations. Recent critics, like Ake v. Ström, admit the truth of some of them and relegate others to the domain of allegory.[32] It is enough for us to refer to the Church's attitude. Now the *Shepherd* of Hermas enjoyed great authority in Rome toward the end of the second century. The *Muratorian Fragment* mentions it in the following terms: "Quite recently, in our own times, Hermas wrote *The Shepherd*, when his brother Pius was sitting on the chair of the Church of Rome; that is why it should be read, although it cannot be read publicly in the church, nor among the prophets whose number is complete, nor among the apostles at the end of the seasons. But we reject everything of Arsinoe, of Valentine, or of Meltiades." [33]

The way in which this celebrated *Fragment* speaks of the *Shepherd* of Hermas allows us to assume that its purpose was to counteract a tendency to accept the *Shepherd* as a canonical book. Why was this dignity refused it? One reason alone is indicated—its late date. It was not contemporaneous with the Apostles. It says it was but recently, under the bishop Pius, that it was written. There is nothing to indicate that it was considered false or heretical. On the contrary, its reading was recommended. A curious thing is that its style has no elegance, no more than has, for instance, the noble simplicity of the letters of St. Clement. Its author, of modest standing, as he himself says, seemed to enjoy considerable prestige. This slave, who was freed by a lady, was not presented as the Pope's brother, but the Pope is called his brother. How can this be explained other than by the great respect afforded to Hermas in his capacity of a prophetic man, the bearer of revelations useful to the Church? If the community at Rome had not believed in post-apostolic revelations, it would never have recommended the reading of the *Shepherd*. Moreover, this was the first time that a book was rejected as being non-canonical although its reading was recommended. This compromise was something new.

It is easily understandable that the *Shepherd* should have been translated into Latin at an early date and that there existed a "vulgate" version of it available to anyone. We can scarcely exaggerate, therefore, the importance of this attitude of the Church of Rome. Was a like welcome reserved for the *Shepherd* in the other churches?

When Tertullian wrote his treatise on prayer (*de Orat.*, XII), he seemed to put the *Shepherd* on the same footing as Scripture. Certain people believed that they ought to take off their cloaks to pray and they felt obliged to go to bed after prayer. They founded their first belief on II Timothy 4: 13, and their second on the *Shepherd* (introduction to the precepts). Tertullian found such an interpretation of authorized texts ridiculous. From this passage we may conclude that Tertullian, whatever may have been his personal opinion of the *Shepherd,* assumed that his readers considered it to be a holy book.

But here is a testimony which carries even greater weight than that of Tertullian: St. Irenaeus considered the *Shepherd* as Sacred Scripture. Wishing to establish a scriptural argument for the creation of the world and of man by God the

Father, in the same way as other texts drawn from the Bible, he quoted in the *Adversus Haereses*, IV, 20, the *Shepherd* of Hermas which he explicitly called *Scripture:* "It is, therefore, fitting that Scripture says, 'Before all else believe that there is one God alone who created and organized the universe. . . .'" [34] This text reproduces word for word the opening phrases of the first precept of the *Shepherd.* Immediately after this, Irenaeus quoted Malachias 2: 10, Ephesians 4: 6, Genesis 2: 7, etc., employing for them the same introductory formula: "It is, therefore, fitting that among the prophets Malachias says. . . ." Introducing Genesis 11: 7, he wrote: "It is concerning this that Scripture says. . . ." It is obvious that St. Irenaeus would not have spoken in this way if competent men in Gaul had not shared his high opinion of the *Shepherd* of Hermas.

This opinion was no less high in the Church of Alexandria. Clement, the outstanding personality of this community, often quoted, in his *Stromata* and elsewhere, the book by Hermas. "But the *Shepherd*," he wrote, "the man of penance, says to Hermas, in respect to the false prophet: 'Certain words in fact are true, but the devil filled him with his spirit in order to procure the fall of a just man.'" [35] Later on Origen, like Clement, accepted the *Shepherd* and quoted it on many occasions in his book *On Principles*, but already he was referring to some opposition—certain people were rejecting Hermas's book.

Since the Church of Antioch was still in the third century in agreement with that of Alexandria, we may conclude that Hermas was in favor throughout the entire Eastern Church. One must wait for a long time before seeing the *Shepherd* begin to decline. Eusebius of Caesarea, who died in 339, spoke of it thus: "Since the Apostle Paul, in the final salutations of the Epistle to the Romans, makes mention, among others, of Hermas, of whom it is said that the book *The Shepherd* is his (sic), it should be known that this book is disputed by some, who would not rank it among the accepted books, but that others consider it very necessary, especially for those who need an elementary introduction. That is why we know now that it is read publicly in the Churches and I have established that certain of the earliest writers made use of it." [36]

St. Athanasius declared himself wholly in favor of the *Shepherd*. In his famous letter "Pascale" of 367 he ranked it among the books which, although not canonical, were recommended for spiritual formation and reading. He distinguished these books clearly from other writings which the Greeks called apocryphal. These were: *The Wisdom of Solomon, The Wisdom of the Son of Sirach*, Esther, Judith, Tobias, the so-called *Teaching of the Apostles* and the *Shepherd*.[36a] Thus the *Shepherd* was in good company!

After this, one is not surprised to find the *Shepherd* figure in the famous *Codex Sinaiticus* as if it were a canonical book. Zahn hardly exaggerates when he writes in his *History of the Canon:* "At the end of the second century the *Shepherd* passed for a sacred writing in the West as well as in the East. . . . The *Shepherd* was inserted into the cycle of sacred writings wherever it was recognized as an announcement of revelations destined for all Christianity." [37]

Undoubtedly the scriptural canon was still in the course of formation. It might be said that the authority enjoyed by the *Shepherd* was accorded to it through the mistake of the faithful in believing that it belonged to the apostolic age. But this belief was, it would seem, far from being general. And there had been other books which went back as far as the apostolic age and yet were not accepted as sacred books. However, all that is of little importance. What does matter is to establish that, if the sole question had been one of date, the *Shepherd* would have been rejected as soon as the late date of its composition became clearly known.

Now, nothing of the kind happened. In Rome, in that Church which was most important and doctrinally most balanced, the *Shepherd* was recommended although it was

known that it had been written under the pontificate of
Pius. Let us not forget that we are dealing with an apocalyptic book, the texture of which is formed by revelations—a
book, therefore, which was very vulnerable since it was not
protected by infallible canonicity. An example of this is furnished by the *Apocalypse of St. Peter* which the *Muratorian
Fragment* accepts with certain reservations as canonical—a
privilege never extended to the *Shepherd*—but which had
been ranked early with suspect books and which, having
completely disappeared, was only retrieved in 1880.

Hermas based his work, as Bardenhewer is bent on emphasizing, upon revelations, upon a divine mandate. "He presents himself as a prophet inspired by the Spirit of God.
Certainly he wished to give more force and a higher consecration to his warnings and his communications. The risk
of this causing scandal was small enough, for he wrote his
book at a time when there was still a general belief in the
permanence of the prophetic charism." [38]

It is for no other reason than this that for a long time
people continued to see good reading in the *Shepherd*. St.
Athanasius ranged it, as we have seen, among the books to
be read for Christian instruction like those, for example, of
Esther and of Judith. As for St. Jerome, it has been said that
he rejected the *Shepherd* in commenting on Habacuc (1, 14).
But it is doubtful whether his commentary referred to the
Shepherd, which is not named and which calls the angel in
question Hegrin and not Tyrus. However that may be, when
St. Jerome spoke *ex-professo* of the writers of the Church
he described the *Shepherd* as a "truly useful book." [39]

When the Church finally placed the *Shepherd* among the
apocrypha she did not at all desire to say that it was condemned or necessarily false. Tertullian, in so far as he was
a Montanist, owed it to himself to condemn it, which he did,
calling it "apocryphal and false." The word "apocryphal"
had at that time the meaning which it still retains—a book
which appears to arrogate to itself a divine authority, or one

formerly held to be sacred, but which in fact has not been accepted in the list of Sacred Books. The description does not, therefore, according to another and fairly common acceptance of the word, mean books of uncertain origin containing many false items mixed up with some true elements. It is by no means certain that we could apply either of these two meanings of "apocryphal" to Hermas' book. Indeed, the judgment of Dom le Nourry, in his introduction to the Latin version of the *Shepherd* in Migne, amply bears this out: "The common opinion of the Fathers, which seems more in conformity with the truth, is that they consider this book very useful and very suitable in the formation of a man recently converted to the Christian faith." [40] To emphasize its value, it has been called an "ecclesiastical book."

3   THE "NEW PROPHECY"

Origin and aim

At the moment when the *Shepherd* by Hermas was reaching the pinnacle of fame in the West, a powerful prophetic current was being released in the East. This occurred toward A.D. 172. Here is how a contemporary, the anonymous polemicist quoted by Eusebius, described its origin: "There is, it is said, in Mysia, on the frontier of Phrygia, a town called Ardabau. It is there, by all accounts, that first of all one of the new faithful, called Montanus, when Gratus was proconsul of Asia Minor, gave the enemy access to his soul through an immeasurable ambition for the highest places. Stirred by the spirit (of evil), he suddenly became as though possessed and seized by a false ecstasy, and he began, in these transports, to speak, to utter strange words and to prophesy in a manner wholly contrary to the traditional usage which is preserved by the old succession of the Church. Among those who at that time heard these spurious discourses, there were some who, importuned by him as by a frenzied demoniac and as one possessed by the spirit of error which agitated the masses, reproved him and hindered him from speaking, recalling the teaching of the Lord and His warning concerning the vigilance which must be maintained against the advent of false prophets. Others, on the contrary, as if exalted by the Holy Spirit and the charism of prophecy, and above all puffed up with pride and forgetful of the Lord's teaching, incited the frenzied spirit, the flatterer and seducer of the people, who were charmed and misled by him to the stage where they could no longer be compelled to be silent." [41]

Among those who were in this state of exaltation were to be found women. Two of them, Priscilla and Maximilla, soon began to manifest the same symptoms as Montanus. The activities of all three of them were mainly centered in the plain of Pepuza in Phrygia. They called this place Jerusalem, meaning by this the new Jerusalem of the Apocalypse. They spoke with such persuasion that their listeners were completely captivated by them, and the ecstatic and convulsive agitation took on such dimensions that it could not fail to have tremendous repercussions.

The "new prophecy," as it was soon called, made followers everywhere. It penetrated all the provinces of Asia Minor; whole communities were carried away by it and all the churches suffered at its hands. As early as A.D. 200, according to Von Harnack, the names of the new prophets were known among the Christians of Syria, in Egypt, in Rome, in North Africa and Gaul, as well as in Phrygia and Asia, and thousands of Christians from East and West received the message from Tymion and Pepuza with the same faith as if it had come from Nazareth or Jerusalem.[42]

We have no reason to challenge the testimony of Eusebius' anonymous polemicist upon the origin of the "new prophecy," for he was a contemporary of the first Montanists. But the affair he described was more complex than he would lead us to imagine. The constant invitation of the Montanists to a more ascetic life is proof that the need for this was felt in the Church. The *Shepherd* of Hermas, around A.D. 150, complained of moral laxity, and the book showed the need for penance. The elegant Greeks, and the Romans, disciplined and full of themselves, readily sneered at the Phrygians as poor, awkward, timid and ignorant people. But on the testimony of the historian Socrates, these Phrygians abstained from the circus games and controlled their passions better than all other peoples, hiding beneath a rather somber manner an ardent mysticism.

Christians, for whom the culture of the soul is the soul of all culture, ought to have had respect for them. Besides, Phrygia had been a country of predilection for St. Paul, who brought it the Faith and who loved to pursue his apostolic labors there (Acts 13; 14; 16: 6). Did not the Montanist preaching present itself as a recall to the teaching of the great Apostle and to the evangelical life? Further, the insistence placed on the parousia seemed to agree with the teaching of St. Paul and undoubtedly gave more pungency to this preaching.

But beneath this exaggerated asceticism were hidden more disquieting aims. The Cataphrygian prophets arrogated to themselves an authority higher than that of the bishops. The prophetesses assumed a large part in the government of the churches. All the doctrines of the Montanists, their organization and their tactics, were sustained by one conviction—the Trinity had opened Itself to humanity: this was now the great manifestation of the Holy Spirit! Didymus of Alexandria recounts this utterance by Montanus: "I am the Father, the Son and the Holy Spirit." [43] And Eusebius of Caesarea relates that zealots had the temerity to boast of Montanus as the Paraclete (*Hist. Eccl.*, v, 16–17).

There was a question here, we believe, of an identity which did not go beyond the psychological plane. At the very least Montanus believed that he was visited by the Holy Spirit in a unique and definitive way. That much the Montanists affirmed, Bible in hand. Besides, they always took care to note the links which united them with the past. Had not Christ promised to send the Paraclete (John 15: 26)? Had He not foretold: "When (the Paraclete), the Spirit of truth, is come, he will teach you all truth" (John 16: 13)? And had not the prophet Joel announced to the children of Israel that *in the last days* their sons and daughters would prophesy (Acts 2: 17)? Here in fact was the true meaning of Montanism: understood in the strict sense, as Père de Labriolle says, it was not simply a "tendency," a "spirit," a simple "moral direction." "It was belief in the mission of the Paraclete embodied in the person of Montanus—subsidiarily in the person of the prophetesses—and in the absolute value of his pronouncements." [44] Tertullian, turned Montanist, emphasized this basis of the prophetic movement of Montanus.

Reaction in the Church

This pseudo-prophetic trend was quickly stigmatized as "new prophecy." The term prophecy was used because the Cataphrygians spoke in the name of God. But this type of prophecy seemed new, that is to say, anti-traditional and therefore false in the eyes of the defenders of the orthodox Faith.

New, first of all, was the manner of prophesying. The traditional prophets did not prophesy, as did the Cataphrygians, in a state of ecstasy comprising obnubilation, even an eclipse of reason. In their case the agitation, the convulsions, the unknown words uttered in a state of delirium such as one observes here were unknown; they kept the use of their reason and understood everything they were saying.[45]

This aforesaid prophecy was new as regards its content and its principles. New was the claim, says Hilgenfeld, that the fullness of the Spirit had not come through the Apostles, nor even through Christ, but solely through Montanus and his companions, and that with them alone the time of true charisms began. Neither is the origin of the Montanist schism to be sought in the disciplinary regulations issuing from the Paraclete, but in the fundamental conception of the Paraclete as the last and supreme source of Revelation, to which the whole Church is subject.[46]

Montanism was not solemnly condemned by the Church. Regional synods, however, were organized to fight it. The different churches combated the error in proportion to the extent that it affected them, and all of them reacted in a wonderfully balanced Catholic manner. Now that the hierarchy was solidly established, it would have been easy to condemn all prophecy under the pretext of effectively fighting the "new prophecy," but the churches did not succumb to this temptation.

In the Eastern Church one of the first defenders of orthodoxy was the anonymous polemicist of Eusebius. He wrote: "The false prophet, in the false ecstasy which is accompanied by impudence and daring, begins with voluntary abandonment of reason and then reaches, as has been said, involuntary delirium of spirit. They cannot point to a single prophet, either in the Old Testament or in the New, who has been filled with the Holy Spirit in this manner. . . . If indeed, as they claim, according to Quadratus and Ammia from Philadelphia, the women who surrounded Montanus received through succession the prophetic charism, let them show some among the disciples of Montanus and of his women who have inherited it. For the Apostle considers that the prophetic charism must exist until the final parousia. But they would have no one to show since the death of Maximilla fourteen years ago." (*Hist. Eccl.,* v, 17, 4).

Later, at the end of the fourth century, St. Epiphanius, with still more force, spoke in the same way. While he did not always treat the heresies with suitable shades of difference, he replied pertinently to the "Phrygian pseudo-prophets." He did not blame them when they said:

We also have a duty to welcome charisms. For the Holy Church of God welcomes them, too, but (in her case) these are truly charisms, authenticated for her by the Holy Spirit. . . . (But) note that the very thesis which they defend convicts them of not being able to attain the object which their jealousy desires. For if we must welcome charisms, and if there be need of charisms in the Church, how does it come about that since Montanus, Priscilla and Maximilla they have no more prophets? Has grace then lost its force? *It has not come to a standstill, however, in the Holy Church; God forbid.*[47]

The saint expatiated upon the contradiction in which the pseudo-prophets imprisoned themselves—they propounded the law of the permanence of charisms, but at the same time they denied it by saying that after them there would be no more prophets. Epiphanius did not miss the point. So he stood up against the Alogi who sought to demolish the "new prophecy" by doing away with the Gospel of St. John upon which the disciples of Montanus believed they could build their teaching.

"These people," he wrote, "not accepting the Holy Spirit, are judged from the pneumatic point of view as understanding nothing of the things of the Spirit. They want to speak in conformity with reason and they do not recognize the charisms which are at work in the holy Church." [48]

At the time of which we are speaking, it was known that the Church in Gaul was in touch with the Eastern Christians. The Phrygian movement had scarcely been born when it was being talked of in Gaul. It was in A.D. 177 that the Christians of Lyons and of Vienne, who were held in high esteem because of their martyrs, wrote their famous letter "to the brethren in Asia and Phrygia." It is a testimony of very high spiritual worth. It mentioned Vettius Epagathus, who was "bubbling with the Spirit," and called him "the 'paraclete' of the Christians, possessing in fact the Paraclete, the Spirit, more fully than Zachary." But he manifested it through "the fullness of charity" [49] and not in the manner of the Montanists.

The attitude of St. Irenaeus is noteworthy. This Eastern Christian living in Lyons became the defender of the gift of prophecy at the very time when the Montanists were vaunting themselves as its chief beneficiaries. It is undoubtedly the Alogi, the extreme anti-Montanists, whom he is censuring when he writes in his work, *Against the Heresies,* composed between A.D. 180 and A.D. 192:

> Others, in order to suppress the gift of the *Spirit* which "in latter times, according as it has pleased the Father" has been poured out upon the human race, do not admit this form of the Gospel which is according to St. John and in which the Lord promised that He *would send the Paraclete;* but they reject both the *Gospel* and the prophetic *Spirit. They are indeed unhappy spirits who, because they do not wish to admit false prophets, would drive out the grace of prophecy even from the Church.* In that, they are like to those who, because of a few hypocrites to be found in the Church, refrain from even associating with the Brethren. It goes without saying that these same spirits no longer accept St. Paul. For in his first Epistle to the Corinthians he spoke in detail of the prophetic gifts and he knew men and women who "prophesied" within the Church. . . . Thus, by their whole attitude they sin against the "Spirit" of God and fall into the "unforgivable" sin.[50]

And no one could testify more explicitly than St. Irenaeus that there still existed men of the type the Apostles called spiritual, "these just men who have received the Spirit of God." The Bishop of Lyons continues:

We have heard speaking in the Church many brethren who possess the prophetic charisms; they speak by the Spirit in all languages and they reveal men's secrets. Heretics, it is true, claim to do as much; they even think that they are surpassing the Master. But what they are performing is Magic: through their tricks they delude the foolish. . . . The true disciples of the Son of God perform their charisms in His name for the good of others: some of them drive away demons, others have knowledge of things of the future, see visions and hold prophetic discourses, others cure the sick by the imposition of hands. . . .[51]

Individual heretics looked upon the Gallic Christians, including Irenaeus, as Montanists! In fact, they had simply been careful not to allow to escape that fraction of truth which was hidden in this heresy. They thought as Catholics.

Moreover, before he wrote his celebrated treatise, Irenaeus had presented himself before the Pope on behalf of his Church. And since he expressed himself so lucidly, there can be no doubt but that he was certain of the conformity of his doctrine with that of the Church of Rome. Precise indications allow us to think, indeed, that in Rome at this period the attitude to prophecies and revelations was favorable.

We are at the time when the *Shepherd* of Hermas was enjoying great authority there. Now we have seen that the *Shepherd* was a prophetic call to penance; it sought to awaken lukewarm and skeptical souls by heavenly messages. The *Shepherd* was, after all, looked upon as a phenomenon parallel to Montanism yet compatible with orthodoxy. When the "new prophecy" reached Rome, then, it found a favorable atmosphere. A text from Tertullian—and this is our second indication—confirms this. In the first chapter of the *Adversus Praxeam* he makes a sharp comment about Praxeas. This man, he says, accomplished two diabolical acts in Rome: "He drove out prophecy (the new!) and brought in heresy. He drove out the Paraclete and crucified the Father." [51a]

In fact, what happened? It is certain that the Pope showed himself favorable, at least at a certain time, to Montanist representatives. Tertullian went so far as to say: "He has already recognized the prophecies of Montanus, of Priscilla and of Maximilla and by this action he has brought peace to the Churches of Asia." The destructive work of Praxeas would bring this action to naught. But even if Tertullian was exaggerating, it is clear that the Church of Rome had knowledge, as had the other Churches, of the "new prophecy" and that it had displayed in this respect a lively sense of the permanence of the gift of prophecy in the Church.

4   IN THE AFRICAN CHURCH OF THE THIRD CENTURY

We cannot speak of the African Church of the third century without reference to Tertullian; his testimony has, however, a relative value only, especially with respect to the problem with which we are concerned. Many in Africa did not share his opinions, even before his separation from Rome which took place later, in A.D. 207. In Carthage the majority of the faithful remained united to the great Church; they continued to believe in prophetic charisms, in visions and in revelations, without, however, adhering to Montanism. One of the best proofs of this is provided by the *Acts of the Martyrdom of Sts. Perpetua and Felicitas.*

The Passion of Sts. Perpetua and Felicitas

Visions form an important part of the *Acts.* There are five of them. All are revelations also. In the first vision Perpetua succeeds in climbing a ladder guarded by a dragon. She finds herself in an immense garden where an old man, dressed as a shepherd, says to her: "It is well you are come, child." When she awakens she understands that she will not be set free and that she will have to endure martyrdom. Through the second vision, in which she recognizes her brother, dead for some time, seeking without success to quench his thirst, she learns that he is suffering and that she can help him. In the third vision she sees her brother Dinocrates drinking and amusing himself like a carefree child. On awakening she is convinced that her brother is no longer suffering. The fourth vision—experienced as before during sleep—apprises her that her victory is assured. She sees herself struggling against a terrible Egyptian. After her victorious struggle a majestic giant says to her: "Peace be with you, daughter!" Saturus, a prisoner like Perpetua, is likewise assured of the happy outcome of his martyrdom.

The *Acts* assure us that Perpetua and Saturus themselves wrote the account in their prison. Visions which are detailed and interpreted as revelations are an easy mark for criticism.

The account itself was placed between a prologue and an epilogue of which this is the substance: If former examples of faith and of divine grace were written down in books for the honor of God and the comfort of man, why should not the same be done, for the same ends, in regard to more recent happenings? Times change; but the strength of the Spirit remains the same. The prophets of Scripture, in regard to the latest times, teach us that the new deeds should surpass the old in the abundance of grace. That is why we recognize and honor the new prophecies and visions and we consider that they are at the service of the Church along with other resources of the Holy Spirit.

It is weakness of faith which makes people think that only the ancients were worthy of martyrdom or of revelations. God carries out what He has promised. That is why we are telling you what we have heard and what we have seen (1 John 1: 3), brethren and sons, so that you who were witnesses of them may not forget the glory of God. And the editor of the *Acts* insists in the epilogue: "He who adores Christ should read these examples, which have no less value for the edification of the Church than those of the early martyrs and saints. Thus there will be proof of the fact that the Holy Ghost, always one and the same, continues to perform new works right up to the present time." [52]

For a very long time critics attributed the *Acts* of these martyrs to Tertullian. But this opinion is not very tenable because the content of the account is not characteristic of Tertullian, inasmuch as at this period there was current belief in visions. The testimonies on this point are innumerable; Père de Labriolle himself recognizes this even though he shares the opinion which we are disputing. The principal argument of the critics is, moreover, rather weak. Identity of words does not always prove identity of author, especially if one considers the richness of Tertullian's vocabulary and the scope of his work. Tertullian was read closely by members of the clergy in Carthage; the editor of the *Acts* was probably one of these. We know how very easily the usage of words becomes general in an identical milieu, in the same city. Then the style is solid and solemn. One could classify it as official and as typical of someone in authority. The editor speaks like a bishop when he says: my brethren and my sons. . . . We are far away from the mastery of style and the tricks of rhetoric of the born lawyer which Tertullian was, who expresses himself in images, antitheses and in the play of words. But he lacks that simplicity which characterizes the *Acts of Perpetua and Felicitas*.

Besides, if Tertullian had edited this account, why did he not later on make more of these facts, known to all, and facts which would have been of great service to his ends? He mentions them only once and even then is confused. In the *De Anima* (chap. 55: P.L., 2, 789) he attributes to Perpetua the vision of Saturus. Is not this incomprehensible in the light of the hypothesis of which we are speaking?

Let us note that even those critics who believe Tertullian to have been the editor of these *Acts* admit that they are not characteristically Montanist. Furthermore, in view of their date—the latest is A.D. 204—Tertullian would have had to draw them up before his break with Rome. In any event, even if it could be proved that Tertullian put them together in his Montanist days, the value of the sources which he transcribed would remain intact. And the work itself would retain its value; for it has been accepted by the whole of Tradition. Anyhow, these martyrs who appear in the canon of the Mass among the very rare non-Roman saints, were not Montanists. Here is the opinion of an exacting judge upon the subject. Delehaye, who sees in the *Acts* in question "the masterpiece of hagiographical literature," writes: "The Passion of Perpetua presents itself to us not as a manifesto of Montanism, but as a faithful narration of what passed in a community where the new doctrines had made their influence felt."[53]

This moving Passion is psychologically and theologically authentic. In it are united vivacity of impressions, clarity of exposition, and a great warmth of feeling, all of which could only be those of an author who had just lived through what he was describing and did not have to search for words.[54] It so happens that we have the opinion of a psychologist in favor of the authenticity of an account which can only be understood by a believer. "The general impression," we read in a study edited by Jung, "does not permit us to reduce these visions to literary fiction. From the psychological point of view one may further note that there is no one purely Christian theme running through all the visions; there are only archetypal images. . . . If anyone had wanted to invent these images for the purpose of edification he would surely have used obviously Christian themes."[55]

Besides, as notes Adolf von Harnack, for whom the *Acts of Perpetua and Felicitas* are "the pearl of the early martyrs," it would have been easy to refute them.[56] The events were, in fact, known and they occurred prior to Diocletian; the circumstances did not as yet allow of embellishment.

The testimony of Tradition with respect to the Passion of St. Perpetua is more important than these commendations. The attitude of St. Augustine will be sufficient for us to show that this testimony is favorable. Augustine must certainly have handled a complete edition of the *Acts* for he quoted a number of details which could have had no other source. He spoke frequently of Perpetua and Felicitas whom he calls "saints." He preached in their honor on many occasions. We learn from his writings that these *Acts* were well known, commonly accepted and highly valued, to such an extent that the Bishop of Hippo felt obliged to state that the book was not canonical. He did so in replying to the monk René who was using the Passion of Perpetua as a theological argument. Augustine did not criticize him on this point; he himself made a long theological reflection on the theme of the struggle engaged in by Perpetua in her dream about the horrible Egyptian. He exalted the Passion and the "divine revelations" of these celebrated saints and he bore witness to the religious respect with which their exhortations were accepted in his time.[57]

St. Cyprian

Critics have said that the hierarchy practically obliterated the gift of prophecy in the Church in its fight against Montanism. It is quite enough to read at random through the writings of St. Cyprian to be convinced of the falsity of this assertion.

A remarkable thing is that this saint, who was a veritable champion of the episcopal authority to which he assigned a central position in the Church, as did St. Ignatius, believed nevertheless in private revelations. Sometimes he even re-

lied, in the exercise of his episcopal power, upon communications which he stated he received from God.

St. Cyprian noted revelations in his entourage. In Epistle
16: 4, he wrote: "Amongst us, innocent boys receive from
the Holy Spirit, not only nocturnal visions but others in the
daytime, and in ecstasy see with the eyes and hear and utter
things by which the Lord deigns to admonish and instruct
us." [58] We note the fact that heavenly communications were
received not only by the children in Cyprian's entourage, but
also by Cyprian himself.

Many examples of them could be quoted. In a circular letter to his clergy on prayer, Cyprian, dwelling upon the subject of particular revelations, said:

> You ought to know that what has particularly urged me to write this
> letter is that the Lord deigns to show and to reveal Himself (*ostendere
> et revelare*). In a vision it was said: "Ask and you shall be heard favor-
> ably." The people began to pray. . . . And behold what appeared:
> The father of a family was seated and a young man came to sit at his
> right hand. This young man appeared disturbed and grieved, even
> affected by a certain indignation, and sat, his chin on his hand and
> with a grave air. Another, seated at the left hand, carried a net and
> threatened to fling it out and gather in the assembled crowd. And as the
> one who saw this watched in amazement, he was told that the young
> man on the right was saddened and grieved because the Command-
> ments were not observed, while he on the left was rejoicing at the
> opportunity which the father of the family would give him to inflict
> punishment. . . . And we see the realization of this vision, for when
> we ignore the precepts of the Lord and do not practice the salutary
> commandments of the law, the enemy obtains the opportunity of de-
> stroying and of gathering into his nets those who are least armed and
> least able to defend themselves.[58a]

We are dealing here with a classic vision—the Father is in
the middle, Christ on the right, Satan on the left. Even in his
pastoral ministry St. Cyprian relied upon revelations. He
officially defended, in a long letter addressed to Caecilius
the tradition according to which the Eucharist should be

celebrated with wine and not with water. Before coming to the biblical arguments, he said:

> Do not think, dear brother, that we are writing to you of personal and human things, or arbitrarily upon our own initiative, for with a humble and discreet moderation we remain always in the common condition. When God inspires and ordains (*Deo inspirante et mandante*), the faithful servant must obey the Lord. Everyone understands, then, that it is not that he is impudently arrogating anything to himself but that he should fear to offend the Lord by not doing what he is commanded. Know then that we have been admonished that in offering the chalice the tradition of the Lord is respected (note 1). He returns to this latter theme at the end of his letter: If someone among our predecessors through ignorance or for some other reason did not observe what the Lord taught us . . . he may be pardoned, but we, we will not be excused; we may no longer *now* ignore what we have indeed been admonished and instructed, that we offer the chalice of the Lord filled with wine, as the Lord offered it.[58b]

Not everyone favored Cyprian's insistence upon revelations. He had written to Florentius: "I remember what was shown to me. . . . He who has graciously wished to show and to reveal different things has also added this: 'He who does not believe in Christ who instituted the priesthood will begin later on to believe in Christ the avenger of the priest.' " Cyprian added: "I know that dreams seem ridiculous and unseemly to some, especially to those who prefer to believe in opposition to the priest rather than to believe the priest."[58c]

The Bishop of Carthage had enemies. This forceful personality would not seem to have been elected by a very large majority. This possibly explains the criticism of his attitude toward revelations. But it may be that this criticism had deeper roots and that it was bound up with the anti-Montanist reaction. Ever since this crisis, as a matter of fact, there have always been tendencies in the Church for and against particular revelations.

A curious fact is that there are Protestants who admire Cyprian in that he was able to unite in himself the bishop and the prophet, the hierarchy and pneumatism. On the other hand, there are Catholics who are ready to connect the prophetic aspect of Cyprian with the Montanism of Tertullian. It is possible that "among the factors which went to form his religious knowledge the subjective element assumed a large and rather abnormal role." But this is not proved. Before passing judgment, account must be taken of the situation of the Church in the third century and of Cyprian's situation in particular. Absent for a long time from his church, which he had left under orders from God—according to his biographer—and finding himself in a situation which made decisions very difficult because of persecution, Cyprian had been able to receive visions which, in more regular circumstances, he would possibly not have received.

In his hiding place he had unceasing recourse to God in prayer, which in his letters he earnestly recommended to his followers. It would be instructive to study the letters which the associates of Cyprian sent him, for example, those of Lucius or of Felix. In the first, one reads this: "By your words you have taught us something we know so little of, and you have strengthened us to endure the sufferings which we now undergo, certain of heavenly reward, of the crown of martyrdom and of the Kingdom of God, as the result of the prophecy which, filled with the Holy Spirit, you have given us in your letters. All this will happen to us, dearly beloved, if you keep us present in spirit in your prayers." [58d] It is safer to believe with the martyrs in the holy bishop's prophetic gifts than to judge them as did Florentius, who calumniated Cyprian by reproaching him with sins of impurity. He also was on his guard against pseudo-prophets.[58e]

One may have reasons to be skeptical about the authenticity of his revelations. But the fact remains that tradition has generally accepted them, as also the collection of his writings. It is not the authenticity of such revelations which counts here, but the attitude of the Church toward revelations in general.

5   ST. AUGUSTINE

If it is surprising to see a man of action of the stamp of St. Cyprian so strongly influenced by revelations, it is no less so to observe the insignificant role played by miracles and revelations in the personal life of St. Augustine. When one considers the delicate sensibility of this African, his outstanding holiness and his immense influence on Christians right down to our own day, one would expect a life interwoven with, or at least accompanied by, all sorts of charisms.

The miracle, writes Bardy, held practically no place in his life. Possidius, his biographer, attributes to him the cure of some people possessed by the devil and he relates with some detail how in the course of Augustine's last illness he restored health to a sick child. And that is all.

The amazing thing is that even legend has respected St. Augustine, so intensely human did he show himself despite his sublime eminence.

So revelations held little or no place in his life. It is true that in Book 8, chapter 12, of his *Confessions* we find this account of a children's song which led him to the decisive reading of his life: "I said that (Until when? Tomorrow? . . . Why not now? Why not immediately finish with my shame?) and I wept in all the bitterness of a broken heart. And immediately I heard coming out of a neighbouring house what sounded like the voice of a child or of a young girl who sang and frequently repeated: 'TAKE AND READ! TAKE AND READ!'"

But it is not certain that we are here dealing with a revelation. That is the least one may say. If one wants to take into account what Pierre Courcelle has to say on the matter in his *Recherches sur les Confessions de Saint Augustin* (chap. 5), if the *"Tolle, lege"* of the scene of the occurrence in the Milan garden is not a literary fiction, nor a hallucination, nor an illusion, but a true revelation, it is unique in the life of the Bishop of Hippo.

Its content, in any case, is extremely meager. It is through the Bible and not through a revelation that Augustine learned what he must do. He had nothing of the visionary in him. He did not behave in the least like St. Cyprian for whom revelations were an instrument of his pastoral ministry. It is curious that despite his immense influence on the centuries to come, the great Bishop of Hippo has never enjoyed the reputation of "prophet" in the wider sense of the meaning given to this word. His genius, drawing its inspiration from the Bible and from facts, was simply a reflection upon the world and upon history of divine grace in souls. He displayed severity toward every species of divination and the revelations, even true ones, which they might express. There was here, he wrote in the *Doctrina Christiana,* a very pernicious error (L. II, cp. 23., p. 34, 52).

That is not to say that he rejected a priori all particular revelation. But he thought, as do many experts in this matter, that it was very difficult to distinguish the true revelations from the false. In practice one must have the help of the Holy Spirit—the gift of discretion.[58f] So he recounted that his mother was able instinctively to distinguish true visions from false ones. She particularly desired to know what she ought to do in the matter of her son's marriage; she waited for the light of a heavenly communication. In fact, she did perceive something, but she recognized it as an illusion and spurned it (cf. *Confessions,* 6, 13).

In certain cases St. Augustine frankly admitted special revelations. He took seriously the visions of St. Perpetua, as we have noted. When he recalled the anguished situation of St. Cyprian, exposed to the attacks of his persecutors, here is how he expressed himself: "His heart," he wrote, "was always ready; what is more, he was strengthened by the revelation of the Lord." The context leaves no doubt; he was speaking here of particular revelations: it was a question of divine exhortations.[58g]

One fact which should have aroused the warmth of popular piety in the time of St. Augustine was the discovery of the body of St. Stephen. Now this occurrence was due, according to the Bishop of Hippo and his contemporaries, to a divine revelation. The body of Stephen the martyr, wrote Augustine, "has remained hidden until our days; but recently, at the moment desired by God, it was discovered, thanks to a divine revelation," as happens generally in the case of the bodies of martyr-saints. But it was revealed to the one who was to find these relics and to display them. For their place was shown by miracles performed beforehand and only by revelation was the place found.[58h]

In his correspondence with his confrère, Bishop Evodius, he mentioned the question of heavenly communications. He related, for example, that his "beloved doctor" who was known by everyone had been cured of his doubts regarding the future life by amazing dreams. Although St. Augustine was conscious of the danger of illusion in such cases, he seemed convinced that the instruction given in the dream was a mark of the providence and mercy of God.[58i]

Finally, it is worth the trouble to quote in full a particular revelation which St. Augustine related as an historical fact in the sermon on "the destruction of the city." Beginning with the text from Daniel: "As I prayed and confessed my sins and the sins of my people," he asked himself the following questions: Why have the human race and the people of God been chastised? Why was Rome sacked? Here is his answer: If we look more closely at it, God has spared the city. For the holy souls who died there are in heaven; contented and free from all oppression, they there thank God. In the long run the city is the inhabitants and not the walls. If the inhabitants are safe the city is safe.

To illustrate this theory he gave the following account:

A few years ago, under the reign of Arcadius, did not God want to frighten the inhabitants of Constantinople in order to correct them, convert them and lead them to a purer life? (Many of my listeners perhaps know this episode; there are even some who were in Constantinople at that time.) He revealed (*venit in revelatione*) to one of His faithful servants, a soldier, who remained faithful to him, that fire from heaven would destroy the city. He ordered him to speak of it immediately to the bishop. The latter, when informed, took the revelation seriously and spoke to the people. The whole city became converted to penance as had Nineveh in other times. But to prevent the people from thinking that the soldier had been deceived, or had wanted to deceive others, the day promised by God arrived. All the people, worried and gnawed by fear, were awaiting the end. Then it became almost like night, a cloud of fire arose from the East, small in size at first but swelling as it drew nearer to the city until it covered it completely. The inhabitants were terrified at the sight of the fire which threatened them so dreadfully and at the smell of sulphur. They took refuge in the church which was not very large. They tried to get baptism from anyone who could give it. It was not only in the church, but even in the houses, in the districts and on the public street that people sought to obtain the Sacrament of salvation. They wanted to avoid the anger of God, not now indeed, but for the future life. By this great trial God made known the faith and the revelation of His servant. Then the cloud began to diminish just as it had grown, and, little by little, it disappeared.[58]

It would be interesting to reflect upon this text and to compare it with others of a similar nature which we find in the documents of the following centuries, but we are here treating of the existence of revelations solely in the writings of the Fathers.

For St. Augustine this particular revelation was a fact. The fact was public. The visionary was a soldier, not a pious woman retired from the world. This soldier did not himself disseminate his revelation in any sort of way. He communicated it to the ecclesiastical authority. There was in this a favorable sign. A very remarkable thing was that God determined to make plainly manifest the authenticity of the revelation. The people, when they saw that the city remained intact despite the destruction foretold, could easily have said: "This was a false revelation; in doing penance the whole city has allowed itself to be guided by a seer or someone with hallucinations. . . ." But if God wished to spare the city because of the penance done by its inhabitants, He also desired to show, through the terrible cloud of fire, that the revelation of the soldier was true. Our text says explicitly: "By this great trial God made known the faith and the revelation of His servant" (cf. note 58j).

With these views of St. Augustine we shall conclude our study of revelations in the first centuries of Christianity. The limitations of our study do not require us to pursue them further. We wish only to demonstrate that the charism of revelations did not disappear with the apostolic age or after the Montanist crisis, but that its permanence was subsequently affirmed even after the peace of Constantine. We should like to add the testimonies of the Greek Fathers, but are obliged to restrict ourselves to the framework of our study which is doctrinal and not historical in aim. For the same reason we have not developed the problem of charisms and of martyrs, contenting ourselves with pointing to the case of the martyrdom of Sts. Perpetua and Felicitas which is very enlightening upon this problem. We should have liked to have noted other aspects complementary to our subject, which is immense and very complex, but the testimonies of the Greek witnesses whom we have just quoted retain their value, even if we have not been able to make a complete study of them.

Even with St. Cyprian and St. Augustine, whom we have

studied with more attention, we have presented only those aspects most pertinent to our subject. Except for the passage of the *De cura pro mortuis gerenda* we have deliberately neglected the testimony of St. Augustine when, advanced in age, he showed himself less critical, as at the end of his *City of God* (cf. L. 22, c. 8).

In the final analysis, let us repeat: it is not the authenticity of this or that revelation with which this study is concerned but the positive attitude of the representatives or witnesses of the Church in regard to revelations. Let us suppose that St. Cyprian or even St. Augustine had believed in a revelation which was actually only a pious hallucination; the fact would still remain that their belief is an argument in favor of the affirmation of the prophetic charism in the Church of their time.

If we stop at this point in our study of the Fathers it is because we have good reasons for so doing. No one among them reflected so much upon revelations and apparitions as did St. Augustine, and his attitude toward them was generally adopted by the Fathers of the following centuries. Here, as in other domains, his influence made itself felt throughout the whole of the Latin Church. So his reflections, in particular those in the twelfth chapter of his commentary on Genesis, have inspired in great measure the doctrinal expositions upon revelations which have been formulated from the Middle Ages down to the present day.

If, despite our preoccupation with doctrine, we have tried to note the chief historical facts of the attitude of the Church's representatives in regard to revelations, that is precisely because it was necessary to seek in the first centuries of the post-apostolic age the best proofs of the Church's admission of the existence of revelations. It was a question of proving that if public Revelation came to an end with the death of the last Apostle, God did not cease to communicate with men and consequently that all revelation did not come to an end.

Since the historical parts of this work are only a means of arriving at the doctrinal synthesis which is our aim, we can and must, for the period which extends from the fifth century to our day, content ourselves with pointing out certain guideposts in the history of the attitude toward revelations in order to furnish sufficient evidence to show that this history has developed in the same direction as in the first centuries. We shall therefore touch only upon the most important movements and events which gave rise to doctrinal reaction within the Church.

CHAPTER IV

From the Middle Ages to Our Own Times

1   JOACHIMISM

TOWARD THE END of the twelfth century the intellectual and spiritual life of the Middle Ages was stamped by Augustinian thought. It is true that a new doctrinal orientation was in preparation, but it did not begin to make itself felt until the thirteenth century. We are not thinking of the "baptism of philosophy" which concluded by consecrating the authority of Aristotle. We are referring here to a less important movement, namely, Joachimism.

Joachimism was an apocalyptic movement which had been set in motion by a certain monk called Joachim, born in Calabria, a country where the blood is warm and the faith well anchored in men's hearts, and which is to Italy something of what Phrygia was to Asia Minor. Joachim left his Cistercian Abbey around the year 1191 and founded a monastery in the mountain fastness of La Sila not far from Cosenza—San Giovanni da Fiore.

The "Abbot of Fiore" seems to have been a genuine contemplative. And he loved study without, however, being an

74

armchair theologian. Very soon he enjoyed the reputation of being a saint and a visionary, and in fact conducted himself in the manner of a prophet in attacking the abuses of his time. Due to his writings, his reputation spread beyond the limits of his own country. His errors on the subject of the Trinity straightaway made his influence dangerous, but his theory regarding the periods of the world (*status mundi*) assured him, for all that, a lasting success.

He divided history into three periods. The first extends from the origin of the world to the coming of Christ; the second from Christ's coming to the year 1260; the third from then until the end of the world. The first period is that of the Father, the second that of the Son, and the third that of the Holy Spirit. On the ecclesiastical level the periods correspond respectively to that of the laity, of clerics, and of monks. In each period one draws from a certain source. In that of the Father this source is the writings of the Old Testament; in that of the Son it is Christ's Gospel; in that of the Holy Spirit it is the "eternal Gospel."

What is this gospel? It is that which St. John saw in the Apocalypse: "And I saw another angel flying through the midst of heaven, having the eternal gospel (*euangélion*) to preach unto them that sit upon the earth, and upon every nation, and tribe, and tongue, and people" (Apoc. 14: 6). It is not a matter of a third written Testament, but of a gospel which emanates from that of Christ as the spiritual content emerges from the letter. It is spiritual intelligence (*intellectus spiritualis*) given by the Holy Spirit. Thus the eternal gospel emerges from the Old and New Testament as the Holy Spirit from the Father and the Son. "In the letter of the Old Testament, which is, so to speak, primitive knowledge, we must recognize the image of the Father," wrote the Abbot of Fiore textually, "in the letter of the New, which is the letter of the letter, we must recognize the image of the Son, and in the spiritual understanding which proceeds from both, the image of the Holy Spirit." [59]

Everything written is temporal. In the period of the Holy
Spirit the letter passes, like everything which is temporal,
carnal, material. The Church remains spiritual, and the Holy
Spirit works fully in her through the eternal gospel and the
sacraments. It is natural that only the spiritual men, that is
to say, the contemplative religious of the third period, should
preach the eternal gospel. They represent, in fact, the image
of the Holy Spirit who "commences in all truth." [60]

This doctrine is not expressed so succinctly in the writings
of Joachim. It is wrapped up in indisputable facts and formulated in such vague and symbolical terms that one can understand the surprising indulgence of religious opinion and
ecclesiastical authority toward the Calabrian abbot.

Equally explicable are the false interpretations of this doctrine, above all if one realizes that at this period apocalyptic
ideas were in fashion and that the religious and secular development of life seemed to herald the imminence of great
upheavals. In addition, a coincidence was bound to give a
further impetus to this outlook. Very shortly after the death
of Joachim, the mendicant orders were founded with immense success and this fact could have appeared to be a
justification of the predictions of the Abbot of Fiore. Seeing
the new horizons of their apostolate in a changing world,
fervent religious found it difficult not to be impressed by
this apparent fulfillment. They also might have found a personal interest in being considered as the spiritual men of this
last period of the world.

In fact, some mendicant religious did exploit the prestige
of Joachim to achieve ends of which he himself would never
have dreamed. They mixed ideas of the celebrated abbot
with others which had a certain affinity with them. They
saw new revelations in his vague interpretations of biblical
prophecies; they made his authentic utterances suit their
own line of thought; they ascribed to him pseudo-epigraphs
which more or less altered his ideas. It is not surprising that
among the religious who adopted what was later to be called

Joachimism there were some Franciscans. Since large numbers of these were still laymen, they were, by their cult of poverty and their way of life, more opposed than others to the traditional boundaries of society; they formed a nucleus which was more disposed to receive the "eternal gospel."

Thus the Franciscan Gerard de Borgo San Donnino in 1254 published his *Introduction to the Eternal Gospel.* But this gospel is no longer simply the full understanding of Christ's Gospel, but a new canonical writing for the third period of the world. Henceforth Holy Scripture has three parts: the Old Testament, the New Testament and the eternal gospel. This latter is composed of three main works of Abbot Joachim—the *New Apocalypse*, the *Harmony of the New and Old Testament,* and the *Harp with Ten Strings.*

According to Father Gerard, the Franciscan Order was raised up to preach the eternal gospel. And St. Francis, who had nothing in common with Joachim, as Fioberti and many others prove, became the angel of the revelation. Some were less adventurous though they still allowed themselves to be swept along by the movement: it would seem that for Peter Olivi the third period had been revealed to Joachim and that St. Francis was the apostle of these latter times. Joachimism was bound to have a remarkable influence which extended very far into religious history.

It is a fact that the *Introduction to the Eternal Gospel* was condemned by Alexander IV, but we should not forget that it was published six years before the year 1260, the date when the period of the Holy Spirit was to begin! A religious epidemic broke out then—remember the Flagellants. It was also around the year 1260 that there appeared in Milan a woman named Wilhelmina, who soon acquired a great reputation for sanctity. A group of disciples followed her and were convinced that she was the incarnation of the Holy Spirit in female form as Christ was the incarnation of the Son in masculine form. After her death her disciples awaited her triumphal reappearance and the inauguration of the reign of the Holy Spirit over all mankind (D.T.C., VIII, p. 1447).

Joachimist ideas fashioned the Fraticellians, the Beghards and the Beguines. It has even been said that it was these ideas which urged Dante to write his masterpiece. However that may be, the great poet who wrote the line: "Rabano is here, and at my side the Abbot Joachim of Calabria, endowed with the prophetic spirit, sheds his radiance," [60a] certainly had a high opinion of the Abbot of Fiore. And from the thirteenth century to the present day a multitude of "prophets" and of sects, in the style of the "vintrasiens," have owed more than perhaps they realized to Joachimism in which the views of the Montanists reappeared.

What we have just said about Joachimism throws light not only upon the question which concerns us now, but also upon other aspects of our study which we shall examine later on. If we have lingered over this movement, it is chiefly because of the reaction which it engendered. We again note that the traditional teaching regarding particular revelations was confirmed and made more explicit at the very time when a big prophetic movement deviated from orthodoxy and when an infatuation for revelations did considerable harm in the Church.

The reaction against Joachimism came quickly. It is unnecessary to describe it in detail. It is sufficient for us to say that the Church which condemned Joachim's teaching upon the Trinity refrained from doing the same with respect to his other teachings, and that the most competent doctors have emphasized the persistence of revelations in the history of the Church. The most authoritative theologians even among the mendicants were too clear-sighted to fall into Joachimism: the attitude of Alexander of Hales, of St. Bonaventure and of St. Albert plainly demonstrates this; but we shall confine ourselves chiefly to David of Augsburg and St. Thomas Aquinas.

David of Augsburg was a Franciscan. Totally dedicated to

the formation of his friars and to the evangelization of the people, he reacted with vigor against the apocalyptic tendencies in the milieu in which he carried on his ministry: "The revelation of things which are hidden or are still to come," he wrote, "seems to be the achievement of many. But many are the victims of illusion—as in the visions which already have been questioned—and attribute to the Holy Ghost what they have invented in their own minds or under the influence of a spirit of error. That is why we are flooded to saturation point (*jam usque ad fastidium repleti*) by all sorts of prophecies upon the coming of the Antichrist, signs of the judgment to come, the destruction of religion, the persecution of the Church, the defection of Christians, the calamities which are bound to fall upon the world, et cetera. There is no shortage of serious and pious men who have given an exaggerated adherence to all this; the same is true of the writings of Joachim and of others who prophesy by interpretations of all kinds." [61]

But while David of Augsburg was convinced that the majority of people were misled by revelations and visions, he equally declared that thanks to them others were turned toward the truth.[61a] And he wrote in his third book, *On the Exterior and Interior Formation of Man* . . . some masterly pages on revelations and visions. He laid down a classification of revelations, emphasized that other charisms are superior to them, and indicated the reasons for illusions in this matter, etc.

St. Thomas, who surely had nothing of the visionary about him, was familiar both with Joachimism and the excessive reaction it provoked, especially among the secular clergy. He stood out against this. He mentioned Joachim, who was not, in his eyes, a heretic. The Abbot of Fiore was neither a pseudo- nor a genuine prophet: he spoke of mysteries and revelations, but he lacked a solid theological training.

In any event, St. Thomas, who loved the great sources and who saw everything *sub specie aeternitatis,* accepted the prophecies and the revelations which they assume, as facts which never cease to occur in the history of the Church: "In every age men have been instructed by God as to what they should do, according as it was expedient for the salvation of the elect" (*Sum. Theol.*, II–II, 174, 6) ". . . and at every period there have never been lacking men having the spirit of prophecy, not, in truth, for developing a new doctrine of faith, but for directing human activity" (*ibid.*, ad 3). We shall see in the third part of our study the importance of this latter statement.

In his many works the Angelic Doctor speaks quite often of prophecy upon which he gives us a whole treatise in his *Summa Theologica*. He says not only that all prophecy supposes a revelation, but for him the most perfect prophecy is that which is communicated by dialogue between two people who see one another, as is typically the case with apparitions (*Sum. Theol.*, II–II, 171, 1 ad 4; 174, 3). He even thinks that, in certain cases, God sends an angel to reveal the Christian truths, for example, to persons who cannot be reached by the preachers (*Sum. Theol.*, II–II, 2, 7 ad 3; 172, 6 ad 1). And in the *Prima Secundae* he asks himself if it is possible to know whether one is in a state of grace. Then he replies: Man cannot arrive at this knowledge by himself. He can attain to only a certain conjectural knowledge by the examination of certain signs. There remains one other method— revelation. "In this manner one can know if one is in the state of grace: God reveals it, in fact, sometimes to certain people through a special privilege" (*Sum. Theol.*, I–II, 112, 5; I, 23, 1 ad 4).

There is no doubt upon this matter. For St. Thomas, God has not remained silent ever since the death of the last Apostle; but He continues to communicate with men, not only through grace, but also through revelations in order to guide the moral and spiritual life of men according to the designs of His providence. The great theologian based this teaching upon the facts which he had been able to observe in his own time and in the past. It was later to be confirmed, as we shall see from the following paragraph.

2   THE REVELATIONS OF ST. BRIDGET

In the Church women are excluded from the priesthood and the entire preaching function is denied to them. One might be tempted to deduce from this that they have nothing to say in the Christian community, especially since certain facts might seem to confirm this first impression—no woman has ever been the bearer of public revelation and no book of Scripture has been written by a woman. Yet is not St. Teresa considered a doctor of the Church? And is not her book *The Abodes of the Soul* comparable with the *Treatise on the Love of God* of St. Francis de Sales or the *Ascent of Mount Carmel* by St. John of the Cross? The doctrinal authority of St. Teresa is, in fact, recognized by the Church.

These facts are beyond any question; nevertheless, it can be stated generally that any important doctrinal influence exercised by a woman in the Church has always been based on the conviction that her doctrine was not purely acquired but was due at least in part to divine revelation. Thus this influence is chiefly explained by the role played by prophecy among the people of God or in the Church.

In fact, the Old and the New Testaments both mention prophetesses of renown. And it seems plain that the prophecy of Joel quoted by St. Peter on the day of Pentecost, "Your sons and your daughters shall prophesy," applies to the whole Messianic period. If the Church, especially after the crisis of Montanism, showed a certain reserve with respect to prophetesses, she nevertheless was not hostile to female prophecy—the reasons given in its favor by the Montanists had a scriptural foundation—but merely felt obliged to condemn the importance and the privileges which were being attached to this prophetic character.

Throughout history we observe how often, thanks to the gift of prophecy or of revelation, women became lights in the Church and, as a result, comparable with men charged with a hierarchical mission. If St. Hildegarde of Bingen, who died in 1179, was able to become the counselor of great numbers of poor people and notables, if she was a source of knowledge and wisdom for her contemporaries, if she did so much for the edification and the reform of Christian people, it was because she lived continually from her childhood in the world of visions. And if God made her His "messenger, His explorer of consciences," it was because she had the gift of revelation, as her biographers state. She wrote upon the order of God: "Ember of embers," we read in her writings included in Migne's *Patrology*, "dust of dust, say and write what you see and hear" (P.L., 107, 383).

If St. Gertrude is called "the Great," if she has had a powerful influence on the intelligences and hearts of the faithful, and if that influence is still felt—she has been called "doctor and prophet of the interior life"—it is thanks to the revelations she received. They were published under the title *Messenger of Divine Love* (*Legatus divini amoris*). Moreover, as she herself relates, it was through a vision of Christ, on January 27, 1281, that she was converted.

We could cite equally Catherine of Genoa, Catherine of Siena, Magdalen de Pazzi, Angela da Foligno, Margaret Mary Alacoque and other saints. In the interests of our study we will examine a particular case in some detail, and have chosen as an example the revelations of St. Bridget.

Bridget of Vadstena, born in 1303, belonged to an illustrious Swedish family. She was married at fifteen years of age and had eight children. This was a case of a strong-minded woman married to a weak man. Not only did she carry out her duties as mother and wife, but she also displayed her ability in the administration of her great possessions and in her duties at the royal court. As first Lady to the Queen, Blanche of Namur, she had the opportunity of observing the political life of Europe at close quarters. But what interested her most was the spiritual life.

With the aid of theologians, she studied the Bible and the religious literature of her time. In 1340 she abandoned court life, and with her husband made a pilgrimage to the shrine of St. James of Compostella. After their return her husband died. She then, in 1344, left her house at Ulvasa and retired as an oblate into a guest house of the monastery of Alvastra. It was there that she began to receive the revelations which were to have such immense repercussions in the Church.

She was initiated into her mission as God's messenger in a fashion which recalls the vocation of the great prophets. In an ecstasy she saw a radiant image and heard a voice: "I am your God who wishes to speak to you." She was terrified; she feared that it was the devil, and an illusion. But she heard the voice again: "Do not be afraid. I am the Creator of all things, not the deceiver. Know that I do not speak only for you alone, but for the salvation of Christians. Listen then to what I say." (*Revel. extravagantes,* cap. 47; see note 62).

From this time on Bridget often received revelations. Editors separate them into four periods: the Swedish, the Roman, and two others marked by pilgrimages in Italy and in Palestine. These revelations were addressed to everyone: to the poor, to the noble, to kings and to princes of the Church. They had as their subject Swedish sovereignty, the indifference of Christians, the Church, the Blessed Virgin, etc. There were messages for Pope Clement VI at Avignon, urgings for the Pope's return to Rome, and quite often re-

proaches of the Lord such as those we find in the first pages
of her revelations:

. . . Then I wished that this hallowed body would be bruised from the
soles of the feet to the head, nailed to the cross, for the sins of all men.
It is this too which is offered every day upon the altar, which should all
the more increase man's love for me and reawaken his recognition of
all the benefits which I have lavished upon him. Instead of which I
am now totally forgotten and neglected, despised and like unto a king
who has been driven from his own kingdom. In my place they have
chosen a wicked robber and have honored him. In fact I wished to
establish my reign over man; I should be, by right, his King and his
Lord, for it is I who created and redeemed him. But behold, he has
broken and defiled that fidelity which he promised me at baptism; he
has violated and scorned the laws I had pointed out to him. He loves his
own will and refuses to listen to me. He places above me this evil robber
who is the devil and he has given him his loyalty.[62]

Confronted by these revelations, Bridget was incredulous.
She asked herself in great anguish if they might not have
come from the devil. The Lord reassured her (*Rev.*, I, 4; III,
10) and told her to submit them to the judgment of her directors, which she faithfully did.

The revelations of St. Bridget exercised a great influence
on Christians towards the end of the Middle Ages. The
Council of Basle had to reject a proposal to assimilate them
into Scripture. The saint's secretaries were, indeed, called
evangelists (*Revel. extrav.*, cap. 49).

Obviously not everyone received these revelations with
enthusiasm. They did not form part of public revelation, and
they freely attacked abuses among Christians of every walk
of life. In the circumstances of the period these attacks inevitably aroused political resentment. A great many ecclesi-
astics at that time were political figures. In addition to this,
the revelations were published in a Latin translation made
by theologians who undoubtedly interpreted the original

text according to their own theological formation. Every translation involves an interpretation.

So these revelations provoked a debate, the most important and most solemn debate which had taken place in the Church on the subject of particular revelations. The most prominent theologians were to display their competence in the course of it.

The Council of Basle had put on its program the examination of the revelations of Bridget of Vadstena. In view of this examination, Gerson composed his treatise *On the Discernment of Spirits* (*De probatione spiritum*), as he said himself in his fifth Consideration. He wished to recommend prudence to the Fathers of the Council. Fifteen years previously he had composed a treatise, *On the Distinction Between True and False Visions*. Therefore he knew his subject. "In this latest hour," he wrote, "at the coming of Antichrist, the world is in a delirium, like some old man. Imaginings and illusions are assailing it like dreams. All sorts of people are saying: I am Christ. Someone foretells who is going to be the future Pope, et cetera." [63]

Gerson pointed out five signs which distinguished true revelations: humility, discretion, patience on the part of the visionary, the truth of the revelations, and finally charity or love of God.

Now he was able to give good advice to the Fathers of the Council. "Try the spirits!" This, he said, is an order from St. John. But everyone cannot try the spirits; only he who receives the gift of the Holy Ghost can do so. There are, in fact, two methods of procedure. The first is doctrinal and rests upon an exact and religious study of the fact of the revelations. Unfortunately it is scarcely possible, humanly speaking, to pass judgment on particular cases through pursuance of general rules. There is another method of trying the spirits. This is the experimental method upon which Gerson insisted. It is based on interior inspiration, upon a certain spiritual taste or a divine illumination. The two methods, research and experiment, should unite in an effort at discernment.

After emphasizing the psychological and even the physiological difficulties—see the eighth Consideration—he made a pathetic appeal for reserve in regard to revelations. And he recalled the following example of a certain holy father. The devil appeared to him disguised as Christ, and said to him: "I am Christ; you are worthy of seeing me in person." The holy father, closing his eyes, replied to him: "I do not wish to see Christ; I will be satisfied to see Him in His glory."

And Gerson insisted: *Expertis crede:* believe those who have experience, especially St. Augustine and Bonaventure, for there is scarcely a more destructive, more pernicious pest than a yearning for revelations." [64] Gerson said plainly that he had no inclination to believe silly women: he made an allusion to Bridget of Sweden and Catherine of Siena, who had become advisers to the Pope.

But the Swedish bishops and the preaching friars vigorously supported the revelations in question. John of Torquemada, Master of the Sacred Palace, became the champion of the defense. In his *Defense of the Revelations of Blessed Bridget* he endeavored to prove that they proceeded from the Holy Spirit. As arguments he advanced also five characteristics (*signa*) which differ little from those of Gerson. These are:

1. The opinion of competent men, specialists in the matter
2. The effects of the revelations—humility, the piety of the visionary and the glory of God
3. In regard to the object of the revelations: truth
4. In regard to their "form": conformity with Scripture
5. In regard to their subject: holiness [65]

And the celebrated theologian determined to resolve all the difficulties by replying point by point to 123 articles written against the revelations of St. Bridget. This detailed "defense" fills more than a hundred columns of the *Collection of Mansi:* xxx, 697–814.

This is not all. Cardinal Torquemada addressed a solemn letter "to all the faithful" on the subject of the revelations in question and he declared that he submitted himself in everything to the Church, to the favorable judgments of Gregory XI and of Urban VI. We should bear in mind that these things were going on at a time when the authority of the Holy See was passing through a crisis. What is remarkable was that men of different tendencies showed themselves well disposed toward the life and works of the great Swedish mystic. Not only were the popes whom we have just mentioned favorable toward her, but Boniface IX had canonized her after an examination of her revelations. And this canonization was confirmed by Martin V at Florence on July 1, 1419.

In the bull of canonization, before solemnly "declaring and defining" that Bridget was a saint, he recalled among other facts that "this widow, by the grace of the Holy Spirit, merited the power of communicating to many the knowledge which she had of their private thoughts, their intimate affections, their most secret attitudes, of hearing and of seeing numerous revelations, and of making numerous predictions under the influence of the prophetic spirit." [65a]

It is not surprising, therefore, that Cardinal Lambertini, later Benedict XIV, included the revelations of St. Bridget among the "private revelations which are approved by the Apostolic See." [66]

One can hardly exaggerate the importance of St. Bridget in the history of revelations. Her work occasioned the first systematic expositions upon the discernment of revelations, formulated by Gerson and Torquemada.

These debates show clearly that the existence of revelations did not pose a problem. The manner in which criteria of discernment were established assumed that the fact of revelations was generally accepted. The repercussion throughout the Church of the revelations of St. Bridget was characteristic; it showed how revelations were appraised to-

ward the close of the Middle Ages; it also denoted a crisis
and provoked a reaction which became radical in the new
situation created by the Protestant Reformation.

3   DURING THE REFORMATION AND
              COUNTER-REFORMATION

The position of the Reformers

The Reformation exploded over the matter of indulgences.
A certain use of indulgences was inspired by a superficial
spirit which attached to secondary religious practices more
importance than should have been attached to them. The
indulgences favored pilgrimages to venerated places the
renown of which was often based upon a particular revelation.

Luther, in his violent attack upon "faith in works," condemned along with the abuses these religious practices themselves, as well as the revelations which to him seemed to be
incentives to sanctification by works. In the same way, in the
matter of the ascetism of monks, he again attacked particular revelations (*heimliche or sonderliche Offenbarung*): God
does not want these solitary saints—*Winkelheiligen*—who
separate themselves from the rest, take themselves off to a
desert or into a convent and, seated in their cells, await a
particular revelation from God or from an angel sent by Him.
"Revelations are to be found everywhere, in every corner:
God speaks to me from the chair of truth; He talks through
my neighbor, my friend, my colleague, my wife, my husband, my pastor, my servant, my father and my mother. . . .

My word and yours should also be as powerful as if they came from God." [67]

And, by means of caricature, Luther attempted to make revelations ridiculous. "A sister," he related, "withdrew from her community into her cell. As her fellow sisters in the community wanted to see her, she replied from within: 'Softly, softly, my spouse Christ is with me and is talking to me.' And she added: 'Do you not see how He has clothed me royally?' Her fellow sisters then looked through the keyhole and saw that she was in a wretched condition, dirty, unkempt, and tattered. This then is what the demon of visions does! Through them he misleads people by such things as pilgrimages in the name of Mary and the dead saints. He has succeeded in misleading a great man like Pope Gregory; why should he not pull us into his trap, too, we others who are asleep?" [67a]

The principle of justification by faith alone seems to have pushed Luther to the denial of revelations. But this principle is still more directly defined by the principle of *sola Scriptura*. The Scripture comes from the Holy Spirit and the Apostles whom He inspired. The same Spirit who communicated Revelation, Revelation which was preached by the Apostles and set down in writing, enlightens the faithful who read or listen to what the Apostles have written. "Now that we have their Scripture there is nothing more to be revealed besides what they wrote. We have no further need of any new particular revelation, nor of miracles. . . . That is why we should abide by this revelation or kerygma of the Holy Spirit who alone will tell us what we ought to know, who is our prophet and who will show us the future." [68]

Several texts from St. John of the Cross show him to be as critical of revelations as Luther was. The latter, however, went too far, for he would not accept the aim and spiritual content of revelations. He did not seem, however, always to reject all particular revelation. There are two kinds of prophecies, he wrote in 1537, in his commentary upon chapter 16 of St. John: [69] "The first has for its object profane, temporal things (*etliche betreffen das weltliche Regiment und zeitliche Sache*); it has nothing to do with the spiritual life of Christians. Let anyone who possesses it make use of it as of a gift of God. The second kind of prophecy is solely revealed to Christians: it concerns the persecutions, the sufferings, the heresies (Antichrist, the fall and the resurrection of the faith and of the churches). This spirit of prophecy," said Luther, "still remains in Christianity. But it does not allow us like the Apostles to predict and to know what is going to happen. Fundamentally it is not a matter of particular revelations as we understand it, but only an interpretation of the books of the Apostles. In short, if there is a particular revelation of any spiritual value it is, it seems, the light which the Holy Spirit gives to anyone who reads or hears the Scripture. It will soon be commonly called the 'inner testimony of the Holy Spirit.' "

This is what Calvin wanted to inculcate into Christians:

We must be content, without craving for new visions, for God to teach us by His word. There are many unstable spirits who would like the angels to come down from heaven, who would desire that some revelations should be given to them. Now in that, not being content with the fact that He declares Himself so privately to us, they do great injury to God. For when we have the holy Scripture it is certain that nothing can deceive us: above all, in the clarity of the Gospel we have, as St. Paul shows us, perfection of wisdom. Since that is so, therefore, those who are still titillated with a vain desire to have visions show very well that they have never understood what holy Scripture is. Let us be content with the fact, therefore, that it has pleased God to reveal so much to us through His prophets, as also through our Lord Jesus Christ His Son, knowing that He made therein a final end without going further. And in fact we see what they have come to who have been willing to go astray and to fly beyond these limits; look into what horrible confusion the Papacy has fallen; look upon what the Pope bases all his doctrine, for he says that the Apostles have not declared everything which was useful for the Church and that the Holy Ghost is come so that they can propose new articles and insist upon holy councils. Inasmuch as the Pope and all his accomplices have not held to the purity of the holy Scripture, it needs must be that God has blinded them. . . .[70]

Biblicism dominated everything and revelations were dismissed along with tradition. Luther and Calvin assumed that people were putting these on the same level as Scripture. A priori they saw conflict therein. They went no further than the abuses and did not distinguish between false and true revelations. The Council of Trent, however, clearly recognized the fact of particular revelations within the Church.

In chapter XII of the decree on Justification this Council taught that here on earth no one can arrive at the certainty of being predestined to save one's soul. "For we cannot know who has been chosen by God unless through means of a special revelation (*nisi speciali revelatione*)." And canon 16 upon Justification was no less explicit: "If anyone says that he is certain, with an absolute and infallible certainty, that he will possess the great gift of final perseverance, unless he has learned this from a special revelation—*nisi hoc ex speciali revelatione didicerit*—let him be anathema" (Denz., 826).

In the preparatory discussions upon these doctrinal decisions the Fathers employed the expressions "special revelation" and "explicit revelation," and they rejected the word "inspiration." [71]

Among theologians

Just at the time when Luther was beginning to propagate his new doctrines, in the year of the encounter at Augsburg between himself and Thomas de Vio (Cardinal Cajetan), the latter published his commentary upon the *Secunda Secundae* of St. Thomas. In regard to the whole of the first article he asked himself in what sense primary truth is the formal object of faith. It cannot be so in an absolute fashion, he said. Why? Because there are many things which one can believe with respect to primary truth which do not enter into theological faith. A limitation is imposed on the object of the faith; this limitation does not bear upon the formal object, the revealing truth, but upon the things revealed, the material object (*ex parte rerum dictarum*). "And so it happens that God, although He reveals many things to certain persons . . . He is not considered as the revealer of all that; but the believer believes of his own accord (*sua voluntate*) that God has revealed them" (in II–II, q. 1, a. 1, n. IX).

While Cajetan was severe in his attitude toward revelations, in the matter of their existence he had no doubts at all. In his commentary on the treatise upon prophecy he affirmed the permanence of the prophetic gift in the Church. Despite his unhappy experiences with pseudo-prophets he declared that at all times there have been prophets. The prophecies are there for the benefit of the Church. He asked himself simply how far their significance and their authority extend. Should they be listened to? Yes, said Cajetan. Not, to be sure, when, in principle at least, there is a question of public acts (*spectant ad publica officia*), but when they touch the private life of persons (*actus humani privatarum personarum*) and provided that they do not offend against the morals and the customs of the Church. He thus interpreted the opinions which St. Paul gives to the Thessalonians (I Thess. 5: 21–23): "Despise not the prophets who arise in our days (*prophetas qui de novo apparent*); but be prudent and on your guard that you do not allow yourselves to be diverted by them to evil; hold fast to that which is good" (*Sum. Theol.*, II, q. 174, a. 6, n. v).

The most celebrated theologians of the sixteenth century returned to and developed, in their treatises or commentaries upon Faith (*de fide*), the problem posed by Cajetan. These were chiefly the Dominicans Cano, Soto and Dominicus

Bañez, and the Jesuits Salmeron, Suarez and de Lugo. These latter increased the importance of revelations by insisting upon the identity of their "object" (*objectum formale*) with that of faith: in both cases it is God who is revealing; whether the object of a revelation be proposed publicly by the Church or in a private manner matters little. Suarez, for example, established the following thesis: "The private revelation, upon whatever subject it bears, if it is adequately propounded, has everything it should have to induce an assent of faith of the same nature as the other assents of Catholic faith: such a revelation may, therefore, be the formal object of faith." [72] Melchior Cano did not admit this. For him, particular revelations concern neither faith nor the principles of theology.[73]

The theologians of the sixteenth century did not speak generally about revelations except in their treatises or commentaries upon faith and prophecy. Following them, the majority of theologians remained on the same level and reproduced their thought. Some, however, wrote upon revelations with the aim of discerning them. In 1638, the Dominican Gravina, consultor to the Holy Office, published his *Touchstones for Distinguishing True Visions and Revelations from the False.* This is an attempt to formulate a genuine and systematic treatise upon revelations; it is the most complete with respect to the scope of the aspects examined, and one of the best of its kind that has been written to the present day. It sketches an outline of the history of revelations, seeks to lay down a definition and establish distinctions, examines the object and the subject, the circumstances, etc. It did not fall into oblivion any more than did the *Norms* (*regulae tutae*) on revelations written by Eusebius Amort in 1744. The latter is a curious book. Like a well-prepared dossier, it collects all the teachings of the Fathers and theologians into a certain number of norms; it is overdemanding for true revelations; and it presents a mass of details and teachings upon the revelations of the past and, in particular, upon the visions of Maria of Agreda. The author wrote his book with the intention of proving the falsity of these latter.

In 1751, Lenglet de Fresnoy compiled a book with this promising title: *Historical and Dogmatic Treatise Regarding Particular Apparitions, Visions and Revelations*. This book does not supply what its title promises. Nevertheless, one may see in it a serious attempt at synthesis.

Among the mystics

The writings of the mystics had prepared the way for and assisted this effort at synthesis. While Bañez, for example, mentioned revelations as a corollary in this question of the object of faith, his penitent, Teresa of Avila, saw them from another point of view.

The career of this saint is inexplicable without revelations. She was tremendously strengthened in her spiritual life by heavenly communications; she was encouraged and guided by revelations to found her convents. In her writings she could not pass over in silence an element of such importance. It was her own experience which she described, classified and analyzed with rare psychological insight; she sought to determine not only the criteria of discernment, but also the dangers and the fruits of revelations in the spiritual life. Certainly they are not essential to this life, but they may enter it, as a very great grace.

Disciple, friend and also confessor of St. Teresa, St. John of the Cross, who devoted half of the Second Book of his *Ascent of Mount Carmel* to revelations, did not seem to be of this opinion. Here is what he said, for example: In the Old Testament it was normal to address oneself directly to God. His answers, the revelations, had for their aim faith or things which concerned faith. But now that the faith is founded in Christ, "there is no further reason for us to consult God, nor for Him to answer us as heretofore. From the time that He gave us His Son, who is His Word, He has no other word to give us; for He has no other word. He has told us and revealed to us all things on one single occasion through this only Word, and He has no more to say. . . . According to the Apostle, God has become, as it were, silent." [74] That is why the person who would demand revelations must offend Christ. He would not have faith in Him; he would be offering an insult and even an injury to God; he would be committing a sin despite all his good intentions. The same would hold true for the confessor who would allow such demands. We have reason and the Gospel. That is sufficient to guide us. We have Christ and the Church with her visible ministers —that is where we shall find the remedy for our ignorance. To stray from this path is to act from curiosity, is to be guilty of great presumption (Col. 2: 3; 1 Cor. 2: 2). In short, the keynote is—revelations should not be admitted (*no admitir*).

One finds passages in the works of St. John of the Cross which seem to vie in severity with the judgments of the Reformers upon revelations. Competent spiritual writers have asked themselves how one is to explain the differences which exist upon this subject among the Carmelite mystics. People have tried to reduce these to differences in method which do not affect the doctrinal basis—John of the Cross proceeded scientifically by analyzing everything, by treating of the essential aspects; Teresa of Avila sought to describe her own experience and mingled the accessory elements with the essential aspects. This is to draw a legitimate distinction.

It is true that the former student from Salamanca was more methodical and more systematic than the enclosed nun from Avila who, during her formative years, devoured the romances of chivalry. We look in vain in the writings of St. Teresa for emphases of the kind we find in several instances in the *Ascent of Mount Carmel:* "It is indispensable that the reader should not lose sight in each of these books of the aim we propose" (Book III, chap. 2, note 1). Or, this is the way John stated the aim of the second book in which he spoke *ex professo* of revelations: "The reader must always recall the intention and purpose which I set before myself in writing this book, namely, the directing of souls in the midst of all natural and supernatural cognition and keeping them sheltered from illusions and difficulties in purity of faith in order to arrive at divine union."

If the author had intended to jolt unbelievers out of a sense of false peace or to awaken the faith of those Christians who do not take their responsibilities seriously, he would undoubtedly have expressed himself otherwise. But systematically following his aim, he had to show himself severe (Book II, chap. 28, note 1).

If one looks at the mystical life from this viewpoint, it is necessary to be on one's guard with respect to revelations. The attraction of novelty and the character of revelations, mostly of a kind perceptible to the senses, constitute very large sources of illusions. For the devil, who cannot directly influence the spirit, does exert his sway in the domain of the senses. St. John of the Cross knew this well. And what is more, he must have known well, and detested, the ravages wreaked in souls as a result of the epidemic of visions which raged throughout Spain during his time. So he was driven to emphasize one aspect of the doctrine without insisting upon another and complementary aspect.

This "Doctor of the Absolute," whose standard was "nothing-everything" (*nada-todo*), apparently did not want to express appreciation of secondary values. Just as he vehemently denounced the exaggerated cult of images, so too, in holy anger and on intransigent principles, he took his stand against the dangers which revelations entail for the spiritual life of many souls. In order to urge mystical souls to union with God he wanted to make use only of the great methods and to lay no stress on those which ran the risk of being more harmful than useful.

Teresa of Avila, whose spirituality was more human, more

"incarnate," once amiably criticized the radicalism of Father John of the Cross: "It would cost us dear if we had to find God only when we are at last dead to the world. . . . God preserve us from these people who are so spiritual that they want to transform everything into perfect contemplation, come what will." [75]

So too we must be on our guard against exaggerating the significance of some of the very severe pages which we read in the *Ascent of Mount Carmel*. They were not written for everyone, but for souls advanced in spirituality. Concerned for their progress, St. John of the Cross considered particular revelations in the light of their reaction upon these souls and not in their charismatic aspect. He did not approach the question of revelations as, for example, a theologian would approach it in thinking about Lourdes. We know how he insisted upon the danger of those gifts of God which might hinder direct union with God. The contemplative above all should be able to renounce the gifts of God for God Himself.

Besides, the severity of the saintly Doctor was directed more against the desire for revelations than against revelations themselves. He described revelations and distinguished them with an insight never equaled before. At all times he accepted their existence and occasionally expressed himself clearly in their favor. He ends chapter 22 of Book II of his *Ascent of Mount Carmel* with the following admonition: "We have shown great rigor in order that souls might repel these supernatural communications, and that confessors might not favor discourses upon these matters; but in other respects spiritual directors would be mistaken if they displayed to souls any distaste for them, any aversion or disdain . . . since they are a method or a way by which God leads these souls; there is no occasion for scorning them. One should not be surprised or scandalized by them." [76]

And in chapter 17, note 4, we read this: "When the soul is disposed by this natural exercise, God often enlightens it and spiritualizes it still further by certain supernatural visions which are those we here call imaginary and which, we have already said, produce great fruits in the spirit." He is dealing now with revelations which are in no way desired but come on the initiative of God alone. St. Teresa's praise for these was hardly greater than that of St. John of the Cross. Besides, he himself received revelations and knew by experience their best results.

After the death of the two great Spanish mystics, Gregory XV, in the bull of canonization of March 23, 1622, acclaimed St. Teresa a new Deborah and solemnly declared that Our Lord had favored her with numerous visions and revelations and that Jesus Christ Himself had often appeared to her.[77] And for the Pope this was just another recorded fact in the uninterrupted series of heavenly communications which, since the Ascension of Our Lord, God has addressed chiefly to the obscure and humble for the greater good of the Church.

After the Spanish mystics of the sixteenth century, spiritual writers soon began to consider revelations and apparitions, in relation to the spiritual life, as mystical epiphenomena. This was true of Cardinal Bona in his book on the discernment of spirits (1674) and Scaramelli in his *Mystical Directory* (1752). This was the subject of the little treatise which Cardinal Lambertini (Benedict XIV) inserted into his summary on the canonization of servants of God and which has exercised the greatest influence down to our own day. Even though he wrote as a canonist, he put emphasis upon the spiritual point of view in order to explain the relationship between sanctity and charismatic or mystical phenomena among which are ranked revelations.

4   THE GREAT APPARITIONS OF
RECENT CENTURIES

After the Middle Ages and the Reformation, under the rationalizing pressures of Jansenism, of the Enlightenment and scientism, we might have expected a diminution, if not indeed an eclipse, of revelations as an animating force in the life of faith. But, far from disappearing, revelations have continued to play their traditional role in the Church. Their influence has become even more important on occasion, than it had ever been before in the history of Christianity. It does not enter into the scope of our study to prove this historically. We shall make only some observations upon the public character of the great apparitions of recent centuries: it is precisely because of this public character that we have given them the name of "great."

Among these must be counted the apparitions of Paray-le-Monial during the years 1673–1675. The facts are well known. Here is the most important revelation, communicated in the last great apparition, during the Octave of Corpus Christi: 1. The heart of Jesus revealed His great love for men and demanded "the return of love." 2. He complained of receiving in recognition only coldness or scorn, and He was particularly sensitive to this ingratitude among individuals consecrated to Him. 3. He urged reparation for all these sins.

The apparitions of Jesus Christ to St. Margaret Mary were revelations in the most perfect sense. They comprised a dialogue between persons who saw one another (*Sum.*

Theol., II–II, 174, 3). Relative to faith, they showed the important role of particular revelations of which they were a typical example. A revelation, in fact, should teach us something which we did not know. It cannot establish a new doctrine but it should supply something new, whether in a domain other than faith or in the sense that it causes to be understood in a vital way some Christian teaching which has been somewhat forgotten or is only vaguely known.

Devotion to the Sacred Heart had been practiced to a certain extent well before the time of St. Margaret Mary. Its basis is actually to be found in the Gospel. People always knew the dogma of the Communion of Saints with its practical consequences. But at Paray-le-Monial these things were mentioned in a persuasive, personal way, with insistence upon the "Heart" which is sensitive to the attitudes of men, to such a point that these apparitions bore a novelty which was shocking to Christians branded with the frigid dignity of Jansenism. After the patched-up peace of Clement IX in 1669, Jansenism, which had seemed to comply with the sanctions of the Church, broke out in worse form than ever and its mentality was to persist for a long time in the Church. The devotion to the Sacred Heart and the facts of Paray-le-Monial were not to be fully recognized for 200 years after the death of St. Margaret Mary. One significant fact is that the book by Jean Croiset, *Devotion to the Sacred Heart*, published in 1691, was put on the Index and not withdrawn until 1887.

A particular revelation, by its very nature, is exposed to attacks, but if it is intended that it should "edify" the Church, it will do so at the time desired by God.

Thus God wished that the apparitions of the Blessed Virgin to St. Catherine Labouré would immediately bear abundant fruits. Even before the general public knew of them, the Miraculous Medal was arousing or increasing Marian devotion everywhere. Its design had been shown in 1830 in an apparition which may be considered as a prelude to the great Marian apparitions of the last two centuries. Sister Catherine saw the Blessed Virgin seated in an armchair before the altar of the convent chapel. The Apparition told her how she should behave in her own difficulties, and, according to notes drawn up forty-six years later, complained of the laxity of the community: "I am grieved," Our Lady said. "There are great abuses. . . ." And in predicting the victims in the different religious communities and among the clergy of Paris, she had tears in her eyes, and with great grief she spoke of the evils which would fall upon France and the whole world.

This theme was repeated by the Apparition of La Salette on September 19, 1846. But it was repeated under so new a form and in a context so charged with meaning that this apparition immediately had a very considerable repercussion throughout the world.

At La Salette the Blessed Virgin not only foretold chastisements as a consequence of sins, but also blessings as the fruit of the conversion of Christians. She urged prayer and penance. What is remarkable was that she dwelt upon the situation in which her people stood in relation to God and to herself; and she indicated a secret drama which was being enacted between her Son and herself because of us: "If my people do not wish to submit, I shall be forced to let my Son's hand fall; it is so weighty that I can no longer restrain it. How long have I suffered for you all! If I wish my Son not to abandon you I must beg this of Him unceasingly. And you do not set any value upon this. However hard you pray and work you will never be able to requite the pain I have suffered on your behalf."

La Salette was for Mary what Paray-le-Monial was for Jesus Christ. The same situation was described in this apparition from the point of view of the Mother, and in the other from the point of view of the Son. It is precisely those who belong to them, those for whom they have given the full measure of Their love, who were disrespectful, disobedient and indifferent toward them.

Conscious of being sovereigns in the kingdom of love, Jesus and Mary now showed themselves in these two apparitions as making the greatest efforts to reconcile their people with God.

But while it is possible to establish a certain parallel between the two apparitions in the matter of their content, it is useless to want to do the same thing from the point of view of the form and the circumstances of their presentation.

The apparition of La Salette did not take place at night as did that of Paray-le-Monial, nor in a chapel or a convent like the most important revelations of past centuries, but in the afternoon of a sunny day, in the open air, in a mountain pasture. The Blessed Virgin did not show herself to a nun nor to a pious person withdrawn from the world, but to little shepherds: two children without any religious training. They barely knew the Our Father and the Hail Mary; they went neither to Mass nor to catechism classes. Prior to the apparition they had no desire to see the Blessed Virgin, as had been the case with Sister Catherine Labouré; more than that, despite the splendor of the beautiful Lady and the other circumstances, the globe of fire, for instance, which gave to the encounter the very clear character of an apparition, they did not think that they had experienced one. They thought at first that the person whom they had just met was a lady from the district, a mother, as Maximin says, who had been upset at home and had fled into solitude to weep. At La Salette the Blessed Virgin did not appear standing, as was almost always the case in other Marian apparitions, but was seated, not in an armchair as in the Rue du Bac, but on a rock, her elbows resting on her knees and her head in her hands. Mélanie said that she saw tears running down the Lady's face during the whole time she was speaking.

We are still holding back one interesting detail. In the very place where the Apparition wept, a spring which had dried up during the summer began to flow again, and has never ceased to flow since this event. Pilgrims carried away a little of this water; it aroused in many of the faithful a living faith in the intercession of the Blessed Virgin and produced miracles which were confirmed by reports of officials sent by the Bishop of Grenoble long before the happenings at Lourdes. And there is a curious thing—in all the great Marian apparitions which have taken place since that of La Salette there has been a question of a spring, and water has played in each of them the role which we have just described.

If we have dwelt at some little length upon La Salette it will be understood that it was not with the intention of exalting this particular apparition at the expense of many more famous ones. But from the historical point of view, the apparition at La Salette ushered in the type of particular revelation to which the great Marian apparitions of our times have all belonged. Everyone knows, for example, about the apparitions at Lourdes and Fatima. There is no need to dwell upon these, but in order to understand them it is a good thing to place them in their historical context, of which the apparition at La Salette forms an important element even from the point of view of the circumstances. At La Salette we see assembled for the first time certain characteristics which were to recur in subsequent apparitions—they have taken place in the open air, always in the daytime; the visionaries have been no longer religious or adults, but children with little education; water has played a part in them.

They have had still other things in common. Secrets were communicated almost every time and, what is even more important, all these apparitions have one general characteristic: they were all addressed to the whole world. At La Salette the following order was even repeated: "Tell this to all my people!" It is true that the apparitions were sometimes concerned also with the personal affairs of the visionaries; but it is evident that in general they were intended for the whole world.

The very propagation of these apparitions has emphasized their public character. The revelations made to St. Margaret Mary Alacoque at first remained the secret of a few people; little by little her community came to know of them, and when they penetrated to the outside world they progressively spread throughout France and elsewhere. Sister Catherine Labouré fulfilled her duties as a Daughter of Charity during a period of forty years without even her own immediate associates knowing anything whatsoever about the apparitions she had seen. These remained the secret of the authorities.

With the apparition at La Salette everything changed. On the following day everyone was more or less aware of the event related by the children. It was spoken of at the communal council. A first report was made in writing. On the day following the mayor himself accompanied the children to the place where the apparition occurred, to reconstruct the event. The curious and the pilgrims began to arrive. Then, very soon, the masses gathered. The children had to repeat continuously what took place. Reports and accounts were set down in writing. The civil and ecclesiastical authorities got to know of the affair. The government and the Pope were informed. Publicity came into the business. And very soon the whole of Europe and the world knew the facts. In no time books were published. In 1847, one year after the event, there appeared in France the *New Account of the Apparition of the Blessed Virgin upon the Alps Mountains,* by Msgr. (later Cardinal) Villecourt, and in the same year a book in German, *History of the Apparition of the Most Holy Virgin on the Mountain of La Salette* by Lorenz Hecht, a Benedictine Father from Einsiedeln.

Quite soon a whole polemic was launched for and against the apparition. It was being talked of to such an extent that the London *Times* thought it necessary to take a stand. This paper, at that time the most influential in the world, was extremely scandalized by the importance which the press was attaching to this apparition. On September 7, 1852, it wrote of what it labeled "the grossest credulity and the most contemptible kind of superstition," "the most monstrous and disastrous absurdities." It saw "in this case something more than a system of extravagant and erroneous doctrine, a deliberate attempt to obtain money from people on the most crude and false of pretexts." What degradation for those who accepted such fictions—worthy of monks from the Middle Ages.[78]

Is it not suprising to note that these apparitions of a frankly popular character began at the very moment when atheistic communism was being sketched in outline? At La Salette the place of the apparition and the visionaries were immediately at the disposal of the people, of the "crowd," of the "masses" without distinction of class. The Blessed Virgin spoke of potatoes, of corn. She showed that no detail of the working day escapes her, and the plebeian expression used by the Blessed Virgin, "They go to the slaughterhouse like dogs," was at the time considered in certain quarters to be language so unworthy of the Queen of Heaven as to constitute an argument against the apparition.

Let us recall certain dates: It was in 1841 that Ludwig Feuerbach, of whom Karl Marx was a disciple, published *The Essence of Christianity.* In 1847 there emerged from the press *The Poverty of Philosophy* in which for the first time Marx scientifically listed the essential data of atheistic socialism. The following year the famous *Communist Manifesto* was read in Brussels. In this context it would perhaps be useful to recall that in 1842 Auguste Comte finished his course in positivist philosophy and that starting in 1845 he began to exalt positivism to the stature of a religion. After 1846, the date of the death of Clotilde de Vaux—for him a positivist saint—Comte would consider himself as the high priest of the new religion.

The popularity of La Salette was very soon far surpassed by that of the happenings at Lourdes in 1858. Here it was no longer a question of a single apparition, but of eighteen. It was no longer just to two isolated children on a mountain that the Blessed Virgin manifested herself. She appeared to the visionary in the presence of the crowd. This attendance of people at heavenly visitations on days fixed in advance was an unusual spectacle in the history of the Church. The slightest reactions of the visionary during her encounter with the heavenly visitor could be studied. Mary appeared, it is true, smiling and attractive as the Immaculate. But let us not forget how anxious she was to convert sinners: "You will pray to God for sinners," she required of Bernadette. She wished actions to be added to prayer. "Go and kiss the earth in penance for sinners," and she launched her urgent call: "Penance, penance, penance!"

It is unnecessary to recall the importance and the influence of the Lourdes apparitions which are commemorated by an official feast throughout the Church. If they had not already been known by the whole world, they would have been so after all that was done to mark their centenary. Pope Pius XII determined to emphasize their importance by an encyclical letter, *The Pilgrimage of Lourdes,* which he published for the centenary. He recalled in this the favorable attitude of his predecessors toward Lourdes and associated himself with the homage which St. Pius X had rendered to it: "The special glory of the sanctuary of Lourdes is to be found in this fact—that people from all parts are drawn by Mary to adore Jesus Christ in the Blessed Sacrament. . . ." [79] Lourdes is truly a Church fact.

In the year in which the Communist Revolution broke out in Russia, Mary manifested herself at Fatima. The procedure was similar to that of Lourdes. An immense crowd attended the last apparition at Fatima. These happenings aroused great movements of devotion: a world crusade in favor of the rosary was formed, and twenty-five years after the apparitions the Pope consecrated the world to the Immaculate Heart of Mary, as the Apparition at Fatima had asked. The pressing call to sacrifice and prayer also has had considerable success among Christians.

At Beauraing the facts occurred in a like manner. The crowd was present during the majority of the apparitions which were addressed in the open air to five children. The apparitions are known: serious books have appeared and such reviews as the *Études Carmélitaines* and the *Revue du Diocèse de Namur* have published articles in which theological and psychological arguments are advanced to oppose or to support the authenticity of the apparitions of Beauraing which have been recognized by the ordinary of the place, Bishop Charue. The apparitions of Banneux have also been recognized by the diocesan authority.

To conclude this first part of our work, we may remark that all the writings on particular revelations have been in a certain sense directly occasioned by them, and that everything which has been written has taken as a starting point the facts themselves. Here is a paradox of our times—despite critical and scientific trends, despite the thirst for proofs in the field of religion, theologians are more and more taking revelations seriously.

This, it would seem, is one of the results of the Marian apparitions which have acted publicly and fruitfully upon Christians. The Church could not remain indifferent to this. Not only have theologians written books in favor of the approved apparitions, but they are beginning to consider particular revelations as a subject in themselves. It is no longer a question of treating them solely from the point of view of dogma, of exegesis, of mysticism or from any other particular point of view. The point is that the theologians are seeking to determine their particular purpose and we await a theological synthesis on revelations.

We find such an attitude in the articles by Congar in *La Vie Spirituelle* of 1937, and of Msgr. Ranwez in the *Review du Diocèse de Namur* of 1950. These articles attempt to draw the best fruits from certain traditional data. . . . So too does Colombo in *Scuola Cattolica* of 1948 and Oddonne in his pamphlet *Visioni ed apparizioni* of the same year. Staehlin, in his book *Apariciones, Ensayo critico* of 1954, touches upon some elements of the theology of revelations, but he does not take the trouble to confine them into a theological synthesis. There is a bit of everything in his work and the solutions of the problems he deals with differ widely in value.

Much more profound is the book on *Visions and Prophecies* by Rahner, published in 1952 and republished in 1958. But he restricts his reflections to certain aspects of revelations: he treats of the possibility of revelations, of the problem posed by the psychological data of visions, of the principle of discernment, etc. What seems most important to us is that he tries in his book to give a true theological meaning to revelations.

In the same sense the article "Les révélations privées" by J. N. Nicolas, published in the *Supplément de la Vie spirituelle* of 1953 is noteworthy. Father Nicolas sees in revelations subsidiary signs, means which are extraordinary yet normal, which lead of themselves to the Faith. All the faithful benefit from revelations to the extent to which they give rise to "a pastoral act of the Church." The pastoral point of view is developed in a fairly practical way by L. Lochet in his book *Apparitions* (Paris, 1956). And G. Tempère, in a manuscript dissertation of 1956, discussing the problem "Revelations and Dogma" emphasizes the necessity for considering revelations in themselves according to their particular theological aim.

All these studies and many others affirm or assume the existence of particular revelations, but they always warn against pseudo-revelations.

This attitude toward revelations has been constant, as we have noted throughout the first part of this book. Summing up, during the whole history of the Church there has been belief not only in the existence of revelations, but also in their permanence in the Church. Obviously they have not always happened in the same way. During the first centuries they were addressed most of the time to representatives of ecclesiastical authority who were often priests and prophets; throughout the long period of the union of throne and altar it was chiefly, it would seem, upon religious, and especially women, that God conferred the charismatic gift of revelations; since the beginning of laicism, it has been chiefly the humble and the ignorant who have received them for the edification of the Church. In all that there is nothing exclusive. God distributes His gifts when He wishes and as He wishes. But He is faithful to His own word which was revealed to us by the prophet Joel and which was repeated by the Prince of the Apostles on the day of the birth of the Church: ". . . your sons and your daughters shall prophesy. . . ."

It is as an accomplishment of this prediction of the prophet and as a strong affirmation of the permanence of the prophetic gift in the Church that we may interpret these words of Pius XII: "We feel the need to speak once more, to remind Our sons and Our daughters of the Catholic world that the Saviour has not ceased to repeat during the course of the centuries in His revelations to privileged souls (*non ha cessato di inculcare attraverso i secoli nelle sue revelazioni ad anime privilegiate*) whom He has deigned to choose as His messengers: appease the punitive justice of the Lord through a crusade of expiations launched throughout the entire world. . . ." (A.A.S., 38 [1946], 259).

PART TWO

THE DISCERNMENT OF REVELATIONS

FROM ALL we have said, this much at least is clear: The Church, while teaching that official Revelation concluded with the death of the last Apostle, believes that God continues to manifest Himself through revelations. But while she affirms in principle the existence of these revelations, she does not recognize, at least not solemnly, the authenticity of this or that revelation in particular. It is true that she has given guarantees for certain ones, and the magisterium has, on many occasions, declared in favor of the authenticity of this or that apparition. But we are dealing here with a "permissive" attitude. No one is obliged to believe in any particular revelation. If a Christian accepts it, he does so on his own initiative. He should ponder his reasons for belief. More often than he realizes, he is led to make some effort of discernment in the matter of the revelations he is considering. It is useful, therefore, to know what procedure the experts follow in this matter.

In this section, we shall try to give an analytical and structural insight into the discernment of revelations as practiced by the Church. With this object in view it will be necessary to deal with a few general considerations before treating of the criteria proper of discernment.

CHAPTER V

General Considerations

1   PSEUDO-REVELATIONS

WHILE ADMITTING revelations, the Church is fully conscious that there are imitations of them. Pseudo-revelations appear with such verisimilitude and frequency that anyone investigating them might end, if he has not taken the trouble to make a thorough study of some particular revelation which is authentic, by rejecting on principle all particular revelations.

It is a fact that each of the great Marian apparitions has been followed by a huge number of fraudulent imitations. False revelations are as old as the true ones; they are certainly considerably more numerous. Pseudo-prophets were the contemporaries of true prophets, and even while the Gospels were being spread, apocrypha were being diffused everywhere. We have had occasion to mention many pseudo-prophetic movements. The Sacred Books denounce some of them. Here we shall transcribe the first detailed accounts of a pseudo-revelation which we find in Tradition.

Firmilian of Caesarea wrote to St. Cyprian: "I want to tell

you a story of something which has happened here among us and which concerns our subject. About twenty-two years ago, at the time following the death of Alexander Severus, plagues and trials in dire profusion fell upon all the populations here, and in particular upon the Christians. Repeated earthquakes destroyed buildings in Cappadocia and Pontus. The very cities disappeared, swallowed up in the craters. . . . Now suddenly there arose a woman who, going into an ecstasy, professed to be a prophetess and behaved as though under the inspiration of the Holy Spirit. She received so compelling an influence from the leading demons that for a long time she attracted and duped our brethren as the result of the amazing prodigies she performed. She even announced that she was going to shake the earth or disturb one of the elements. Sometimes the evil spirit, understanding and foreseeing that an earthquake was going to occur, made it seem that he was the author of the thing he knew was going to take place. These lies and extravagant boasts had subjected many spirits to him: people obeyed him and followed him wherever he wished. . . . Due to him this woman, in the midst of the coldest winter, walked barefoot through snow and ice without suffering any harm." [79a]

It is surprising to realize how extensive the influence of pseudo-revelations may be. Wonders, strange coincidences whether artificial or real, authentic spiritual benefits, insistence upon certain arguments and unvarying silence about others, an irresistible emotional need, the suggestion of the crowd, the influence of individuals they love and admire, may impel Christians to assume attitudes which at first sight are inexplicable. These attitudes, which turn a minor aspect of religion into a leading element in Christian life, are not to be found solely in the so-called ages of faith and of ignorance, but even in our own day, when science might seem to be triumphant in many spheres of life. They are in fact flourishing vigorously at present, a fact that may be partly explained by the efficiency of modern methods of communication which permit the immediate diffusion of news of the slightest event throughout the Church.

The situation is so serious that the highest administrative authorities of the Church have deemed it necessary to react against a tendency so injurious to Christian life. Cardinal Ottaviani, in the article already quoted (page 5), which he published in the *Osservatore Romano* on February 2, 1951, made this surprising statement: "Who would have imagined fifty years ago that the Church today would have to put her sons, and even some priests, on their guard against so-called visions, against fictitious miracles, in short, against all those events regarded as preternatural which, from one continent to another, from one country to another, practically everywhere attract and excite the masses? . . . For many years we have been observing a recrudescence of the popular passion for the miraculous, even in the religious domain. Masses of the faithful flock to places of presumed visions and fictitious wonders and, on the other hand, they neglect the Church, the sacraments and preaching."

This article shows in a masterly manner at what point the faithful may be deceived if they do not apply the true criteria of discernment when confronted by pseudo-revelations. It is also to be noted that never in all her history has the Church explicitly rejected such a large number of false revelations as in our own twentieth century. In the last thirty years alone she has condemned at least fifteen of them.

A sure discernment of true revelations assumes a penetrating knowledge of pseudo-revelations.

Anyone who knows the structure and the sources of these is better enabled to estimate the value of the positive criteria of a revelation. Every revelation is a communication from one person to another. In our case it is a communication from God to man. That is why it is easy to understand the lapse from a revelation to its counterfeit: an individual is never completely knowable even when he is quite open and frank. This is all the more true when God is concerned in the matter. God remains always a mystery, even when He manifests Himself. Despite grace, He is never comprehensible to man in his earthly condition.

It is not surprising that the man who thinks that he has received a divine communication might be mistaken. For he has no evidence of the divine presence which spoke to him. Certainly God, in revealing Himself to man, may give the certainty of His presence. But this is a grace granted to the visionary who cannot transmit to others this personal guarantee. There must, then, be reliable criteria of discernment for everyone.

That is not all. God may speak to a man through an intermediary. This makes no difference to the nature of the revelation. He may address Himself to us by means of His creatures. As a matter of fact He has frequently chosen angels, His "messengers," as the instruments of His communications.

Finally, if God speaks to man personally, or through an intermediary, He is expressing Himself in a human manner and man can only grasp the divine communication through the means and the method of human knowledge. In such conditions the danger of confusing a revelation with its imitation is intrinsic in the event itself. The principal danger lies in man himself who in certain psychological states may believe that God is speaking to him whereas in reality he is speaking to himself. But, when a true communication is objectively received, it does not necessarily proceed from God; the creatures, in particular the fallen angels, are capable of giving it. There are, therefore, two sources of confusion which make discernment very difficult, namely, the human psyche and the interference of the demons in the life of man. In this matter, then, certain principles must be remembered before a study of the criteria for discernment is undertaken.

2   THE ROLE OF THE
PSYCHE IN DISCERNMENT

The insertion of revelation into the psyche

Every revelation is a divine word which reaches man, but
it is known to us only through and in the human psyche
where it is received. To discern it as such we should be able
to determine if it is subject to any changes from the fact of
its insertion; one should also know the nature of such change.
Certitude here is impossible. Here is how opinions stand in
regard to this matter:

According to some, the revelation which the visionary
transmits to us comes integrally from a heavenly person; it
is this heavenly person, so to speak, who composes its text.
Each word comes from above and penetrates the human
psyche. We are dealing with an encounter between two persons: a heavenly person "has come," "has visited the earth."
Happy are the eyes which saw him, and blessed the place he
sanctified by his presence! The expression of the face, the
demeanor, the dress are objective details which are clothed
with symbolism. Once heavenly intervention has been admitted, the entire event is clothed in an objectivity equal to
that of other facts.

This attitude toward revelations seems very "naive" to
others. According to them, God makes use of the psychological realities which He has placed in man. To believe that
He performs miracles in order to accomplish something
which does not exceed the limit of human possibilities is

"miracle-hunting." God likes to work through secondary causes. He is able to make use of imagination, of the realities of the subconscious projected into the transsubjective domain. This projection is a normal fact of psychology as hallucination also is. Why should not God make use of it as a means of communication? He may use it, just as the devil may abuse it.

There are religious hallucinations, as there are diabolical hallucinations. There is no purpose in dwelling upon the clear consciousness of an objective perception which the visionary says he has had. Hallucination also carries an impression of perfect objectivity.

In every revelation there is psychological co-operation. It is minimal, according to the first opinion. But according to the second, it is so developed that one may ask if the revelation is not turning into a fiction. It is not surprising, then, that others put forward a solution midway between the two, which is that the content of a revelation comes wholly from God, but that it enters deeply into the psyche which expresses it more or less in its own way. The revelation comes back to the individual and undergoes a change in the sense that it receives an explanation from the intellect. And when not only inspiration or thoughts, but words themselves are given, then these undergo a trivial change here and there which does not affect the substantial content of the revelation. What is true in the case of the Scriptures may well be the same for particular revelations.

There are no errors more like the truth, more seductive, more widespread, than the exaggerations of partial truths. This is the case in the question with which we are now dealing. Any of the three theories proposed does not give by itself a satisfying explanation of all the facts. The first seems to explain some of them, the second, the majority. With regard to the third, it is necessary first to resolve a problem which it raises before saying anything else on the subject.

To begin with, let us not minimize the value of the first

solution. It is as dangerous to underestimate the value of a theory as it is to exaggerate it. It is too facile a procedure to write off an explanation as unsatisfactory because it seems to us to be "naive."

Certainly the visionary is not a mechanical transmitter of words which he may hear; he is not a parrot. But neither is that to say that God always makes use of all the layers of the psyche. On the contrary, there are many clear indications in favor of a restricted use of the psychic capacities of the visionary.

Let us recall, for example, this moving fact of the story of the apparitions at Lourdes. On March 25, 1858, Bernadette received a revelation which she did not understand: "Que soy era Immaculado Concepcion!"[80] Generally speaking, these words are considered to be the most important revelation of the apparitions at Massabielle. They formulate the mystery of the Grotto, the message of Lourdes. In order not to forget these words which the heavenly Lady had communicated to her in a very impressive way, the visionary never stopped repeating them the whole way along the road which took her to the Curé. Her whole concern was to forget none of them so that she could transmit them to her pastor exactly as she had heard them. Bernadette had to concentrate all her efforts in order to sustain one psychic faculty, namely, the memory. It has even happened that visionaries transmitted the whole of a discourse in a language which they hardly knew, and the meaning of which escaped them.

But there are Christians who pay considerable attention to the findings of psychology and reject the first explanation. They would find "naive" an objective apparition who was said to speak as a human presence. Possibly they would ask themselves this: Why should God perform such an extraordinary miracle, why should heavenly personages put themselves out in this way, if Heaven can achieve the same result by setting in motion the resources of the subconscious and the psychic possibilities which we mentioned earlier? We

shall discuss this question further on. For the moment it is
sufficient to state that one finds, at least in one category of
revelations, facts which are not to be explained by this
theory.

In the apparition at La Salette this is what happened:
Maximin, the little shepherd boy, twirled his hat on his staff
while the "beautiful Lady" spoke, and rolled little stones
toward the Apparition. Mélanie, the other witness of the
event at La Salette, reproached him afterward for lack of
repect. Here is an account: "Mother Superior told me yes-
terday," we read in Mademoiselle des Brulais's record dated
September 12, 1849, "that a few days earlier the two children
were taking their recreation in the presence of the Sisters
and she had to rebuke Maximin for his lack of manners (he
was sitting on the floor in the passage). 'Oh,' said Mélanie,
who on this particular day was more excited than usual and
a little naughty, 'why would you want him to behave himself properly, Sister? He could not behave himself in front of
the Blessed Virgin.' 'What? He did not behave himself properly in front of the Blessed Virgin? What did he do, then?'
'Well, first of all he had his hat on his head; and then he took
his hat off his head and put it on his staff and he made it
spin around on his staff like this (she mimed the action); and
after that he put it back on his head; then he took his staff
and he pushed stones with it so that they rolled toward the
feet of the Blessed Virgin!' 'Oh,' interrupted poor Maximin,
'don't believe that, Sister. Only one stone rolled as far as the
Blessed Virgin!' 'But you made the stone roll.' 'Yes, but only
one struck the Blessed Virgin. That's for sure!' " [81]

All this took place during a normal conversation. The two
visionaries were obviously not in a state of ecstasy or trance.
The apparition was not a dream; it is difficult to see a hallucination in this, or any parapsychological phenomenon.
Phenomena of this type assume a total concentration, an
extraordinary attention; the visionary is absorbed by the
imaginary object. But here, in the middle of an apparition,

the two children who saw it simultaneously were distracted at the same moment. Mélanie noticed that Maximin was rolling the little stones and Maximin was perfectly conscious of what he was doing, since after this unheard-of event in his life he remembered just how far he rolled them!

The Bible too seems rather favorable toward objective apparitions. St. Luke relates, for instance, that an angel of the Lord appeared to Zachary "standing on the right side of the altar of incense." The angel introduced himself: "I am Gabriel, who stands before God." After the account of the apparition and its consequences we read: "And in the sixth month the angel Gabriel was *sent from God (apestalè)* into a city of Galilee, called Nazareth, to a virgin . . . named Mary. And the angel *being come in (eiselthon) said* unto her: Hail . . ." (Luke 1: 26–28). The Evangelist, having established the dialogue between the angel and Mary, adds: "And the angel *departed from* her" (*apelthen*, Luke 1: 39).

The Scripture, then, states explicitly that a specific angel, Gabriel, was sent by God to a specific place, Nazareth, and he entered Mary's home, spoke with her and went away. If it is not improbable that God would have desired to choose a method of apparition which seems "naive" for this very important revelation which was made to Mary, why should this method be excluded, on principle, from particular revelations? There is nothing to indicate that God has changed the method of revelations since the death of the last Apostle. If the revelations related in the Bible have an advantage over the others, it is perhaps because of the content and certainly because of the guarantee of authenticity deriving from Inspiration; but the method is not to be overlooked.

St. Thomas is entirely positive on the question of the real presence of heavenly persons who manifest themselves to man. In the third part of the *Summa* (q. 57, a. 6) he wants to establish that the Ascension of Christ is in a certain sense the cause of salvation. In the answer he states that if Christ, by a particular disposition, sometimes descends corporally to earth, as was the case when He appeared to St. Paul (Acts 9), this is not contrary to the right and the merit He has acquired to live eternally in heaven. With regard to eucharistic visions he believes that it is not always a matter of subjective phenomena; according to him, these apparitions are sometimes forms which may be seen in a manner of reality existing outside the subject.[82]

Obviously it is very difficult and even practically impossible to determine with certitude if in such and such a particular revelation there was a personal presence in persona; but it is almost as difficult to prove that there was not. It is very probable that on the majority of occasions the revelations are inserted fully into the psyche in the sense of the third solution outlined above. Now, in this case, hallucinatory elements slip in almost normally. Certain features stand out in relief, a color leads to a complementary color, during a specific noise words are easily articulated. Theologians admit in general such "weaknesses" of human perception, even in some particular revelations recognized as authentic, on condition, however, that the substance of the content is not affected. When it is a matter of real hallucinations, the situation is not the same and another problem arises.

Hallucinations and revelations

Here we are considering in particular "corporal" and imaginative revelations. These, in fact, play a fairly important part in the devotion of the faithful and therefore in the pastoral work of the Church. But they are very much more exposed to fraudulent imitations than are purely spiritual revelations. In a thousand ways material elements may deceive or falsify the transmission from spirit to spirit. It is easy, too, to take for revelations phenomena which are purely psychic, or even communications which come simply

from man or from the devil. There are such things as occultism and spiritism; there are all sorts of metapsychical phenomena such as telepathy, clairvoyance, etc., which may
resemble revelations to such an extent that despite the best
criteria their discernment becomes difficult. But the most
perfect imitation of revelations is achieved in hallucination.
Depth psychology has done nothing to change this fact; it
enables us only to understand hallucination very much better and especially to discover its sources and the reasons that
lead up to it. One must endeavor to define the nature of hallucination before trying to resolve the problem which it
raises with respect to revelations.

Hallucination is "perception of objects with no reality."
This is an old definition, sometimes criticized but invariably
returned to, even by the most recent and best qualified
writers. It is paradoxical. Taken literally it seems to express
an impossibility: if there is no object there is no perception.
But if properly understood, it indicates the two essential
characteristics of hallucination. The first, expressed in the
definition by the word "perception," is exteriority. Hallucination causes the subject to feel all the characteristics of
true perception which has its source in objective space. It is
in this sense that Fröbes can say of true hallucinations—as
distinct from pseudo-hallucinations—that they are physical
perceptions.[83]

They cause the subject who is undergoing them to experience all the characteristics of true perception: the feeling of
presence and of immediate reality, the impression of complete objectivity, a vivid, precise, and spontaneous representation. This is the mark of the exteriority of the perception.

The second mark of hallucination is the absence of the
real object which the sensory perception presents to the subject in an incoercible manner. This perception obviously has
an object, but it is a subjective phenomenon; it is not to be
found where the perception places it, namely, in spatial

objectivity. In principle, it has not even its source in the transsubjective world. Hallucination is really a perception without an object, just as is understood by the definition. One can define it in a more positive way by saying that it is a sensory representation containing an apparent objectivity and reality. It is not surprising that psychologists place hallucinations among the pseudo-perceptions.

In fact, all these phenomena mislead, yet they are distinct from one another. Pseudo-hallucinations do not have the first mark of real hallucinations, namely, exteriority, and illusions do not have the second, namely, the absence of a real object. It is true that pseudo-hallucinations may be vivid, precise, and spontaneous representations, but they do not give the feeling of presence and of reality which essentially make up the mark of exteriority; they do not create, as do hallucinations, the appearance of an objective reality. In practice it is not always possible to indicate the limits of either of them. A representation may intensify so as to become truly hallucinatory. It may create an illusion of a reality, a certain spatial exteriorization, later recognized as such.

Illusion is pure perception of a partially real object, to which are joined subjective representations and hallucinatory elements. It is the perception of a distorted object. If while listening to a discourse I retain words imperceptibly added to those which are spoken, or if in the dark I take a post to be a man, I have an illusion, but if, in absolute silence I hear voices and am perfectly convinced that they are reaching my ears from outside, then I have a hallucination. This is how to distinguish between the two definitions.

But here, as elsewhere, there are borderline cases. Illusion is the partially real perception of a distorted object. Might we not find this particularly in the very slight alteration of some detail, as for instance in correcting mistaken impressions unconsciously formed while reading an interesting book? It seems not, since the integral object as such has not been altered or distorted. This is a matter of tiny and common errors of normal perception. These borderline cases are found not only between illusions and wholly true perceptions, but also between hallucinations and illusions. In hallucination, the felt presence of a reality is an invention of the subject suffering from hallucinations—that is, provided that the hallucination remains truly the work of the psyche. It is not to be ruled out that this work may suppose some excitation from outside. But normally such excitation does not provide the content of the hallucination.

One may ask if a simple metesthesis (a sensory perception appearing after the presence or the action of the real object) is a hallucination or not. We think it is. Certainly the content of a hallucination comes from outside; but this is not in virtue of the actual perception. This latter is "without an object" in the sense explained earlier, and to it applies the definition of hallucination. The time of this appearance is of little importance, so long as the real perception has ended. One may likewise count among hallucinations the eidetic phenomena. These phenomena are visual hallucinations set in motion by true perceptions; one finds these chiefly in children, and in particular children from the country.

Here is a type of eidetic hallucination encountered in a psychological clinic. A little boy is looking very attentively at a vividly colored picture projected in a dark room. The picture represents a small cat prowling around a jar full of marmalade. The cat dare not lick it because, let us suppose, it is too hot. The picture is then removed from the little boy. A short while later he bursts out laughing. When he is asked why he is laughing he relates that the cat has just knocked over the jar and that the marmalade is spilling out over the floor. In vain he is told that this is not true. He protests: "But it is. I see it." And he relates in detail how the cat overturned the jar. There was nothing at all of this in the picture.[84] This was a hallucination provoked by a true perception which preceded it.

Numerous questions are raised if we confront what we

have just said about hallucinations with the nature of those revelations defined in our introduction. Do not revelations belong to a certain category of hallucinations called "divine hallucinations"? For, from the point of view of phenomenology, do revelations differ from hallucinations? Is the person suffering from hallucinations not just as certain as the true visionary of what he has seen and heard? It is true that objectivation is not objectivity. A hallucination does not have the objective reality that it holds for the person who has suffered it, but is the revelation necessarily founded upon objective reality? Is not the dream a subjective phenomenon like the hallucination? Now it is a fact that God reveals Himself through dreams. Why should He not do so through hallucinations? Some writers, in fact, answer this question by saying that He does. "Induced by illness, this hallucination is a mental disturbance; induced by the devil it is diabolical, induced by God it is divine. When God causes it He quickens our aptitude for dreaming, making us see not Christ but a physical likeness of Christ," writes Quercy. This hallucination is divine as the result of its cause, but through its matter and its neurological origin it is identical with that of the damned or the mad.[85]

Dr. Lhermitte is of the same opinion, but he expresses himself less categorically than Quercy. "With St. Teresa," he writes, "with St. John of the Cross, we do not doubt that exterior and impressive manifestations may come from a supernatural source and appear divine in their first cause; we have only to ask ourselves if, physiologically and psychologically, the visions and the divine words are not human actions set in motion by a power which surpasses us and which we call God." [86] In these manifestations the mechanism of the visionaries in no way differs from our own. If God wanted to create mechanisms for every case, He would have to engage in a perpetual miracle. "In each of these a similar mechanism is involved, and only the principle which

brings them to light turns out to be distinct in its consequences." [86]

There are good reasons for sustaining this position. But
the question is not so simple as one might think. The hallucinations caused by God are divine—nothing could be
clearer. But on reflection, one queries the meaning of the
expression, God *causes* hallucinations. What causality is in
question? Is any causality whatsoever sufficient to make hallucinations divine?

Divine causality is at the base of all activity. Its power is
no less in phenomena of religious value. First of all, let us
consider the case of naturally explicable visions and apparitions which make fruitful the life of a Christian who accepts
them as coming from God and who values them as a grace.
It may be admitted that mystical souls who contemplate the
lives of Our Lord, of the Blessed Virgin and of the saints,
may have visions which are profitable and desired by God,
but which may be the effect of psychological laws, of hallucinations. Maréchal writes quite reasonably: "Here the
hallucinatory character—which is often only accidental and
dependent upon the nervous constitution of the subject,
much more than upon the immediate intention of Providence
—does not necessarily lessen the value of edification, which
may even be reinforced. For it is important not to confuse
the two problems—vastly different—of religious value and of
psychological mechanism: one easily conceives a providential intention and even a special intervention by God in
visions in which the psychological mechanism would belong
in other respects to the category of genuine or psychic hallucination." [87]

That does not prove that there are divine hallucinations,
which would have to be caused by God. Now this is not the
case. It is only through their finality that they have a relationship with God. If their content is religious it derives from
the psyche. The hallucination remains human.

The following case would appear to be less simple. The

supernatural action of God reveals itself in an indirect way. One may think of the indwelling of God in the souls of the just, but also of the infused contemplation which does not touch the psychic faculties. Let us think, for instance, of that spiritual light, the *"luz espiritual"* spoken of by St. John of the Cross. It is, he says, a general knowledge, which communicates itself with such purity and simplicity and in such complete detachment and remoteness from all intelligible forms, from characteristic objects of the understanding, that the understanding does not feel it, does not see it. Sometimes indeed, on the contrary, when this knowledge is more pure, it blinds the understanding by depriving it of its normal lights, of its representations or images. The understanding at that stage is well aware of the shadows in which it lies. In such cases the psychic faculties, especially the imagination, may form words and representations which do not come from God, but which are induced by a kind of spreading of light which penetrates or which has penetrated the "extreme point of the soul."

It does not come within our scope to emphasize here the inevitable defectiveness inherent in the translation of a spiritual occurrence into the language of the intellect or of the senses. The mystics invariably complain of being unable to describe their mystic experience in a satisfactory way. It is only a question of determining whether the hallucinations which would lead to the making of this translation, might be divine hallucinations. One might be tempted to consider them as such. There is, in fact, a casual connection between divine action and the hallucinatory phenomenon. But this connection, in our opinion, is not sufficient to make a hallucination divine. It is humanly fashioned in forms in no way prompted by divine action. Neither does it possess any divine guarantee protecting it from erroneous expressions.

If divine hallucinations exist, one finds them only in the following case: the visionary is impressed by an object or an action which does not come from outside, as, for example, by a real person whose external appearance is reflected upon the visionary's retina and whose words reach his ears. It is God Himself who produces the physiological stimulation of the sensory faculties, it is from Him that what the scholastic calls *species sensibilis impressa,* or at least its effect, comes. If this *species* is incited or even produced by God, it can take very different forms: perception, hallucination, eidetic vision, as also representation and pseudo-hallucination.

One may certainly ask whether it is good to talk of divine hallucinations, since purely psychological hallucination implies, after all, a fraud, for it shows that which is not, or makes disappear from the subject that which is. But this is not the case if one is assuming a divine hallucination. The cognitive form comes from God, even if it seems to come from outside. Fundamentally there is no fraud. Let us take the example of a certain son to whom his dead father suddenly appears and asks him to have Masses said for his intention. Let us suppose this to be a hallucination desired and induced by God. Certainly the father was not present, but one may be sure that, through God's permission, the father's wish has been transmitted.

This would here be something analogous to what passed between Jacob and the patriarch Isaac in the matter of the blessing of the first-born. When Jacob said: "I am Esau," from a certain point of view, which could be called phenomenological, Jacob deceived Isaac, hence Esau's violent reaction after the benediction had been given to Jacob. But in God's design, and as a result in reality, Jacob became Esau in so far as he became the first-born. The rights and the fruits which are normally the consequences of the physical act of birth were transferred to another in virtue of the will of God. That is why St. Augustine could say of this event: this is not a lie but a mystery.

Moreover, there would be in a divine hallucination something which would recall the mode of knowledge belonging to the angels. They do not possess knowledge under the influence of the object, but under that of God Himself who directly communicates the forms of knowledge to them.

To sum up, it seems preferable not to speak of divine hallucinations. They have an analogous meaning only. And since "hallucination" is a psychological term and commonly used as such, the expression "divine hallucination" could too easily create equivocation. But taken by itself, in its analogous sense, it is justifiable.

Discernment between revelations and hallucinations

How, then, can we discern revelations from hallucinations? It must be admitted as a fact that the compelling sensation of a present reality may be as strong in hallucination as in external sensation. The most developed and complete hallucination, the hysterical hallucination, proceeds in a very autonomous way. It may fabricate something out of nothing and succeed in giving a certain unity to the whole invention. This achievement is greatly facilitated by depersonalization, or by a split in the personality which allows an imaginary personality to take possession of the psychological faculties. Everything may then seem normal and every invention appear as real. Hysterical hallucination has, indeed, and quite rightly, been called "the great simulator." Hysteria has all the hallucinatory range at its disposal: visual and auditory hallucinations, hallucinations of touch, of smell, diabolical hallucinations and mystical hallucinations. Hysterical hallucination gives a personal character to everything and if under its inspiration imagination freely enters into play, visions are also clothed with a charm and a dazzling beauty which surpasses everything one can see in a normal state.

It might seem, therefore, that we must accept the following conclusion: even the most beautiful apparitions and the most detailed revelations can be naturally explained. But such a conclusion is imposed upon only a superficial observer. We do not claim that discernment is easy or that one may reach it through purely psychological means, but impartial and detailed psychological observations are sufficient to prove the contrary to those who maintain that discernment is impossible.

If we are dealing with pure visions or visual hallucinations, discernment is certainly difficult. We are not attempting to do so because it does not enter into a study which has revelations as its subject. In certain given circumstances pure visions may serve to reveal something, but there are no revelations properly so called except those received through the medium of words. Visual data, that is to say, visions or apparitions, are not considered here, as we said in our introduction, unless in conjunction with a revelation properly so-called.

The only hallucination susceptible of discernment is the auditory-verbal hallucination. Every hallucination implies a certain psychic disturbance, a weakness, which is not the case with ecstasy, the result of a great effort of concentration, or else simply a gift from God. According to the experts in this matter, no hallucination assumes more disorganization of the mind than the auditory-verbal hallucination. Dr. Lhermitte, whose severity with respect to supernatural phenomena has more than once been criticized by doctors and theologians, writes: "The person suffering from auditory-verbal hallucination is already evidently disordered, while the person suffering from visual hallucination may keep his lucidity intact throughout the evolution of the strangest phantasies, can laugh at them, be amused or irritated by them, as any ill person may grumble about some symptom which is irritating because of its persistence or its recurrence." [87a]

The most carefully studied data demonstrates that auditory-verbal hallucinations reproduce the thoughts and feelings of a sufferer whose mental powers of expression have been deranged by illness, and have become a kind of autonomous activity alien to the personality of the subject. It remains to be estimated to what extent these hallucinations reveal a deep disturbance of the personality and how easily they may be accompanied by psychic disintegration and the dissolution of the links by which the unity of the ego is ensured. "All psychiatrists since Séglaz have recognized that hallucinations of language appear among subjects whose personality is more or less severely affected; that most frequently their indefinite persistence coincides with a disintegration of the ego." [87a]

These hallucinations are also the most complicated. Animals do not seem to have them; they do, however, suffer from visual hallucinations of every kind. Hallucinations of language imply an intellectual activity conditioned by the illness; it seems that there is an intellectual transformation of psycho-sensory phantasms. The word is made in the likeness of its efficient cause, namely, man. It is perfectly material; it extends in the dimensions of space and time. But it is also immaterial, being the likeness and the emanation of the mind. It is understandable why in the Bible, that wonderful story of the communications between God and men, "the word" takes such an important place. It is often personified in the Old Testament. It carries out the will of Yahweh, it leaps forth like a warrior in the midst of the land of perdition. In the New Testament the Person of the Son is called the Word. It is not surprising that an entire philosophy, the "Thou Philosophy" of Ferdinand Ebner and Martin Buber, could be founded upon the fact of the word.[88]

In this context it is easier to understand that verbal hallucination assumes a splitting of that which makes the unity and the greatness of man, namely, the person. Now this splitting, this disintegration of the self, is a contestable fact. The simulation reveals itself as such to a thorough medical examination.

This is the case, in particular, of the hysteric who allows a hallucination to run its maximum course. But from the fact that the hysterical hallucination is capable of simulating everything, or almost everything, one cannot conclude that revelations are not discernible. A simulation is, by definition, different from the reality simulated, and this difference renders discernment possible in principle. But in practice the method of discerning simulation from reality comes to us from the very nature of the hysterical hallucination: it is accompanied by pathological symptoms. These are not only of a psychological kind; cerebral lesions may, according to the statement of doctors, explain the supervening of auditory-verbal hallucinations. All this belongs to the domain of debate. Discernment, therefore, remains in principle possible.

In the quest for discernment the believer and the theologian, for whom God and the saints of heaven are persons as real and present as the men who surround them, are naturally inclined to see revelations in manifestations which are presented as such. But the psychiatrist, who is dealing only with persons whose extraordinary manifestations are of a pathological kind, has a tendency to resolve the case of a revelation as if it were also pathological, since his experience of similar or "identical" cases is so great. There are the addicts of miracles and there are the addicts of psychology. In the field of revelations the inflation of hysteria is a fact. Every time that there is a question of discernment, a serious diagnosis must prove that symptoms of hysteria are not present and a study must be made of the whole behavior of the subject. It has happened that doctors have noted and emphasized symptoms indicating hysteria, and that symptoms completely contrary to hysteria have remained unobserved.

What we have just said of hallucination in relation to the supernatural is equally valid in the case of other psychic phenomena. Before beginning the quest for discernment with which we are concerned here, and before forming a judgment, we must have a thorough knowledge of the results on the psychic life and the spiritual life in general of psychic or parapsychic phenomena and of God's communication with souls which may bear some resemblance to these phenomena. But we would have to go outside the scope of our study if we were to try to give a synthesis of problems which have already been treated at length. Doctors and psychiatrists on the one hand and theologians on the other have done their most fruitful work in this field during the last twenty years. Their work has thrown much light upon the relationship, so hard to determine, which exists between the nature and the activity of the psychic and spiritual domains, and have made clearer the teaching of St. Paul on "psychic" and "spiritual" man.

At this point we shall try to formulate some principles which touch more directly upon the quest for discernment.

1. In order to discern the true from the false in our sphere one must be free from all prejudice for or against psychological or supernatural solutions. The prejudice in favor of the supernatural is the more dangerous, for the risk of mistaking a pseudo-revelation for a revelation is greater than doing the opposite; but with everything otherwise equal, the prejudice of the doctor in favor of a psychological solution is normally stronger and more natural than that of the theologian in favor of a supernatural explanation. From the theologian's point of view, the domain of nature's forces remains in principle accessible, but the same does not hold true for the doctor or the psychologist in regard to the supernatural. Psychic phenomena are within everyone's range; supernatural phenomena are not. The doctor and the scientist are tempted to think there is a scientific explanation for those supernatural phenomena which are beyond them and this temptation is all the stronger because supernatural phenomena contain certain analogies with natural phenomena.

The attitude of Immanuel Kant in this matter is surprising.

Although he was an enemy of mystic or psychic manifestations, of revelations, of mysteries, of clairvoyance, telepathy, etc., he did not condemn them, according to a letter addressed to Mademoiselle Charlotte von Knobloch: "In order to prove this impossibility, one should know the nature of the spirit. Now, of this we know so little." Kant rejects such phenomena (*Erscheinungen*) because they had not been sufficiently proved. He rejected them also because of their incomprehensibility and their pointlessness; also because so much irresponsibility, so many difficulties and deceptions prevailed in this domain. Nevertheless, he refrained "from blindly rejecting the prejudice in favor of apparitions and visions as the result of another prejudice." [89]

2. Another principle compels attention: The different circumstances of such an occurrence must be carefully observed and they must be retained in the memory just as they were observed. It is very easy to collect a great many details of the same kind while allowing others to escape attention, or, if they are observed, not to take them into account when forming a judgment regarding the whole. The dictum of the psychologist Jung on the attitude of people, even educated people, in regard to metapsychical facts is significant: "They deny the testimony of their senses. In a specific case they sign an official report of a meeting, and, as has happened on more than one occasion, withdraw their signature later on, thinking that what they observed and confirmed was impossible—as if a perfect knowledge of what is possible could be attained." [90]

All discernment is falsified if all the special characteristics of an occurrence are not taken into account. What happens in the scriptural sphere may happen here—that is, when two things possess some similar elements, one may run them both together. One finds certain elements of the Book of Genesis which resemble those to be found in Babylonian stories, but this does not make Genesis merely a systematic transcription of Babylonian traditions. It is clear that the use of this method would make it possible to reduce all revelations to a set of psychological circumstances and vice versa.

3. As a practical application or as a consequence of the second principle, one may deduce a third: A doctor or a psychologist, finding only scientific data in an occurrence which is represented as a revelation, still cannot affirm that the occurrence is solely a psychic affair. The doctor may establish "a perception without an object" with all the characteristics of a hallucination and consider that he is dealing with one, but is he sure that no force superior to the psyche may not have set in motion what he calls a psychic hallucination? He may object: I have faithfully and fully analyzed the event and I found in it only the effect of psychic (or physiological) forces. Obviously he cannot find God there, any more than a biologist can find a soul by analyzing a living body. Every scientist seeks the explanation within his own sphere; a biologist will explain by a bodily condition what a psychiatrist will explain by the psyche: the physical acts upon the physical and the psychic upon the psychic. But the psychic elements may act upon the body; the spirit may act upon the psyche, and God may act upon the spirit, the psyche and the body. It is a very mysterious activity. In this activity the superior reality knows its own task, its own movement and that which it is inducing in the inferior reality, but not vice versa.

4. In line with the third principle we add a fourth: The theologian does not have to establish that the occurrence in question has no specific psychic characteristics in order to discern the authenticity of a revelation. The psychic structure of a revelation may be identical with that of a hallucination. They differ only in their efficient cause. But God, the absolutely spiritual cause, is not psychologically verifiable. In this domain, therefore, one may only conclude that God may be present as a cause. For revelations are not miracles in the strict sense. These are characterized by a reality perceptible to the senses, a sign of the invisible action of God.

Thus revelations do not have the same purpose as miracles. The latter manifest the omnipotence of God: the former His omniscience. It is more difficult to exclude all probability of a natural solution in the discernment of revelation than in that of a miracle.

5. So we hold as a principle: It is not necessary to establish the absence of all probability in favor of a natural explanation in order to discern a supernatural cause in an occurrence which presents itself as a revelation.

Among the principles we have just formulated, this last probably lends itself most readily to criticism. There was a time when the following thesis was still fairly generally accepted: As long as the slightest probability in favor of a natural explanation subsists, the supernatural cause of some occurrence must be excluded. This thesis was formulated at a time when apologetics had to defend the Faith against rationalism, and so the rational aspect of the Faith was exaggerated. Among the majority of theologians an almost rationalist prejudice prevailed against revelations and apparitions. And since these could not be "sufficiently proved"—that is to say, reason could not entirely elucidate all the details of these manifestations—they were rejected.

Even if particular revelations attained the convincing force of prophecies which, together with miracles, are the "very certain signs of divine revelations," according to the Vatican Council, they would remain in the sphere of signs and not of evidence.

Furthermore, why should one demand criteria in the discernment of particular revelations which are not demanded of the revelations contained in Scripture? Rationally and psychologically speaking, it would be easier to explain the revelation of the angel to Zachary as a psychic hallucination than certain post-apostolic revelations about which we know a mass of details, all confirming their authenticity.

From the standpoint of an antirationalist apologetic which has sought its weapons too much in rationalism itself, the principle of economy has been invoked and applied as a criterion of discernment of revelations. This principle may be a working hypothesis, but it is nothing more. The principle of economy demands that one exclude a special divine action in a wonderful event, if such divine action assumes a causality more complex than in the case where such action is missing. Certainly one should not uselessly multiply or complicate things. But one may ask if the principle of economy is obligatory in human researches. In any event, when the action of God is involved, it is not demanded. It is a fact that in the work of the Creation and of the Redemption God did not always act according to the principle of economy. God could have saved us, for example, by a simple pardon, but He chose a more complex solution, that of the Incarnation, of the Cross and of the participation of men in the priesthood of Christ.

Once again, it is always good to apply the principle of economy as a working hypothesis, but it cannot be a criterion of discernment. That is not to say that one should become involved in "miracle-hunting." It is essential to estimate carefully the different factors which play a part in any occurrence.

6. We hold the following as the sixth principle: If in the infra-spiritual domain of man, pathological elements are discovered whose power is evident just where the revelatory action of God is said to be inserted, one cannot pronounce in favor of the supernatural quality of the occurrence in question.

Certainly it is admitted today that morbid elements may be mingled with charismatic graces and mystical epiphenomena. When these elements touch just the point where the divine gifts enter the psyche, discernment becomes impossible.

7. Throughout the quest for discernment this next principle must never be forgotten—it is the last we shall propose in the restricted scope of our present work: Although it is

necessary to consider that all the aspects of an occurrence must be examined, certain aspects of a particular character may assume a decisive importance in discernment.

These aspects are by preference if not exclusively in the realm of theological criteria. Strictly speaking, a spiritual process by itself may be sufficient to discern the true from the false in judging revelations; fundamentally these are spiritual realities. A spiritual reality cannot be judged finally by doctors, psychiatrists and psychologists.

What St. Paul said in a much wider context than ours applies to our problem: "But the sensual man perceiveth not these things that are of the Spirit of God; for it is foolishness to him, and he cannot understand, because it is spiritually examined. But the spiritual man judgeth all things; and he himself is judged of no man" (1 Cor. 2: 14, 15).

Conscious of this state of things, André Combes writes: "Neuropsychiatry has strictly nothing to say upon the authenticity of a mystic . . . lack of balance does not constitute any valuable proof contradicting the reality of an inpouring of God into a passive soul." [91] In order not to see exaggeration or even error in this statement, it is essential to understand it properly. It concerns a judgment of principle regarding spiritual data. In this sense, too, we can properly apply to our problem, namely, revelations and the psyche, the conclusion reached by the psychiatrist Karl Stern in his study on psychoanalysis and religion: "We may state, therefore, that the normal criteria of medicine lose all their significance in the sphere of the spiritual life. We have already said that psychiatry, like psychoanalysis, was equally unable to penetrate the mystery of the person, but their radical powerlessness is nowhere more apparent than when confronted by the supernatural realities." [92]

Certainly before reaching any final conclusion regarding spiritual data—which include revelations—the spiritual inquiry should extend to a full investigation of the psychic life and psychic pathology of the subject involved, in order to avoid consideration from a purely spiritual angle of what is merely a psychic phenomenon. This danger may be avoided by relying not only upon science and human experience but also by applying theological criteria, which in the last analysis alone results in the recognition of what comes from God and what does not. Without these criteria it is impossible to distinguish between revelations and diabolical imitations, which we shall describe before studying the value and use of the criteria of discernment in their entirety.

3   DIABOLICAL FRAUDS

The power of diabolical imitations

Let us suppose that in studying a phenomenon which appears to be a revelation one succeeds in establishing that something more than purely psychic reality is involved. Let us suppose even that one reaches the conclusion that there are other supra-psychic factors or agents at work. Obviously one has not the right to draw the conclusion, "This must be a revelation," for the devil may have his share in it. It is not necessary to examine the different categories of deceits which could be involved: the bad faith of the visionaries, their intention to deceive, the possibilities of being deceived by men, in particular by occultism, spiritism, or certain metapsychical practices. The criteria of discernment which we shall treat in the following chapters are methods capable of determining with some certitude whether in a particular case one is dealing with an occurrence desired and caused by God or not. Moreover, even if one were to succeed in proving that the witnesses of a revelation "have not been mistaken, have not wanted to deceive and even had they wanted to do so they could not have deceived," the problem of discernment would not be resolved as certain writers think. What we have just said about the problem of the psyche and revelations must be considered.

But there is the influence of Satan. That is another question, a question which has such importance for our study that certain reflections about him are called for. Satan is the fallen angel who labors in souls against God's reign on earth. The Hebrew word "Satan" signifies adversary. Satan is the supreme adversary of Christ and of Christians. Why should he not struggle against revelations, since these are methods used by God to animate the Christian faith and to strengthen Christ's reign?

His destructive activity is very dangerous because as an angel he still has his penetrating intelligence. He knows how to make the best use of it. What is more, he is a liar and the father of lies (John 8: 44). As an individual, he knows how to deceive people. He very cunningly discredits true revelations and raises up the false ones. His power enables him to deceive. Christ called him the "prince of this world" (John 12: 31), and as such Satan has his co-operators among the men who do not submit to God. The Council of Trent held that man became the prisoner of the devil through original sin (Denz., 788). Certainly Christ conquered the prince of this world; but the latter still retains a certain domination over the world. "This domination of the devil over the world is a governing idea of John's," notes the Jerusalem Bible (Luke 4: 5, note g).

This domination is clearly expressed by the Synoptics in the account of the temptation of Our Lord. Leading Him up onto a mountain, the devil, after showing Him all the kingdoms of the world, said to Him: "To Thee will I give all this power, and the glory of them; for to me they are delivered, and to whom I will, I give them. If thou therefore wilt adore before me, all shall be thine" (Luke 4: 6–7).

The devil was relying here, as in other temptations, upon truths. As it is true that the Son of God has the power to change a stone into bread, it is also true that Satan possesses the world. Without such solid supports these temptations would have had no cogency. So Christ did not protest against the supports of the tempter, but against his suggestions and his unlawful demands of Him. The devil could not have said, "To whom I will I give them," if he did not possess them. He stated clearly that the power and the glory of this kingdom had been delivered to him.

It is true that through the death of Christ "the prince of this world shall be cast out" (John 7: 31). The world has been ransomed by the Blood of Christ; but the world must freely accept this ransom in order to be liberated in fact. Everyone who accepts it becomes the child of God. Now, "Whatsoever is born of God, overcometh the world: and this is the victory which overcometh the world, our faith" (1 John 5: 4). But anyone who does not believe, anyone who sins, remains, even after the Redemption, the slave of the devil: "He that committeth sin is of the devil" (1 John 3: 8). The devil continues to exercise a certain domination over the world inasmuch as sin persists in the world. This implies first of all a restricted power over material things. According to a doctrine generally taught in the Church, the particular powers are governed in the world by universal powers. Thus the lower angels are subject to the more universal power of the higher angels, and corporal things to the angels.[92a]

The fallen angels retain their noble angelic nature and thus superiority of action, as the result of the superior quality of their being. Since through their nature they are superior to men, their domination over matter surpasses that possessed by men to such a point that their actions seem to be miracles. The man who is without knowledge and experience does not succeed in distinguishing these actions from miracles properly so called, that is, the works of forces surpassing those belonging to any creature. So Satan has been called "the amazing wonder-worker." His power is surprising, when he makes use of created means, and surprising too is the power of the people who rely upon him. St. Thomas wrote: "All the facts which in this world come under the experience of the senses may be produced by the demons acting not only through their own energies, but also making use of the forces of nature." [92b] It is, in fact, thanks to Satan that Antichrist is capable of achieving "all power, and signs, and lying wonders" (II Thess. 2: 9). So too the coming of Antichrist will be marked by the "working of Satan, in all power, and signs, and lying wonders, and in all seduction of iniquity. . . ." (II Thess. 2: 9–10).

In the prayers of the liturgy the doctrine of Satan as domination over matter is expressed at least implicitly. The exorcisms said over water, salt and oil assume that he dwells in these elements as he does in his own domain, and that he exercises some domination therein. In the chrismal Mass of Holy Thursday the bishop reads, in blessing the oil for the sick, the following exorcism: "I exorcise thee, most unclean spirit, as also all invasion or illusion of Satan in the name of the Father and of the Son and of the Holy Spirit: depart from this oil so that it may serve as a spiritual unction. . . ." And in the same Mass, for the blessing of the oil of the catechumens, the bishop pronounces this exorcism over the oil: "I exorcise thee . . . so that all the evil power of the enemy, all the inveterate malice of the devil, all violent assault, all trouble and all illusion on his part may be uprooted, cast out and removed from thee."

It may be imagined with what ease our "adversary" is able to deceive us in the sensual sphere. This is precisely the sphere which seems to serve most commonly as the means for heavenly communications. According to St. Thomas, the best form of prophecy is that of an apparition speaking to man. This apparition may have an artificial form. Thus an angel may appear with a human body, and the devil may imitate him. But his influence upon the interior senses is more common and more subtle. A good angel or a bad angel, by virtue of his nature, is able to stir the imagination of man. We have said earlier that corporal nature obeys the angel as far as local movement is concerned. Anything which can be caused by the local movement of some body is therefore subject to the natural power of the angels. It is clear that imaginative apparitions are caused in us by the local movement of corporal influence and fluids. And the disturbance of influences and fluids may be such that types of apparitions may also materialize in the waking state: this happens to those suffering from mental illnesses and to others.

St. Thomas expounds this teaching in the *Summa Theologica* (I, 111, 3); he expresses it very strongly also in *De Malo:* "Evident proofs and experiences show us that the devils may make things appear to men in sensible fashion." [93]

The domination of the devil may even extend to the mind of man. It is true that he cannot directly touch the intelligence or move the will, but he can act strongly upon these spiritual faculties by way of the senses. Through the interior senses, for instance, he can arouse such perturbation in the human spirit that all intellectual knowledge becomes practically impossible. Besides, through the tremendous means at his disposal and through his penetrating knowledge of signs, he can divine secrets and future events. The entire man with all his faculties may even fall wholly under the devil's domination, that is, if he freely gives himself to the devil. He cannot then withdraw himself even if he wants to; he becomes truly the possession of the devil; as a possessed person he is totally at the disposal of the devil: he is the "prophet" of the devil who speaks through him.

It is clear that we now find ourselves confronting the richest and most subtle source of illusions and frauds. When the most beautiful guise is not sufficient to deceive, the devil even propounds truths to attain his ends; he can thus at least create confusion. This is what he did through the mouths of the possessed—who were not the same as the bodily sick—in the presence of Christ: their declarations were revelations, at least for the people who heard them.

When the possessed on seeing Jesus fell down before Him and cried out: "Thou art the Son of God" (Mark 3: 12), and "Son of God, art thou come hither to torment us before the time?" (Matt. 8: 29), they meant what they said. Their words are to be identified in substance with the well known profession of faith: "Thou art Christ the Son of the living God" (Matt. 16: 16). And this was, as Jesus Himself said, a revelation. Moreover, it is significant that Christ's reaction was the same to the revelation of Simon Peter as to the statement of the possessed. After the disciples' profession of faith he commanded that they "should tell no one that He was Jesus the Christ" (Matt. 16: 20). He strictly charged the possessed persons that they should not make Him known (Mark 3: 12).

The context demonstrates clearly that the unclean spirits spoke the truth. This was not a revelation in the full sense of the word: it did not come from the heavenly Father; it was *acquired* perhaps through the interpretation of signs or of heavenly words spoken at the time of the baptism of Christ or after the profession of St. Peter.

Criteria of discernment

In the face of such powerful activity on the part of the devil, do we not lose all hope of being able to discern the true revelations from the false? Jesus Himself spoke of false Christs and false prophets who would produce signs and prodigies so considerable as to be able to deceive if possible even the elect (Matt. 24: 24). There is no situation more difficult for discernment than this. And still it is not impossible. That is not to say, indeed, that one will always arrive at a satisfactory result, but actually one may succeed in discerning the true from the false by making use of the appropriate criteria. It would be difficult to admit that God would not give to His own, to the Church, the means of distinguishing His activity from that of the devil. In fact, God does give such means abundantly here where human means are even less efficacious than in other domains. We shall see the collection of the chief criteria which allow revelations to be discerned from imitations of them, including diabolical counterfeits.

Here we shall only draw attention to the appropriate means which the Church places at the disposal of her ministers for withdrawing from the devil his domination over men and things in particular cases. This is exorcism. While this is applied to interference by the devil in souls, its effects also touch diabolical pseudo-revelations.

In the presence of extraordinary events which are presented as revelations, one first should use the method of elimination. Before assuming the devil to be at work, one should inquire about the presence of human forces or weaknesses such as clairvoyance, hysterical manifestations, split consciousness, etc. A subject suffering from demonomania could perfectly play the part of a possessed person. Violent impulses in opposition to the habitual temperament, the feeling of being a victim of a strange force, convulsive attacks, and so on are not necessarily symptoms of possession, but they may be the effects of demonomania. A subject who manifests them, however, cannot be considered as the bearer of a particular revelation.

Among the criteria of discernment which the experts of exorcism recommend to us is the revelation of occult things. The content of these revelations allows a certain measure of judgment to be reached. If it is a matter, for instance, of things which men could not know, but which have no religious value, at least in their purpose, then one should give up the idea of seeing a particular revelation in them. A certain religious content is obviously not sufficient to prove the existence of a particular revelation. But this content may be so profound and so much in the context of religious events and circumstances that it gives at least a favorable indication of the authenticity of a revelation.

Pierre Thyrré in his treatise on demoniacs, points to the revelation of hidden things as a first sign for recognizing diabolical possession.[94] If it concerns things the knowledge of which could only derive from God, one may then be sure that God has spoken through the mouth of man.

But we shall be dealing with positive criteria of discernment in the next chapter. We are considering only the negative criteria here, that is to say, knowledge of the measure and extent of *created* forces which keep us from taking certain natural effects for signs of a supernatural revelation.

Let us suppose that someone reveals to us, as coming from God, things which are in fact outside the scope of human knowledge, and that the question must be asked whether the matter is of the devil or of God. The question then arises: "Are there criteria which allow us to deduce the presence of the devil?" Certainly there are, but they are more rare than those mentioned in earlier treatises upon the possessed.

We are not concerned here with debating the worth or the weakness of these criteria. Those who laid them down knew less than we do about what the forces of man can achieve. The criteria which belong properly to the religious domain are not in danger of losing their value because of the progress of science, especially of psychology. We shall limit ourselves to the description of two: the application of holy things without the knowledge of the subject who seems to be a visionary or a prophet, and his compulsive obedience.

If, without the knowledge of the subject in question, one actually applies holy things—holy water, a crucifix, relics, etc.—and observes agitation, horror or anguish in the body of the subject, or if, immediately after the application of these things, the person flees, one may rightly conclude that

the devil is at work. Holy water seems to be the most effective method of driving out devils. The Church moreover
mentions this purpose in the prayers of blessings. So, too,
St. Teresa of Ávila writes in her *Autobiography* (chap. 31,
note 4): "I have seen many times in my own experience that
there is nothing more effective than holy water for repulsing
the devils and preventing them from returning. The cross
also puts them to flight, but they return. The strength of holy
water must be very great." And St. Bernadette Soubirous, in
order to make certain that her vision was not a diabolical
phenomenon, sprinkled the Apparition with holy water. The
Apparition did not disappear, nor give any sign of disturbance; but her "only response was a smile." [95]

The other criterion we mentioned seems surer to us. It
was applied by Our Lord Himself. The possessed who were
a terror to the people and whom no one succeeded in con-
trolling—who even broke the chains which people had man-
aged to put on them—immediately obeyed the orders of
Jesus Christ like slaves without strength or personality.

If, in a doubtful case, one applies exorcism to the subject
in question and if the person reacts by compulsively and
promptly obeying orders whose execution demands super-
human or "preternatural" agents, one may be morally sure
that he is dealing with a diabolical situation. As in the domain of parapsychology, there are accounts of this type of
thing so trustworthy and so well attested that one has no
right to refuse their authenticity solely because they refer to
things which do not tally with what we know. Very strange
events occur which people hide in order to avoid annoyance.
To the event which Dr. Calmeil recounts in his work on mad-
ness [96] one could add others which are analogous.

Dr. Calmeil quotes a letter in which Père Lacour related
his own experience. As a missionary in Indo-China, he was
called to the town of Chela to exorcise a young man between
18 and 19 years old. The priest, determined to believe nothing if he did not see indisputable signs of possession, went to

find him. He saw him at the hospital, on the ground, slavering and violently convulsed.

After a few attempts at discernment Père Lacour decided to exorcise the young man in the church of the town. The priest commanded the devil in Latin to carry the young man up to the ceiling of the church, feet foremost and head down. Immediately the young man's body became rigid and was dragged from the middle of the church to a pillar and there, with his feet together and his back pressed against the pillar, without any help from his hands, he was carried in the wink of an eye to the ceiling. His feet stuck to the ceiling and he remained there, hanging with his head down. The priest made the devil confess that he was a deceiver and forced him to admit that the Christian religion was holy. The priest held the devil that way over half an hour. Frightened himself at the spectacle, he ordered the devil to put the young man back on his feet without doing him any harm. The devil threw him on the ground "like a bundle of dirty clothes without harming him."

This incident shows that one may at least succeed in a negative form of discernment. May one then deduce a divine manifestation if exorcism has no effect upon a man who claims to have received revelations? No, one cannot arrive at this conclusion with certainty.

The criteria which we have defined so far are not sufficient to lead to a conclusion upon the question of discernment. We have simply been determining the part played by created agents—human or demoniacal—in apparent revelations, with a view to a study of the criteria themselves, which taken together make it possible to discern with certitude the false revelations from the true. That is the study we must embark upon now.

CHAPTER VI

The Intrinsic Criteria of Discernment

WHAT WE HAVE attempted so far in our discussion of discernment has really been merely to clear the ground. We must now make an effort to build. Particular revelation, like all revelation, is a very complex reality—an assumed relationship between human action and divine. It implies intense emotion in the ontological sense of the word. Involved in it are the agent, the content, and the subject who receives the revelation, as also the mode and circumstance of the communication.

The surest discernment lies with the agent, who may have direct knowledge of the divine action. Possessing this, one could dispense with all study of the content, the subject, the mode and the circumstances of a particular revelation. But only in the Beatific Vision shall we have this direct knowledge of God and of His activity. We are able, however, to come to a certain understanding here on earth of the revelatory activity of God, either through experience or through the gift of discernment. The Church has always known and recognized the effectiveness of this gift, which is included among the great charisms enumerated by St. Paul (1 Cor. 12: 10). St. Augustine, as well as so many other authorities with deep reserves of experience, declared that sure discernment does not take place without a special gift (cf. note 58f). In so far as a particular revelation is supernatural it is covered by these words of St. Paul: "For what man knoweth the things of a man, but the spirit of a man that is in him? So the things also that are of God no man knoweth, but the Spirit of God. Now we have received not the spirit of this world, but the spirit that is of God; that we may know the things that are given us from God" (1 *Cor.* 2: 11–12).

For achieving discernment there is the way of charism, but there is also the way of investigation by the man enlightened by the Faith.

In so delicate a sphere it is necessary to assure ourselves of all the guarantees: those of the pure gift and those of investigation. However, the way of charism does not need enlightenment: one possesses this or one does not possess it; it is a special gift which the Church always receives. The way of investigation is another matter. One cannot embark upon it in any sort of manner. Investigation calls for an insight, a certain attitude, that is difficult to acquire. Before estimating the value and the weight of the extrinsic criteria of revelations, we shall try to consider their object, their subject, their method and their circumstances from the viewpoint of discernment.

1   THE CONTENT OF REVELATIONS

The first criterion of discernment is doctrinal in character. In considering a revelation the Church has always asked whether its content corresponded with Catholic teaching. One can a priori disregard any inquiry into such correspondence when the matter concerns trivial or fantastic, useless or profane things.

Here is what is said in "The Messages from Beyond" (*Botschaften aus dem Jenseits*) published by the *Geistige Loge* in Zurich in 1949: "Yes, I [the spirit Joseph], I come today to you all as a real tradesman, so to speak! I have here a big basket full of lovely flowers which I have found for you in the celestial paradise. . . . I have here twice three roses (the medium—Beatrice—extends her two hands as if she were holding them). These two bouquets of roses belong, each of them, to one person present whose life and aura are identical with those of the roses. The aura (*die Austrahlung*) of these persons and the perfume of these roses are equally agreeable and blend into a whole. If I greet these two ladies with the two bouquets of flowers in this way, it is because these roses are formed of their own rays" (p. 41). The spirit Joseph, who communicates such things through the medium, gives us information about the present and future life of the philosopher Kant and of the poet Conrad Ferdinand Meyer. The first is in a spiritual paradise of light, the second in a paradise of flowers; both are purified and will return. Meyer will give a still better form to the poems he has written; he will send them to us. He is looking for a man who will be able to receive his thoughts and the knowledge which he has acquired in the spiritual world (pp. 308–309).

In a case like this the negative discernment can be made at once. It would be pointless to study this affair any further. Every revelation must be rejected a priori if its context is opposed to the Church's teaching. In places where the Scripture speaks most explicitly of the discernment of spirits and where it urges Christians to "try the spirits if they be of God," it gives only one criterion which is of a doctrinal nature. "By this is the spirit of God known: every spirit which confesseth that Jesus Christ is come in the flesh, is of God: and every spirit that dissolveth Jesus is not of God" (1 John 4: 2–3).

The criterion which is based upon the content is not so easy to handle as might seem at first glance. Theological trends, the habit of considering every thing "in itself," and even personal ideas may have a dangerous influence upon the judgment to be made in this sphere.

During the period when society overestimated the value of reason, theologians were inclined to underestimate the revelations concerning the Sacred Heart. If it is so difficult to extricate the true meaning of many matters of universal Revelation because these truths are deeply rooted in the movement of the actual life of a country or of a person, the task is still more arduous and more delicate when we are dealing with particular revelations. For surely no less than universal Revelation they must be considered in their historical context.

Before passing judgment on the content of a revelation one must first ask in what way the divine has been adapted to the manifestation in question. To what end are the details of its content directed? Do the circumstances in any way obscure the truth of the historical fact or at least the true meaning of the words spoken?

God adapts Himself so often and to such an extent to natural facts that we are able to speak of a law of divine adaptation. Christ showed Himself to Magdalen in such a guise that she came to think that He was a gardener. He appeared to the disciples on the road to Emmaus as a traveler. Here and there He has made Himself known. So in the apparitions throughout the history of the Church, an "incognito" has often been used, revealing a certain adaptation to the customs of the period. In the Marian revelations, for instance, the Blessed Virgin made herself known—but she spoke to adults in a way different from that in which she spoke to children, and to Christians advanced in the spiritual life in a way different from that in which she addressed ignorant people. Thus some have found banal the reply of the Apparition at Beauraing when the children asked what she wanted of them—"to be good," she said. And when Our Lady of La Salette complained that during Lent people were going to the slaughterhouse like dogs, certain people found this everyday language coarse and unworthy of the Blessed Virgin.

But we may interpret such things as heavenly adaptations to human life. We do not find the use of learned language in the approved revelations; we search them in vain for a logical system of transitions to underline the movement of thought. The style is normally direct and matter of fact, and the syntax simplicity itself. The content is chiefly expressed by independent propositions, juxtaposed or co-ordinated; it takes varied and personal turns. This was the language of the prophets, of Christ and the Apostles.

The next important thing is to extract the true meaning of the revelation; this, after all, is basically what we want. All the details of content are not of equal importance, yet each should not be considered separately. The point is to apply, to a certain extent at least, the method by which one interprets the parables. The details are to be interpreted within the context of the whole. Eusebius Amort, who is noted for his severity in regard to particular revelations, goes so far as this:

He believes that in the visions of the saints—he speaks in particular of St. Gertrude—the forces of fantasy intervene. And he is wholly convinced that it is with pleasure that God sees these forces at work in the souls of the just. In his opinion God mingles holy insights and spiritual movements with these forces. And it is not solely the forces which please Him; He Himself encourages the fantasy so that it may exercise its activity and enable Him to introduce His lights and manifestations in the soul. It is Amort's conclusion that in such visions of the saints "one must examine and correct what is human." [97]

It even happens, as we may prove from the Bible and the history of the Church, that certain representations coming from God should be interpreted as signs of more profound realities which are basically the content of the revelation.

When Joan of Arc learned in prison that she would be freed through a great victory, she took the word victory in the literal sense in which she was accustomed to hear it in her military career. But the great victory divinely announced was martyrdom.

And when St. Francis of Assisi, praying before the crucifix in the Church of St. Damian, heard a voice which said to him: "Francis, do you not see that my house is in ruins? Go and repair it for me," he thought that the church meant was the old and abandoned one in which he was praying. And he started at once on the work of repairing it. It was not until later that he understood what the revelation really meant, that it referred far more to the living Church than to a material building.

In the examination of the content, it is necessary to consider the circumstances in which this content is finally given or transmitted. Certainly speech is the highest mode of communication, but there are other methods which may at least help in understanding the true meaning of the words. In particular revelations the symbolic language of events and of facts surely exercises no less influence over strictly verbal expressions than is the case with universal Revelation. And the words themselves should be taken as they were first uttered. As soon as they are removed from their context, as soon as they are translated, above all when this translation involves a dialect, there is a risk of passing an erroneous judgment on the meaning of the words, as we have seen from the discussions regarding St. Bridget's revelations at the Council of Basle, and elsewhere.

The criterion based upon the content of the revelations is chiefly of a negative character. It is used above all to establish that a revelation is *not* supernatural. But it may have a positive value. Certainly the fact that a text put before us as a revelation contains nothing opposed to the teaching of

Scripture and Tradition does not constitute an argument for the authenticity of that revelation. So too the *imprimatur* given by ecclesiastical authority for the publication of texts presented as revelation is not an approbation. It is simply an official statement that there is nothing in them contrary to faith and morals. However, the criterion of content may have more than a purely negative effectiveness. When the content in question is not merely correct but of a depth and doctrinal balance which surpasses the capacity of the subject who is presenting it, and when it is, furthermore, simple and original, then one may see in these qualities a criterion which has a positive value for discernment. Obviously, however, this criterion is not sufficient alone to prove the divine origin of the content of the revelation.

This applies to those revelations which have such importance in a life that unless their origin were supernatural one could not explain the facts—either separately or collectively —of that life.

Thus the qualities of the revelation of Blessed Angela da Foligno were such that they formed a positive criterion of discernment. And anyone who wished to deny, for example, the divine origin of all the revelations made to St. Teresa of Avila, especially during the period when she was founding her convents, could not explain her life.

Furthermore, one may find important bases for the criteria of discernment in the life and personality of the one to whom the revelations are made.

2   CRITERIA FOR THE
SUBJECT OF REVELATIONS

By subject we do not mean the object of the revelations but the person who receives them. The criteria to be found in such a person are no less efficient than those we have just seen. It is easy to understand why.

Revelation is true if its content comes from God. But this content is not given us directly by God; it passes through the visionary—the person who receives it. Now there is a universally recognized law which says: "Everything which a subject receives, he receives according to his dispositions." Everything transmitted by human means undergoes some change by the subject who transmits it. To arrive at discernment one must know in a concrete case the extent of the change made in transmitting the message. Has the substance of the content been retained intact? Have we all the content? Is it false or rather a simple imitation of a transmitted message? Has the visionary kept his openmindedness as a witness or not? Here arises the problem of all testimony, the dialectics of which were expressed in the clearest possible way by Christ Himself. "We testify what we have seen and you receive not our testimony" (John 3: 11). "My doctrine is not Mine, but His that sent Me" (John 7: 16): "for I have not spoken of Myself; but the Father who sent Me, He gave Me command what I should say, and what I should speak. And I know that His commandment is life everlasting. The things therefore that I speak, even as the Father said unto Me, so do I speak" (John 12: 49–50).

But we must not forget this: Christ is the ideal witness because He has the same nature as His Father and is His perfect image. The human witness or "prophet" is not in the same position; in every stratum of his being obstacles may arise which could disturb the perviousness which would allow him to transmit perfectly what he has received from heaven, obstacles which may belong to his physiological constitution, to his psychic make-up or development, to his moral or religious attitudes.

The physiological aspect

Those authors who have concerned themselves with the problem of discernment have attached a certain importance to the difference of sex. Amort, relying on Gravina and Gerson, laid down in the *Summarium regularum* (nos. 1 and 12) of his treatise upon revelations, the following criterion: "The revelations of women, if other proofs do not contend in their favor, are very probably false, and these probably false revelations should in practice be considered as absolutely false."

Why should he judge the revelations of women more harshly than those of men? Because women are imprudent and talkative. The woman, says Amort again, is a weak being, unstable and irresponsible.[97a] For the same reasons she is excluded by the Church from public ministry. Besides, is it not a fact that the majority of pseudo-revelations come to us from women?

This is a biased judgment which is based upon an inadmissible generalization and in which various aspects are neglected. It is true that because of their constitution and their more delicate sensibilities women, generally speaking, are more subject to the influence of the sensory world. So, certain passions may arise more easily among them. And defects which do not favor positive discernment may be more accentuated in women than in men. Now it is precisely in the sphere of the senses that the devil, the pre-eminent liar, exerts his influence.

But, on the other hand, any woman who is not warped by education or evil experience shows less difficulty in giving herself than the man. She finds it easier to forget herself and to serve others. Now, experience seems to prove that man is more creative than woman. One has but to think of the difference in the artistic and scientific activity of the two sexes. In the practical sphere it is a fact that women succeed better as secretaries and telephonists than men, who are less suited to pure transmission; the latter are more tempted to inject something of their own into the message. From this point of view we may understand the advantage which women have in the positive discernment of revelations.

The same tendency for giving and abandonment, more pronounced in the woman than in the man, disposes her better to devotion, which consists in the gift of self to God. St. Thomas, who gives this definition (*Sum. Theol.*, II–II, 82, 2, ob. 1), teaches also that man, being better endowed for contemplation and knowledge, is of himself in a situation which favors devotion; but because of these good qualities which are more easily accessible to him there is more danger that he will attach himself to them for his own sake. Thus it happens that in practice one often finds more devotion among simple men and among women (*Sum. Theol.*, II–II, 82, 3, 3). St. Teresa is also of the opinion that women are in general more attached to God than are men. Now God normally reveals Himself by preference to those who are most attached to Him.

If it is true that one finds pseudo-revelations considerably more frequently among women than among men, it is also true that, so far as one may reckon from the Church's history, God has revealed Himself more frequently to women than to men. We have only to think of the holy women Gertrude,

Bridget, Catherine of Siena, Margaret Mary Alacoque among others.

Even in the Marian apparitions of these last two centuries women have the strongest representation among the visionaries. At Lourdes and at Banneux there was one visionary—a woman. And in cases where both sexes were represented, the role of the woman was the more important.[98]

Thus Pope Gregory XV began the bull of canonization of Teresa of Avila by emphasizing the fact that in the post-apostolic era God has revealed Himself by preference to the humble and the unknown.[99] And among these, right up to the twentieth century, may be counted chiefly women. There are theologians who have gone so far as to state that God might have wished to establish a certain balance in the distribution of His gifts by extending that of prophecy especially to women, who are deprived of the graces of the priesthood and of the ministry of the word. Be that as it may, the difference of sex does not require a different use of the criteria of discernment.

From the theological point of view St. Thomas arrives at the same solution: The grace of prophecy is manifested according to the spirit illumined by God; and from this point of view there exists no difference between the sexes [99a] (*Sum. Theol.*, II–II, 2, ad 2). And Benedict XIV approves the opinion of Mattheuccius: "One must not reject apparitions and visions because they have been received by women." [100]

Finally, one should be careful not to exaggerate the difference of sex. At all times in history there have been women who possessed to a high degree the virtues called virile, just as the weaknesses more often attributed to the female sex are known among men. From the point of view of the soul and the spirit (*pneuma*) there is no difference of sex. The suprasensible forces are not necessarily conditioned by the influence of sex. But science is today in a position to explain better certain facts to which we have just alluded. The intensive study of physiology, especially that of hormones, has demonstrated that the difference of sex is not always clearly defined. The constitution of a man, for example, may up to a certain point be feminine and vice versa, so that he feels better if he lives in the manner of the other sex. And thus it happens that individuals after undergoing an operation will change their sex officially. The results of these modern studies make it easier to understand why there have always been effeminate men and virile women.

Other physiological factors may affect discernment, such as the illness or age of the visionary. Obviously, the visionary need not be in perfect health. An illness, even a psychic illness, is not necessarily a proof against the authenticity of a revelation. But there are illnesses which exclude authenticity, such as Parkinson's disease or cerebral lesions which predispose the sufferer to auditory hallucinations.

It is not pointless to consider the age of the visionary. In the case of a child, for instance, the question of split personality could not be assumed; but it would be important to investigate whether or not there are eidetic dispositions. But at this point we enter the psychological domain. We have already examined the relationship of psychology and revelations. Now we will consider the application of psychology to discernment.

The psychological aspect

It is understood that the examination of the psychological make-up alone can never be the basis of a judgment in favor of the divine origin of a revelation. Only by a supernatural process can we in the long run judge supernatural facts. But a medical examination may furnish valuable support for the formation of a positive judgment. If the diagnosis of the doctor affirms the perfect health and psychological balance of the subject who claims to be experiencing revelations in an extraordinary way, then this constitutes positive support for a favorable judgment. But the diagnosis in itself, apart from the other factors, has no positive value for discernment. It can, however, constitute a negative criterion; if it can be established that a person was showing all the symptoms of hysteria at the moment when he received the revelations, a favorable judgment cannot be reached, even though it may not be impossible that God was communicating with him.

Not only pathological symptoms but certain normal facts of psychology may influence the judgment in discernment. They may, in a particular situation, constitute a negative criterion of discernment. One could, for example, more easily consider the possibility of a clever simulation of the circumstances of the "revelation" in question if its subject has a very high intelligence or a fierce determination to draw attention to himself. In the same way, and many writers have called attention to this, one should distrust in advance those visionaries who have a prolific imagination. Further, constitutional instability, hyper-sensitiveness and excessive impressionability in themselves constitute negative (unfavorable) criteria for discernment.

It is significant that experts find in these characteristics the predispositions for the career of a medium. Dr. Maxwell, who is neither a spiritist nor a Christian, but who has no tendency to depreciate mediums, writes in his book, *Mystical Phenomena:* "The chances of encountering a medium will be greater if one searches among nervous people. It seems to me that a certain impressionability or nervous instability is a favorable condition for the successful achievement of the work of the medium."

Paroxysmal states, everything which leads to psychic disassociation, as also the possession of metapsychical powers such as clairvoyance—that precognition which serious minds trained in scientific methods either admit or are inclined to admit—all these constitute negative criteria in themselves.

An unfavorable judgment is also indicated if one discovers that the subject in question has been known to tell lies, since it is obvious that a falsehood could radically change the transmission of the revelation which is being examined. It may be that the lie is only a psychic anomaly, but in a sound and balanced subject lying is always an act in the moral order. It is in the spiritual domain to which the moral order belongs that we find the most certain intrinsic criteria of discernment.

The spiritual criteria

First of all, we ask ourselves in what sense the life and moral virtues of the subject should influence the judgment in discernment. According to the teaching generally accepted by the Church, this judgment is not determined by the moral behavior of the visionary. A morally perfect life is not a requisite for receiving revelations from God. Grave moral defects are obviously unfavorable signs, though generally they do not constitute a negative criterion. But there are particular defects which do constitute negative criteria—the lie, surely, is one, and so perhaps is indiscretion. How could God lay upon a liar the burden of transmitting His plans? The lie radically interferes with the transmission of the divine communication upon which the effort of discernment is concentrated.

But in the life of the Christian the moral act is normally also a religious act. It receives the influence of grace, it forms part of the spiritual life. The three virtues we are about to indicate as being positive criteria of discernment are obviously not purely moral virtues. They form the basis of those criteria more surely because of the grace of the Holy Spirit working in them. And grace is all the more discernible in that these graces must be demonstrated in the visionary to a very high degree. The virtues are humility, obedience and fortitude.

No quality in the subject of a revelation bears clearer testimony to his or her authenticity than does deep humility. All the experts insist upon this virtue. Gerson puts it at the head of five criteria of discernment which he recommends in his treatise upon the distinction between true and false visions. It is not difficult to see why humility is so important for discernment. It is because the man who possesses it is not seeking his own glory; he seeks self-effacement. He is, as a consequence, excellently disposed to receive revelations without including therein anything of his own. Praising humility, Our Lord Himself declared: "He that speaketh of himself seeketh his own glory: but he that seeketh the glory of him that sent him, he is true, and there is no injustice in him" (John 7: 18).

Humility in the Christian sense is not a diminution of man. It has certainly a negative aspect: it takes away false greatness and glory from the person who seeks it. But it is above all the vision and the life of truth. The humble man sees himself as insignificant; he is so as the result of his relationship with God. That is why imposture or lying is not in such a man. That is why the heavenly Father reveals Himself to "little ones" (Luke 10: 21). And history shows that God continues to reveal Himself to little ones, that is to say, most of the time to those who by nature and their own state are little—in any case only to those who recognize themselves as little ones, in short, to the humble.

For similar reasons obedience may constitute a criterion of discernment, or at least provide a strong support to someone already grounded in humility. It is, obviously, less intimately bound up with the revelation itself than is humility. It proves that the visionary, even in the spheres of will and of action, is not seeking his own interests. As Christ said, "I do not my own will but the will of my Father," so the fact that the visionary proves himself to be submissive to the authority which comes from God cannot help but be a testimony in favor of the revelation which he may have had. This obedience may not have been so strongly evidenced before the occurrence of the revelation as was the subject's humility, which predisposed him to receive that revelation, but displays itself effectively during and after this revelation has taken place.

In regard to this matter there is scarcely a more instructive case than the following which is related in the *Autobiography of St. Teresa of Avila* (chap. 29, 5–6) in which she recounts how the Lord manifested Himself to her. She considers the visions which she has received from Him as signal favors from God, and adds that she would not have wished to change one of them for all the riches and pleasures of the world. But since these visions became more and more frequent, her confessors began to see in them the work of the devil.

"They bade me," writes the saint, "to reject them every time by the sign of the cross and by derision, and the devil—for this was he, I was to be certain of that—would return no more; but it was necessary to banish all fear from my soul; besides, God would watch over me and would deliver me. Their command caused me very deep grief. As it was impossible for me to admit that these visions did not come from God, it was a fearful thing for me to obey. I could not wish, as I said before, that the visions should be withheld. But despite everything, *I did as I was bidden*. . . .

"It was for me a most painful thing to make a show of contempt when I was being favored by the vision of the Lord. When I saw Him before me, if I were cut to pieces, I could not believe it was Satan. . . . It reminded me of the insults which the Jews had heaped upon Him, and so I prayed Him to forgive me, seeing that I did so in obedience to him who stood in His stead, and not to lay the blame on me, seeing that he was one of those whom He had placed as His ministers in His Church. He said to me, that I was not to distress myself, that I did well to obey; but that He would make them see the truth of the matter." [100a]

Here we are dealing with a matter of obedience to God in the mystery of Christ and of the Church. To offer opposition to the obedience owed to the Church is to misunderstand this mystery; it is to set oneself upon the wrong path. Disobedience is a negative criterion of discernment and emphasized by theologians. And one of the reasons which bishops and other ecclesiastical authorities have given for condemning this or that apparition has been precisely the disobedience of the visionaries or even of members of the Church who believed in the apparitions in question and disobeyed the instructions given upon the matter, as happened at Exquioga and on other occasions.

Fortitude appears as a criterion only after the occurrence of the revelation. A revelation places its subject—prophet or visionary—in an exceptional situation and thereby necessarily in opposition to ordinary ways of life and normal attitudes to which everything else is referred.

Thus we see throughout the whole history of the people of God that prophets and visionaries were persecuted because they were the bearers of revelations. This persecution sometimes brought its victims to their death. The opposition of parents, the hostility of authorities, the temptations of kindness, the tortures of interrogations and threats of prison —all these things the visionaries of the great Marian apparitions had to endure. And these visionaries were always signalized by their strength; it was like a law which applied to the very weakest. Even children demonstrated a strength of soul which one finds rarely in adults.

One could quote in this connection many details taken from the story of the children of La Salette, of Lourdes, of Fatima and of Beauraing. Here is what a road-mender of Lourdes, Léon Latapie, had to say about Bernadette: "One Sunday, after Mass, Bernadette came out of the church with two other little girls accompanied by a nun. I took her gently by the arm. 'Why are you taking hold of her?' asked the nun and she began to weep. 'I have orders.' Bernadette said to me: 'What do you want?' I answered: 'You must come with us, child.' Bernadette began to laugh and said: 'Hold me tightly, and [sic] I will escape.' I was close to the little girl and the police superintendent was behind me. The people looked on amazed without saying anything.

"We went along to M. Rives, the magistrate, who lodges with M. Claverie, the notary. M. Rives is no longer in Lourdes. When we went in, the magistrate said to Bernadette, in dialect: 'You have come, naughty child?' 'Yes, sir, I have come,' 'We are going to lock you up. What are you looking for at the Grotto? Why are you making all these crowds run around like this? Someone is prompting you to act like this; we are going to send you to prison.' 'I am ready; put me in and let it be strong and well locked up, and I will escape from it.'

"These gentlemen were not joking. The magistrate said: 'You will have to give up going to the Grotto or you will be locked up.' 'I will not stop going there.' 'I will let you die in prison!'

"At this moment the Sister Superior of the Hospice came in. She wept and said: 'I beg you, gentlemen, spare this little girl; do not take her life! . . .'

"The magistrate released Bernadette, who said as she left: 'I will go there; next Thursday is the last day.' " [101]

One might ask whether there are not other special qualities to be sought in the visionary, such as discretion. Although there may be, we are limiting ourselves to the three which seem to us to be the most certain. They are also the best founded in traditional teaching. Here and there certain testimonies may be found in favor of sensible joy, of peace and of charity, of holiness, but the majority of writers who are qualified to speak on the matter exclude them from the criteria of discernment. First and foremost, peace, a profound peace which passes well beyond the senses and all understanding, is ranked by the mystics among the distinctive signs of true revelations. But since peace is a purely subjective experience it has no value as a sign for non-visionaries and cannot, therefore, be used as a criterion. Ecstasy, indeed, is perfectly visible, but it does not in itself belong to the supernatural domain.

Is the desire for revelations a negative criterion of discernment? Some doctors, like St. John of the Cross, have so strongly condemned it as the expression of indiscretion or curiosity, that there is a temptation to see in it a true negative criterion of discernment. But let us not forget that what is demanded of contemplatives should not necessarily be extended as universal law. It is not only the mystics who receive revelations. Facts do not sustain the thesis that one must consider as illusions all visions and revelations claimed by one whose soul has not yet arrived at mystical transformation and consequently who has never experienced the union of mystical love.[102] We shall return later to this point.

Whether indiscretion be a negative or a positive criterion, it is in any case certain that it is a weighty argument against the supernatural character of a revelation.

3   THE CRITERIA DERIVED FROM CIRCUMSTANCES

We have already insisted upon the importance of details in discernment. From the study of apparently insignificant details may spring forth a light which will uncover the marks of the truth. Hence the importance of the circumstances in

the quest for discernment. By circumstances we understand
the particular conditions which accompany a fact. The fact
is the occurrence of the revelation. It is impossible to treat
all varieties of circumstances in an abstract way. What we
can do is to place the most important in categories and try
to measure the weight which they carry in the decision on
discernment. The true weight of this or that circumstance
cannot be measured except by someone who can examine it
concretely. The play of muscles, for instance, or the gaze of
a visionary at a given moment during his interrogation, cannot be judged as a sign except by the one who is observing
them. Such is the way of all knowledge coming through
empathy or intropathy: *Einfühlung* (Dilthey). The categories
of circumstances which we shall discuss are: the purpose,
form, manner, means, time and place of the revelation.

The purpose

The purpose of a revelation may relate to its content, to
its subject, and lastly to its effects. According to the first consideration, the content is the end or purpose of the occurrence itself (*finis operis*), that is, the aim or the meaning of
the revelation. Thus understood, the content goes beyond
the nature of the circumstances; it forms part of the substance of the occurrence as an element which distinguishes
it. If this meaning of the purpose is not accepted as expressing a circumstance, it is because it is too intimately connected with the very act of the revelation.

In another sense the purpose designates a circumstance of
the subject of the revelation—it is a matter of the intention of
the visionary. It is the purpose of the agent (*finis operantis*).
If the visionary is disinterested, if he seeks only to carry out
what the requirements of the revelation ask of him, going
contrary to his own tendencies and not allowing himself to

be too impressed by sufferings and disappointments, we have a favorable sign in support of the authenticity of the revelation, but not a criterion. But the opposite would be the case if the visionary profited by his "revelation" and sought his own glory, a situation in society, or even material advantages.

The purpose, finally, can show the effects of the revelation. If the effects are the immediate consequences of the revelation, one may consider them as circumstances to be considered in the decision of discernment without having a decisive influence thereon. An example would be the conversion of the visionary, as in the case of Ratisbonne. But if it is a matter of consequences more or less remote from the revelation, that is, from all its "fruits"—miracles of the physical or moral order performed in reference to the revelation, the establishment of institutions, the performance of works —then that is another thing. These consequences are outside the circumstances of a revelation; they no longer accompany the fact but follow it. We shall speak of them when the question of extrinsic criteria arises.

The form

By form we mean the sensible appearance under which a being manifests itself to our senses. A revelation may be communicated under different forms, either through persons or through things. The theologians teach generally that one ought to reject revelations communicated under the appearances of persons or of things which are malformed: every physical or moral deformation, every false attitude, every indecent movement, constitutes a negative criterion.

The mode

One cannot deduce any criterion of discernment from the ways in which God communicates Himself to anyone. Whether God communicates Himself through the exterior senses, through the imagination or again through the intelligence, the problem of discernment remains the same. It is true that suprasensible revelations are, of themselves, more certain for they are protected from all the tricks of the senses which the devil can work. But they escape direct examination. Revelations made through the exterior or interior senses, so exposed to illusions, allow of a certain verification, sometimes even direct.

Revelations made in a dream present fewer guarantees for positive discernment. They demand a more rigorous examination than the others.

The methods

Revelations may be accompanied by a great many things which may considerably influence the decision to be made regarding them. They may take place in the presence of a crowd of people or even of doctors who observe the reactions of the visionary, as at Lourdes. They may be received by one or several persons. The plurality of visionaries makes it possible to determine more easily whether there has been a hallucination or not; but the question of collective suggestion then arises. Wonders may surround the fact of the revelation as did the "miracle of the sun" at Fatima. The examination of these methods and of so many others is useful in the quest for discernment.

The time

No time is reserved for revelations. The Scriptures and Tradition tell us of revelations which have taken place at night and in the daytime. Certainly, all things being equal, the day is more favorable to a positive discernment than the night. Darkness, or at least a diminished light, favors the apparition of metapsychical prodigies. In the séances of mediums light is not favored. The demands of the medium Eusapia Palladino were notorious: they were always for *meno luce, meno luce!* (less light).

The day is a preferable time not only because verification is easier but also because man is less impressionable in the daytime than at night. That Catherine Labouré claimed to have received a revelation from the Blessed Virgin in the dead of night is a fact which in no way encourages one to believe in the supernatural origin of the revelation. However, in the happening at the rue du Bac certain positive criteria were better verified than in revelations made elsewhere in the broad daylight. What may have a certain importance in discernment is the historical moment at which a revelation takes place. At turning points of history, in times of war, in periods of disturbance, the critic should take into account the dangerous increase of the taste for the miraculous which favors the atmosphere of pseudo-revelations. On the other hand, it is also true that at such times there is more reason for particular revelations than during more tranquil times.

In the same sense the context of religious history may have its own importance. Why the revelations of the Sacred Heart in the days of Jansenism? Why the events at Lourdes four years after the dogmatic bull *Ineffabilis Deus*? Anyone who studies closely the historical context of revelations may be confirmed in his positive judgment upon a revelation, but it is necessary to be on one's guard against exaggerations. There are Christians who see in the slightest coincidences the necessary and providential links; they sometimes make connections which are completely artificial.

The place

The place should have no special influence upon the worthwhile judgment of a revelation, any more than the circumstances of time. God has not reserved any place to communicate Himself to men. In fact, the revelations throughout the course of history have been communicated in very varied places—in a house of God, on a mountain, in a prison, etc. Certainly the most suitable place in itself would seem to be the house of God, but since it favors recollection it may also more easily dispose man to pass from prayer to a hallucinatory dialogue. That is why revelations made in other places are, practically speaking, preferable, all other things being equal, when it is a matter of the quest for discernment.

It might be good to indicate, at the end of this chapter, whether the criteria we have mentioned are sufficient to establish the authenticity of a revelation. But since we shall have to pose the same question in respect to extrinsic criteria, we shall try to answer it at the end of the next chapter.

CHAPTER VII

Extrinsic Criteria

NORMALLY ONE FINDS the best proofs for the authenticity of a thing in its own nature. It is sufficient to know it to recognize whether it is authentic. But, as we shall see, the extrinsic criteria for discerning revelations are no less important than the intrinsic criteria. Why? Because the difference between the two criteria is not so accentuated as one might at first think.

Certainly there is a difference from the chronological point of view, since extrinsic criteria such as miracles may not be directly connected with the occurrence of the revelation. But with respect to the agent there is no difference. It is the same God who is the principal agent of both the revelation and of the miracle. And since no one knows a fact better than its author, there are no better arguments for discernment than the judgment of God. In this case we must even say that the discernment is thereby definitely established. In the face of God's judgment there is no further need of criteria.

But in practice the thing is not as simple as it appears. If God came to reveal explicitly that He is the author of a specific revelation, the authenticity of which one is seeking to prove, our human condition would oblige us to ask the question: How can we be sure that this second revelation, which confirms the first, is not false? And even if one assumed another revelation confirming the second, the situation would remain the same.

But we are not in this situation. We assume that God manifests Himself in such a way that there is no need to trust to another revelation. God manifests His wishes through the language of the sign which bears the proof of its divine origin, that is, the miracle. Now, if He speaks, He speaks through the representatives of Christ, who declared: "He that heareth you heareth Me." This means the authority of the Church.

It is true that if the Church pronounced solemnly in favor of the authenticity of a particular revelation, such a pronouncement would no longer be a simple criterion among others. The Church would be the judge whose judgment would not rely in the last analysis upon the criteria of discernment. But in fact she does not judge; the theologians even say generally that she could not do so.

Her attitude, however, may be more or less favorable to a revelation, and this attitude may constitute a criterion of discernment. For while the Church never imposes a particular revelation upon the faithful, her attitude may become an argument capable of determining the assent of a member of the faithful who is seeking to reach a judgment upon a revelation. But what type of assent can result from the application of the criteria and the indications which we have been trying to establish? This is a final question which arises in this chapter; we shall treat of it in two sections:

1. Miracles as criteria of revelations;

2. The authority of the Church and discernment of revelations.

1   MIRACLES AS
CRITERIA OF REVELATIONS

The miracle is a fact apparent to the senses, performed by God and beyond the forces of nature. It is, indeed, essentially a work of God which surpasses the entire power of the creature. But if the miracle consisted only in that, the whole dynamism of grace would have to be called a miracle. It is, besides, a fact apparent to the senses, and this is a secondary but essential aspect of the miracle. This characterizes it in our eyes—*quoad nos*—better than everything else. It is by this means that it succeeds in amazing us, in being the *mirum* indicated by its name.

If we consider the miracle not only in its intrinsic causes, but also in its finality, if we accept the philosophic teaching according to which an action is determined by its aim, and if finally we take into account that the occurrence of a revelation is not a substance but an action—it has to be admitted that amazement (and its consequences) is the principal element of the miracle. From the ontological point of view, however, the miracle has only the value of an effect or a property of divine action.

If we look at the matter from this standpoint we can see in what sense miracles may be the criteria of revelations. Miracles are really extrinsic criteria of a revelation. We may even say that they are the best positive criteria. Besides, no other criterion is supported more explicitly or with more authority in the Church.

Her Founder, our Saviour, has already laid down the principles touching this matter. His will is that all may be saved. But in order to be saved men must believe in the love of the heavenly Father revealed in His Person: "Whosoever believes in Him shall be saved." To arrive at this faith, we receive two kinds of help: First, interior attraction through grace: "No man can come to Me, except the Father, who hath sent Me, draw him" (John 6: 44). There are some who have no need of other aids for belief: "Blessed are they that have not seen, and have believed" (John 20: 29).

Christ, with visible regret but because of the poor dispositions of certain people, points out another help, this an exterior one: works and signs, that is to say, miracles. "If I do not the works of my Father, believe me not. But if I do, though you will not believe Me, believe the works: that you may know and believe that the Father is in Me, and I in the Father" (John 10: 37–38). The two forms of help do not exclude each other: "The works which the Father hath given Me to perfect, the works themselves which I do, give testimony of Me, that the Father hath sent Me. And the Father himself who hath sent Me, hath given testimony of Me. . . ." (John 5: 36, 37).

This pattern established by the Lord is visibly fulfilled in the history of the Church. This constituted a proof for the primitive Church: for the faithful, the Eleven, "going forth preached everywhere: the Lord working withal, and confirming the word with signs that followed" (Mark 16: 20).

The Church has spoken in the same terms. In the constitution on the Faith at the Vatican Council, Session III, chapter III, she declared: "God has chosen to add to the interior aids of the Holy Spirit certain exterior proofs of His revelation, that is to say, divine occurrences, and notably miracles and prophecies. These are signs which are very sure and suited to the understanding of all because they manifest excellently the omnipotence of God and His infinite knowledge" (Denz., note 1790).

It may be objected that these texts do not allude to particular revelations. They concern Revelation. That is true. But, due allowance being made, the same law applies to particular revelations. Their existence cannot be denied. If they exist they come from God—directly, or at least indirectly. If God wishes to act in an extraordinary manner upon men through these revelations, He also gives proofs of this action, among which miracles take an outstanding place.

When St. Thomas treats of the role of miracles in the life of Christ, he first of all expounds a general principle which he then applies to Christ. Here is his thought: Every miracle is a testimony. Sometimes it is a testimony for the truth which is being enunciated; at other times, however, it is a testimony for the person who performs the miracle. Now no miracle is performed except through God. But God cannot be a witness to a lie. Therefore, every time that a miracle is performed in testimony to an enunciated doctrine, it is clear that this doctrine must be true, even if the person who enunciates it does not present morally good qualities. However, these qualities are required if the miracle is performed not in testimony to the doctrine but to the person.[103]

St. Thomas speaks not only of the miracles of Christ or of the Apostles but of every miracle, even those which might be performed by sinners. According to him the miracle is above all a guarantee of the truth rather than of the holiness of the person who enunciates the truth. "God," he writes, "grants to man the power to work miracles for two reasons: the first, which is the chief, is to confirm the truth which someone is teaching. Everything which comes within the realm of faith is beyond the reason of man; it cannot be demonstrated by human proofs; it is necessary, therefore, to have recourse to proofs derived from divine power, so that confronted by works which God alone can perform, men may believe that what is being said comes from God" (*Sum. Theol.*, III, 43, 1). "Miracles are the sensible signs given to manifest a truth" (*Sum. Theol.*, III, 55, 5).

For the same reason, miracles are also criteria of particular revelations. St. Thomas does not speak explicitly of revelations. But what he says applies to them also, for God does not lie. Whether the question is one of a revelation or of the statement of a simple and general truth matters very little; if a genuine miracle is performed in testimony to or in confirmation of what is enunciated, it is a true criterion of discernment. Two conditions are required, therefore, in order that a miracle may be a criterion: the miracle must be genuine and it must be performed in testimony to the revelation. In other words, the matter is one of the authentication of the miracle itself and of its connection with the revelation.

The first condition, the authentication of the miracle, assumes that the miracle can be discerned as such. We do not have to prove that here. In our days we are particularly sensitive to the difficulties surrounding the discernibility of miracles. They can be resolved, however, when the criteria of discernment are faithfully applied and follow the example of the ecclesiastical authority. Miracles are by their very nature more easily discernible than revelations; for they are designated, according to the teaching of the Vatican Council, as "very sure and adapted to the understanding of all" (Denz., 1790). If in our days the difficulties have become subtler, the methods of authentication are also more delicate. Moreover, the Church authenticates miracles with the assistance of the most highly qualified specialists. She does this particularly in the matter of the canonization of saints, but also through her magisterium in the confirmation of an apparition or of a revelation.

The second condition, the connection of the miracle with the revelation, must be quite clear. It is not sufficient for a miracle to occur at the scene of an apparition for it to be considered as a proof of this apparition. The lesson which St. Bernardine draws from the anecdote "San Beninforte" is very genuine. Beninforte, he relates, was a dog so named because he had heroically defended his master's baby against a serpent. The dog was honorably buried and his master erected a little monument in commemoration and gratitude. The faithful began to think of this heroic Beninforte as a saint, and to pray to him. Miracles occurred at the place where he was buried. The miracles could have been genuine, concludes St. Bernardine, despite the error of those who requested them. God wanted to reward the trust of His faithful.[104]

Since the beginning of the era of positivism and of tremendous respect for the exact sciences, not only has more attention been devoted to the authentication of miracles, but there also has been more stress laid upon the connection between revelations and miracles. This period also marks the beginning of the great Marian apparitions of which we spoke earlier.

It has frequently happened that people in desperate need have addressed themselves to Our Lady of La Salette, Our Lady of Lourdes, Our Lady of Fatima, that is to say, to the Blessed Virgin herself, but as she was seen in apparition in these places. And cures have been performed in such a way that experts and ecclesiastical commissions have been able to place them as miracles before the diocesan authorities. Such happenings continue to be established as miraculous. In connection with the events at Beauraing, for instance, miracles have been examined in an exemplary way with the aim of throwing light upon the authenticity of the apparitions. The connection of miracles with the apparition of the Virgin at Beauraing is particularly emphasized.

Here, for example, is the conclusion of a report of the doctrinal commission of Beauraing on the case of Maria Van Laer:

Considering the twofold fact duly established: illness and cure;
Considering the conclusion of the report of medical experts in which they declare that they are unable by the aid of solely natural factors to explain the disappearance of the functional infirmity and of the swelling in the neck as well as in the leg;

Considering that there is nothing to authorize belief in the intervention of preternatural forces of a diabolical kind;

Considering that Mlle. Van Laer addressed herself formally to the Blessed Virgin under the title of Our Lady of Beauraing;

Considering that the general feeling of Mlle. Van Laer's entourage attributed to the Virgin of Beauraing the wonderful cure under question;

We for our part deem that one may prudently attribute the cure of Mlle. Van Laer to the all-powerful intervention of Our Lady of Beauraing and in consequence we decide to submit the present dossiers, reports and conclusions to the judgment of the diocesan authority. Namur, April 4, 1949.

J. Bouchat, chanc. secr., A Monin, E. Ranwez, F. Martens, O. Praem, fr., Cyr. Lambot, advocatus, F. Toussaint, promotor fidei.[105]

The eyewitnesses of the miracle, as also all those who are alive to the importance and effectiveness of an official commission composed of qualified men, can truly see in the miracle thus established a criterion of the apparition in question. But the commission submits its judgment to the ecclesiastical authority. If this latter confirms it, do we not then stand before another positive criterion of discernment? We are now about to attempt an answer to that question.

2 THE AUTHORITY OF THE CHURCH AND THE DISCERNMENT OF REVELATIONS

We have already emphasized that the authority of the Church cannot be ranked among the criteria for discernment, if by this we mean that this authority imposes full acceptance upon the faithful. In that case it is a criterion of the Faith, *regula fidei,* but when the Church pronounces upon revelations she does not commit the faithful. If the magisterium of the Church declares, for instance, that the faithful have good grounds for believing that such and such an apparition is authentic, there is no obligation to believe in it. However, such a declaration is undoubtedly a very solid guarantee of authenticity. It may have a tremendous value as a criterion of discernment. The value of this criterion depends upon the attitude of the Church in regard to revelations in general and to such and such a revelation in particular. We shall give a few examples which we find in the history of the Church and particularly in the reactions of the hierarchy in regard to revelations in modern times.

Attitude of the Church toward revelations before the nineteenth century

In determining the scriptural canon the Church recognized, at least implicitly, the authenticity of all revelations contained in the Scripture. But in the *Muratorian Fragment* we find a striking statement bearing on our subject. We read there: "We also accept revelations, but only those of John and of Peter. However, many among us do not wish for the latter to be read in the Church." [106] And here is what the same document says of the *Shepherd* of Hermas, which it mentions immediately after the Apocalypse: "It should be read, but not publicly in the church before the people." [107]

In interpreting these texts one must be careful not to allow oneself to be too much influenced by the fact that the revelations of Peter and the *Shepherd* of Hermas were later ranked among the apocrypha. The apocryphal idea was at that time multivalent. The term could, it is true, indicate a false scripture, but that was not to say that it was purely and simply false; it may have been so only in so far as it claimed to be canonical Scripture. Moreover, "apocryphal" could also signify secret. Apocryphal might simply be a writing which should not be read in public; its "secret" reading, that is to say, its private reading, was permitted.[108]

The *Muratorian Fragment,* which is generally considered as a Roman document of the second century, proves that the Church admitted revelations which were non-canonical. Although the community at Rome knew that the *Shepherd* of Hermas, a book interwoven with revelations, did not go back to the apostolic age, it nevertheless declared that it should be read.

St. Athanasius who, as we have seen, expressed the same rule, explained why the reading of such books was recommended—it was for instruction and spiritual formation (cf. p. 49).

The Gelasian decree is even more precise in this matter. It distinguishes first of all the "accepted" writings from those which must be avoided. And among the accepted writings it classes those which today we call the canonical books as well as those of the first councils and the Fathers—"those which are accepted in the Catholic Church." It also adds the writings which the Roman Church declares acceptable (*suscipi non prohibet*).[109]

With regard to the *Acts of the Martyrs,* which often mention revelations, the decree holds that these may be admired and highly venerated. But it also remarks that they are not read—publicly, we presume—in the church at Rome; for infidels and certain Christians could find them futile and ridiculous. It mentions accounts of the finding of the Cross and of the head of St. John the Baptist, accounts in which revelations play a decisive role. "These are," it observes, "new accounts which many Catholics read; but when they come into Catholic hands, let Catholics respect the advice of the Apostles: try all and keep what is good." [110]

The decree neither approves nor condemns; it allows the reading of these accounts which fall far short of the documentation of the accounts of the great modern apparitions; everyone must judge with prudence.

It is inexact to say that in principle it is not the function of the Holy See to judge the authenticity of revelations. It is the Holy See which is by right the judge of their supernatural character. We have established in any case that it has made judgments in such matters.

Not only do the facts prove this, but the Church has even made an explicit pronouncement on the subject. The Fifth Lateran Council laid down the following rule at its eleventh session: "We desire that henceforth when divine communications are reported and before they are published or preached to the people that they be generally and legally reserved to the examination of the Apostolic See. Only when there can be no delay and in urgent case, should they be communicated to the Ordinary of the place. Let him examine them carefully with three or four learned and responsible counselors who later, at an opportune moment, may, on the responsibility of their consciences, give permission for them to be published." [111]

The practice laid down by this decree of September 19, 1516, was modified by another of July 5, 1634: The books, it says, which contain accounts of the miracles and the revelations of those who have died with a reputation for sanctity should be supported by the approval of the Ordinary of the place; the latter should summon a council of theologians and experts to examine them and advise him. Then he should send the case to the Holy See and await the reply.[112] These decrees obviously hold good for revelations and miracles which have occurred in the lives of persons whose canonization is not contemplated and for cases where the circumstances do not permit awaiting the death of the person before coming to a judgment in the matter.

Attitude of the Church toward certain
apparitions of the last two centuries

We shall now consider the great apparitions since those at Paray-le-Monial. The ecclesiastical authorities could not await the deaths of the visionaries, who were children, before pronouncing upon facts which, because of their worldwide repercussions, had to be decided upon as quickly as possible.

La Salette "is the first Marian apparition of the nineteenth century open to the general public, which is not restrained from interesting itself therein." [113] It would be instructive for us, by way of example, to examine the details of the approval of this apparition.

Some months after the event the Ordinary of the place organized, as he said in his pastoral letter of September 19, 1851, "a numerous commission, composed of responsible, pious and learned men who would maturely examine and discuss the *fact of the apparition and its consequences*." And indeed a big inquiry was made, and the details and difficulties of the event were studied. The consequences were also examined.

It was about these consequences first of all that the ecclesiastical authority had to make a decision. In particular there was the question of miracles; when the juridical inquiry was concluded, a large list of miracles was presented to the Ordinary of the place where the apparition occurred. The Ordinaries of the different dioceses of France pronounced a canonical judgment upon a miracle.[114] After this official recognition of the miracles, the Bishop of Grenoble sent to Rome not only the whole dossier upon La Salette, but also a draft doctrinal decision. Having received an approving reply from the Prefect of the Sacred Congregation of Rites, Cardinal Lambruschini, dated October 7, 1851, in which he wrote: "Everything is going very well and the reading has left me nothing to desire . . . ," the bishop published the pastoral letter of November 10, 1851. Here are the most important passages of the doctrinal decision which it contained:

Relying upon the principles taught by Pope Benedict XIV, and following the way outlined by him in his immortal work "On the Beatification and Canonization of Saints." . . .

Having heard the discussions from various angles which have taken place before us upon this matter in sessions of November 8, 15, 16, 17, 22 and 29, December 6 and 13, 1847,

Having equally seen or heard what has been written since this period, for and against the event,

Considering in the first place the impossibility we find of explaining the fact of La Salette other than as divine intervention, whatever way we viewed it either in its circumstances or in its essentially religious aim,

Considering in the second place that the wonderful consequences of the fact of La Salette are the testimony of God Himself, manifesting Himself through miracles, and that this testimony is superior to that of men and to their objections. . . .

Having newly invoked the Holy Ghost and the assistance of the Immaculate Virgin;

We declare as follows:

First Article.—*We decide that the apparition of the Blessed Virgin to two shepherds on September 19, 1846, on a mountain in the chain of the Alps, situated in the parish of La Salette, of the archpresbytery of Corps, bears in itself all the characteristics of truth, and that the faithful have good grounds for believing it to be indubitable and certain.*[115]

Thus no one was surprised when Pope Pius XII wrote on October 8, 1945, to the Superior General of the Missionaries of La Salette as follows: "Our devotion to the Most Holy Virgin, to whose heart We have consecrated the Church and the world, cannot but expand at the pleasant prospects which your letter suggests to Us, of the coming centenary of the apparition of Our Lady of La Salette . . . *the canonical process of which, instituted at the time by the diocesan authority, proved favorable*" (A.A.S., 38 [1946], 155. Our italics).

The same procedure was followed for the other Marian apparitions which were approved following that of La Salette. The study of the facts of Lourdes also resulted in a doctrinal announcement in which Bishop Laurence made the following declarations: "We remain convinced that the apparition is supernatural and divine. . . . Our conviction is based upon the testimony of Bernadette, but especially upon the facts of the occurrence which cannot be explained except as a divine intervention. . . .

"The testimony of Bernadette, already important in itself, assumes a wholly new power from, we would even say is complemented by, the wonderful facts which were accomplished after the first event. . . . *We decide that the* IMMACULATE MARY MOTHER OF GOD *really appeared to Bernadette Soubirous on February 11 and on following days to the number of* EIGHTEEN TIMES *in the grotto of Massabielle near the town of Lourdes; that this apparition bore all the marks of truth and that the faithful have good reason to believe it certain.*" [116]

In 1877, three bishops addressed themselves to the Congregation of Rites inquiring what attitude the Holy See was adopting in regard to the apparitions of La Salette and of Lourdes. The reply was clear and restrained: "These apparitions or revelations have been neither approved nor condemned by the Holy See which has simply allowed them to be believed on purely human faith, on the tradition which they relate, corroborated by testimony and documents worthy of credence." Therefore neither approval nor condemnation was forthcoming, but simply a permissive attitude from the Holy See. This text was literally repeated thirty years later in the encyclical of St. Pius X against Modernism.[116a]

Does the attitude of the Church finally rest in permissive-

ness with respect to revelations? Does the Holy See go no
further? At all events the text quoted has not the aspect of
a law. The expression "these apparitions—*ejusdem apparitiones*" does not seem to denote the universality of a law
which would be applicable to all revelations, but relates to
the apparitions of La Salette and of Lourdes. Even if the
text were also applicable to other apparitions of the same
type, it indicates by the use of the past tense—"condemned,"
"approved," "has permitted" (*damnatos, approbatas, permis-
sas*)—the attitude which the Holy See *adopted in fact*. In any
case, it is not conceived according to the forms of a law
setting forth a principle also valid for the future.

Has the attitude of the Holy See always been permissive?
To judge by the facts which we cited in the first part of our
book the answer must be no. Let us recall the declaration of
Benedict XIV: The Congregation of Rites has often examined such and such a revelation, vision or apparition in particular; but this examination has not often resulted in an
approval. . . . "At times some vision, some apparition has
been approved." [117]

The attitude of the Apostolic See was more positive with
respect to revelations in times when Christians were united
as in the Middle Ages. In these latter centuries the Church
has more and more adopted an attitude of prudent reserve.
By this means she avoids certain attacks on the part of unbelievers and non-Catholics; at the same time she preserves
her members from the danger of placing too much value
upon these extraordinary graces at the expense of the ordinary great sources of divine life in men. The essential guarantees are, moreover, given by the bishops who pronounce
doctrinal judgments in virtue of their membership in the
magisterium of the Church.

In our days, however, we note dispositions or doctrinal
tones emanating from the highest legal authority of the
Church which are difficult to interpret as the expression of a
purely permissive attitude.

Even after the document of 1877 which expresses this attitude very plainly, Pope Leo XIII declared in his encyclical *Annum Sacrum* of 1899 that Margaret Mary Alacoque *had received from God* the order to spread the devotion of the Sacred Heart.[118] In the office for the Feast of St. Margaret Mary the Church states without any reserve that "Jesus made Himself visible to her (*conspiciendum se obtulit*) and that He showed her His divine Heart." The fact of the apparitions is reported with fuller details again in the Office for the Feast of the Sacred Heart in which it is said that the Sacred Heart appeared to the Saint (*ostendit*).

Still more significant in our view is the attitude of the Church in regard to the happenings at Lourdes. In our days when the Church generally shows considerable severity in her attitude toward wonders, she has instituted a feast to commemorate the apparitions of Lourdes—and in the office of that feast the fact of the apparitions is recalled without any attenuation: "The Blessed Virgin appeared several times." [118a] Even the details about the method of this heavenly intervention are not omitted.

Certainly one may ask: What value does the second nocturn in the breviary have? One cannot deduce any argument from this source. We are not exaggerating. Obviously the Church has no intention of guaranteeing the historical truth of what the breviary relates of the lives of the saints. Most of the time she mentions in it the simple tradition which has no other guarantees than human testimony. But whatever historians may think of the genuine historic value of certain facts included in the breviary in times more or less remote, in the twentieth century the Church certainly does not insert facts which she has not examined with the modern resources of historical research. Since in the case of apparitions the supernatural resources of knowledge are more important than the others, indeed the only decisive ones, and since the Church has more experience of discernment than ever before, it may be concluded that the particular testimony furnished by the breviary in passages inserted in modern times is not devoid of value—we are not speaking here of mere details or of just any vision or life of a saint canonized in one way or another. We know to what long and rigorous examination such apparitions are now submitted.

In addition, the Sovereign Pontiff Pius XII emphasized in the encyclical *Fulgens corona* the historical fact of the very important occurrence at Lourdes:

> In a village in France, at the foot of the Pyrenees, a simple and inno-cent child saw at the Grotto of Massabielle the Blessed Virgin who appeared to her (*Deipara Virgo . . . se conspiciendum dedit*). The Blessed Virgin had a youthful and friendly aspect; she was dressed in a robe and cloak of white and wore a blue girdle. To the child who in-stantly asked to know the name of her who had deigned to show herself to her, she replied, lifting her eyes to heaven and smiling sweetly: "I am the Immaculate Conception" (A.A.S., 45 [1953], 578).

Is this again a matter of a permissive attitude? Here is one good reason which could justify an affirmative reply to this question: In the testimonies we have quoted the Holy See did not pass judgment upon the apparitions in question. It trusted implicitly or explicitly to the doctrinal judgment of the Ordinary of the place to whom it had given permission to pronounce in the matter. The Holy See mentioned the apparitions as certain facts because they had been declared to be such and duly established by the diocesan authority. The Sovereign Pontiffs also spoke in their commemorative encyclicals in an entirely affirmative way of certain facts which they did not intend thereby to cover with their own authority. They were relying upon data such as forms the basis for certitude of historical facts.

This was also the attitude manifested by St. Pius X when, on March 12, 1904, in the introduction to his encyclical, *Iucunda sane,* he wrote that thirteen hundred years had passed since the death of Gregory I, and announced his intention to celebrate solemnly this thirteenth centenary (*vertente anno millesimo tercentesimo*).[119]

But when the Holy See allows belief in this or that revelation it does not do so simply because data is available for proving the certitude of a particular historical fact. In affirming the fact of a revelation, the Holy See does not base this affirmation exclusively upon the human testimony advanced in its favor, but refers sometimes even explicitly to the canonical judgment of the Ordinary of the place. Something more than a purely natural factor is involved. Moreover, when we read the doctrinal judgments upon apparitions we note their grave tone, their occasional solemnity, and the bishops' insistence on prayer, such as the invocation of the Holy Spirit and of the Blessed Virgin.

All we have said shows that the ecclesiastical authority has not always adopted the same attitude toward particular revelations.[119a] It should be added that this attitude is a very important criterion and, in a certain sense, a decisive criterion for discernment.

Congar is of the opinion that even a negative approval "adds an increased weight to the other incentives which we have for accepting a private revelation." What weight would a positive approval have? That of a criterion of discernment, it would seem. It also adds an incentive for serious and favorable examination.[120] But since this incentive is of a particular weight and since it is added in the end to all the others with the effect of confirming them all, one may consider the positive approval as a decisive criterion.

In fact, as many bishops point out in pastorals which contain a doctrinal judgment upon the fact of an apparition, this judgment is preceded by a consideration of all the elements which might provide criteria for discernment.

It is also a fact that, even among the best members of the Church, there are some who in the presence of proofs which they consider to be solid, still hold back their assent until the Church pronounces in favor of a revelation in question.

3   ASSENT TO REVELATIONS

The criteria for discernment only have meaning if they result in an assent. When they result in this, they achieve their purpose. But of what assent do we speak? The answer to that question will be the conclusion of all that we have just said upon discernment, a conclusion which will serve as the foundation for the last part of our study. The criteria—or norms which guide the discernment of the true from the false—are usually determining principles of certitude. In order to clarify the meaning of assent, it is essential to be very explicit about the nature of certitude.

Precise details about the idea of certitude

Certitude is a firm adherence of the understanding to its object.[121] The distinction is commonly made between subjective certitude and objective certitude.

The first without the second is a fictitious certitude; the second without the first is a potential certitude only. Neither of the two constitutes certitude in its full sense. But full certitude, provided that it be based upon an objective truth, is finally of a subjective character—it is a state of mind, an adherence.

We speak, too, of "spontaneous" certitude, which runs the risk of collapsing upon reflection. This is not the case with "reflective" certitude which is its opposite. In reflective certitude, the mind has verified the basis of its adherence to a proposition.

If one considers as a basis the different dimensions of reality, one can, according to the scholastics, distinguish three kinds of certitude: that which is based upon the domain of being and determined by absolutely necessary laws —this is metaphysical certitude; that which is based upon the reality of nature and determined by its constant laws—this is physical certitude; finally that which is based upon the practical laws of human life—this is moral certitude.

All three are genuine certitudes since they assume the tranquil and conscious possession of their respective truths. But metaphysical certitude alone excludes in advance all possibility of error. And only moral certitude admits the practical possibility of error without, however, allowing itself to be troubled by doubt.

In our case we are dealing solely with reflective moral certitude. But everything is not resolved by these very clear pronouncements of the scholastics. To establish that we have only to look more closely at the meaning of moral certitude.

Why is moral certitude also found in the domain of necessary realities, even absolutely necessary realities? The masters of logic, in fact, admit that these propositions relating to objects in themselves necessary may fall under probability. Certainly the object, if it is not contingent in itself, may be so because of the way in which it is presented or apprehended by the mind.[122] In this way the object in so far as it is a known object comes under contingence and as a consequence under probability. And this latter cannot lay claim to a certitude which exceeds moral certitude.

This is not all. One may go so far as to ask whether, according to the division we have just outlined, one should necessarily consider moral certitude as an imperfect, diminished, relative certitude as it is so often considered. It must be such, one may say, because its object is a contingent reality. A certitude may be perfect in spite of the contingence of its object, if this object is grasped by immediate experience. I may with perfect certitude affirm: I rebel. That is why it has even been possible to lay down this experience as a principle like that of the present activity of the intelligence: I think.

So the ancients and the scholastics who saw perfect certitude only in the domain of necessary reality admitted a certain necessity in the attitudes or modalities of the reality in itself contingent. In every real presence they saw this necessity (*Sum. Theol.*, II–II, 49, 6).

But when this presence disappears into the past it still retains its necessity as a historical fact. The facts in so far as they are past assume a certain "necessity." [122a] For a historical fact remains a fact.

This necessity is such that even God in His omnipotence can change nothing of it (*Sum. Theol.*, I, 25, 4; II–II, 49, 6). Thus one understands why the death of Jesus Christ which is of itself a contingent fact can become, in the order of grace, a very certain truth upon which depends the eternal salvation of everyone who believes in it. Faith has, indeed, the means of directly reaching this fact, which is not possible to nature.

But let us suppose a fact which may not be dogmatic and which by its remoteness in time and space renders personal experience impossible. In that case the question of certitude changes some of its aspect. One is then oriented toward what St. Thomas calls "probable certitude." This is undoubtedly a paradoxical expression. All those, however, who know the idea of probability only from books on morals in use in these latter centuries, have a tendency to minimize the certitude which the expression attempts to designate. Here is what St. Thomas writes: "We must not expect to find certitude equally in every matter. For in human acts, on which judgments are passed and evidence required, it is impossible to have demonstrative certitude, because they are about things contingent and variable. Hence the certitude of probability suffices, such as may reach the truth in the greater number of cases, although it fail in the minority. Now it is probable that the assertion of several witnesses contains the truth rather than the assertion of one" (*Sum. Theol.*, ii–ii, 70, 2).

To begin with, it is clear that this is not a matter of equiprobability. The person who acts for good reasons, even if he sees reasons equally good which forbid his action, is not acting because his action seems to him to be probably good. In that case we would be in doubt. No, if he acts in such and such a way, he has decided that he has valid reasons for so acting. The probable is that which approaches closer to the truth, and does so visibly. In testimony there should, according to St. Thomas, be many witnesses rather than one single witness.

There are moralists who say that it is probably midnight if two watches show midnight, even if according to three other watches, equally good, midnight has already passed.[122b] Probable then indicates a close possibility rather than a probability in the sense which St. Thomas gives to the word. If the meaning of moral probability has been weakened by many modern moralists, it has been overestimated by theologians or metaphysicians who apply to the moral domain the idea of probability itself, which when understood properly belongs to logic.

The word "probable," which comes from *probare,* indicates that it refers to proofs. Now the teaching on proofs belongs to logic. Everything which has been subjected to proof is "proved." Certainly, the probable is opposed to the proved, but probable says more than that. Probable, that is the "provable," designates by its flectional ending a potentiality, an incompleteness of proof. When I say it is probable, I have already tried out the ground; I have already commenced the proof which seems in a fair way to arrive at some conclusion. The proof has progressed to the point where I am in a position to say: I can prove it.

So it is that we declare, after having heard the exposition of a problem: "This is understandable." That is not to say that we have understood everything or that we have admitted everything, but merely that we have surely understood a good portion of the whole or even—not so clearly—the whole. And thus it is in many analogous cases. If, for instance, scientists declare that the moon is *accessible* to us, this means that they have made a close study of the way which leads there and that they have already tried to some extent to survey it. The researches are continuing successfully. We say that they will probably reach it. But unforeseen obstacles may hold up the journey from the earth to the moon.

There are, naturally, degrees of probability. But the ancients had a very strict conception of probability which has never been completely forgotten by the theologians. This places probability at the level of what modern writers usually call the great probability. Probable is everything which is proved by non-demonstrable proofs, that is, by signs or by competent authorities. But since these proofs cannot throw a full light, they are only partial proofs. The probable in this sense is therefore opposed on the one hand to the evidence, and on the other hand to what is doubtful, what is open to surmise or conjecture.

Let us give an example. St. Albert, treating of the syllogism, in the First Book of *Topics,* teaches this: The syllogism is a debate by which we succeed, by means of premises, in grasping something which is not in the premises. Now there are three kinds of syllogism: The first is the conclusive syllogism which is so called because it concludes with evidence. There is also the dialectical syllogism of which the "matter," that is, the premises, is made up of probable propositions (*ex probabilibus*). A third and last syllogism is called "litigiosus" because either its premises are only apparently probable or the form of the syllogism is false.

But what is this "probable" with which the dialectical syllogism is concerned? It is the knowledge which one acquires by the signs and not by the necessary causes of the object of knowledge. Of itself, there is no necessary link between subject and predicate.

Here are the signs upon which is founded the "probable" which is for St. Albert the "likelihood" which he takes very seriously. These signs are sometimes on the surface of things; they are the external qualities, the object of sensible experience: such as the whiteness of snow. At other times the signs of the probable do not appear on the surface, but are found in the interior of things, in the intermediary regions between the exterior phenomena and the essential principles of being, for example, a star at the tail of the Little Bear situated at the Pole. This probable judgment is based both on sensory observation and on reasoning. The signs may be studied still more deeply at the interior of things until they become interchangeable with their essential reasons; for example, the moon which moves in the epicycle contrives to penetrate deeply into the shadow of the earth.[123]

Signs, except those of the first category, are reserved to more or less restricted groups; the general public accepts the "probable" results of the specialists. So testimony mingles with the signs.

It is clear that if one understands the probable in this way, there is no longer necessarily opposition between probability and certitude. In this case one may admit a strong probable certitude.

Our reflections have shown equally that if there are different kinds of certitude, this is chiefly due to the reasons for them. Certainly the object has something to do with it.

Certitude is, in brief, the conscious and thoughtful possession of the object. It is, as Newman emphatically says, the consciousness of the knowledge of a truth; it assumes research and proof, and comprises a particular feeling of satisfaction and intellectual peace.[124] This is attained by proofs

and non-intellectual attractions, that is, through the reasons
for certitude.

It is understandable that a theologian of standing could
write as a conclusion to his researches upon this aspect of
certitude: "The probable is higher than the hypothetical,
higher than the doubtful and . . . it ranks among the arguments capable of convincing objective and serious minds;
indeed, if it is a matter of practice or of morality—prudent
and well-intentioned—the probable leads positively to the
absolute truth." [125]

Assent to revelations with respect to their object

Can we give particular revelations a certain assent? To
answer this question we must examine the worth of the
reasons which might or might not be capable of furnishing
a basis for such assent. Now certitude is established through
its reasons, which depend directly or indirectly upon the
object of the certitude in which these reasons are rooted.
They have no other purpose except to bring consciously to
the mind the guarantees immanent in the object of certitude
by means of the evidence, the signs and the testimony.

The object of certitude in our case is the fact of this or that
revelation. Each fact implies contingence. And since in addition there is the question of a fact which is not exclusively
physical but also and above all human, we cannot consider
for it any other certitude than moral certitude. Evidence is
precluded. As a consequence of this, conclusive proofs are
also precluded. The nature of our object permits the full
entry of testimony. But is this testimony sufficient reason for
establishing certitude? If it succeeds in establishing only a
probable decision, as the majority of moralists agree, there
is no question of certitude. For a decision which does not
exclude serious probability, or even equally strong prob-

ability of the opposite, does not create certitude. So the classical writers, when they say that revelations are accepted as "probable," are using this term in the strong sense of the early writers. In speaking thus they are excluding revelations from the domain of Faith, the certitude of which is more than simply "moral."

Private revelations, writes Cardinal Bona, which the saints have transmitted to us in writing are not approved so that we may give them an assent of divine faith, but that we may accept them as probable.[126] Benedict XIV teaches the same thing: the approval of the Church has not the certitude of Faith; it is meant to open the way only to an assent of human faith according to which these revelations are probable and "piously" credible.[127]

The meaning of probable here has less strength than that attributed to it by St. Thomas in II–II, 70, 2. In the moral verities everything comes more or less under the scope of probability, if there is no support from divine faith. This probability, however, may be very weak, or it may be strong enough to be a basis for a true moral certitude.

A very large number of people, for instance, have never seen Tokyo; but they are absolutely certain that this city exists. Their certitude is based upon innumerable witnesses who for many centuries have affirmed its existence, without there ever having been a single testimony to the contrary. The proportion of witnesses is not just more, that is, many against one, but innumerable against none.

We must, it would seem, exclude a priori this perfect certitude based upon testimony when a question arises of deciding upon the existence of a revelation, for this is by nature more difficult to grasp and usually less accessible to witnesses.

But if the assent to revelations finds relatively weak support in testimony, it can be considerably strengthened by the signs which accompany the testimony. If the existence of Tokyo were not already fully assured by testimony, one could call in the proofs of the sign. The witnesses could produce objects from this city, and in our day especially photographs which people could check and compare with others at their leisure. So it is with revelations. They offer a mass of signs which one may study and compare with other signs. And thus, into the reasons for certitude there enter factors which offer a weight of probability in the strict sense of the word used in the non-moral domain. It is true that signs do not always have the same value; they remain rather on the surface of the fact in question, and they are not always immediately connected with the fact in question. But they are signs. To determine the value of each sign within the perspective of the whole is an essential task in the work of discernment.

The criteria of discernment which we have emphasized are based in large part upon signs. Let us recall the most important. The content may constitute a sign, if in a wonderful manner it acts upon the life or even the teaching of the Church. We may think here of the Miraculous Medal and the devotion of the Sacred Heart.

The attitude of the visionaries during and after the revelation is sometimes a sign which is even more important. From a distance it is easy to account for things as one wishes. But when one is present at the event it is not the same thing at all. There are certain reactions—above all in the case of simple people—which cannot deceive. The insertion of the heavenly and the sublime into individuals so untutored, the fusion of fearlessness and humility, and a great many other facts, may be disconcerting to matter-of-fact individuals who wish to explain everything by natural causes. There are a mass of circumstances which may constitute a sign, if in their great variety they converge upon the same point.

There is the question of an accumulation of probabilities, independent of one another, springing from the nature and the circumstances of the particular case in question; these are probabilities too inconsistent to have a value in themselves alone, too subtle and imprecise to be converted into a syllogism, too numerous and varied, moreover, for any similar logical operation even if they lend themselves to it. To all this is added the surest sign, even though it is extrinsic to the fact itself; revelation is intimately connected with it because it comes from God, the Author of revelation, and that is the miracle. If in fact the Church confirms the authenticity of this sign from God, if she explicitly allows belief in the miracle and if she permits it in its own way to speak and to act as an established fact, then one cannot question that an assent to approved revelations can be a certain assent.

The language of the ecclesiastical approvals agrees in fact with this conclusion. In connection with the apparition of Our Lady at La Salette—"the canonical process of which proved favorable," as Pius XII declared (A.A.S., 38 [1946], 155)—the Ordinary of the place decided in his doctrinal pastoral, article one, that the apparition "carried all the characteristics of truth and that the faithful have good grounds to believe it *indubitable and certain*" (cf. note 115). There was no question here, as emerges from the discussions preparatory to the pastoral, of moral certitude having the same significance as very great probability.[128]

The bishop of Tarbes on his part decided in the first article of his pastoral that the apparition of the Mother of God at Lourdes "bears all the characteristics of truth, and that the faithful have good grounds for *believing it to be certain*." [129] The Ordinary of Fatima declared that the visions of the Cova da Iria were worthy of belief, "dignas de credito." [130]

The act of assent

All that we have just said is based upon the objective realities of certitude—the particular object of the certitude and the reasons which connect it with the subject. But one other proof may be furnished on behalf of an act of assent. We give it as the full confirmation of the conclusion which we draw from our exposition—that we can accept revelations with a certain assent.

What is this act? To reply properly to this fundamental question it is necessary to determine the subject in whom this act is realized. The assent may be given by the visionary or by the person to whom the revelations are communicated directly or indirectly by the visionaries.

1. In the case of the visionary, in former times serious debate was devoted to the question of whether or not an assent of divine faith was demanded. The Salmaticenses wrote: "There is indeed a considerable discussion among the theologians on the matter in question: should we, or at least, may we give to these private revelations an assent of theological faith. . . ." [131]

Before the Council of Trent, Cajetan had excluded any act of divine faith from particular revelations. Melchior Cano and Bañez are of the same opinion. But today when we are confronted by a general opinion in their favor, we may be surprised to find that Vega, Suarez, Lugo and all those who followed them held a different opinion. Suarez, for instance, established the following thesis: Private revelation, if it is "sufficiently proposed," is of the same nature as the Catholic faith and may constitute a formal object of faith . . . (cf. note 72). However, he alone who receives the revelation is obliged to believe in it; for others the general rule holds that the approval of the Church is necessary in order to be obliged to believe.

Here is the decisive reason in favor of this position. It is the same God everywhere who reveals Himself; we must believe in God. The Church, in so far as she proposes the Faith, is only an accidental element of theological faith; she does not enter as an essential condition into the formal object of the divine and Catholic faith.

Suarez must have been influenced by the commentary

which Vega had made upon the decree on justification of the Council of Trent. We may be surprised by a statement made by the majority of the Fathers and theologians of the Council in regard to our problem, according to the résumé of the discussion made by Father Laurence Mazochius: "The majority of theologians and finally nearly all the Fathers (of the Council) decided that without a special revelation no one may be certain with a certitude of faith that he is actually in the state of grace." They said "certitude of faith," the same theologian reports, since they could not have been thinking of certitude of evidence; and probable certitude was admitted as a fact without the intervention of a special revelation.[131a]

It is not necessary for our purposes to enter into the details of the discussion upon the possibility of divine faith in revelations. One thing is certain—through the particular revelation it is possible to arrive at absolute and infallible certitude. Canon 16, upon justification, laid down by the Council of Trent, says that one cannot be certain with an absolute and infallible certitude that one will have the gift of final perseverance unless one has learned this through a special revelation (Denz., note 826). The certitude of Faith does not go further. But it is not necessary that this certitude be the effect of divine and Catholic Faith. God is there and acts very effectively upon the human mind. And it is not solely through theological faith that He communicates certain knowledge to man. There is, for example, prophetic illumination. This attains a very great certitude (*maximam certitudinem*).[132] Its existence is not necessary to illumine the mind upon the mysteries of the Faith, but to communicate facts which direct action, as St. Thomas emphasizes. This is precisely that orientation of action which is the aim of all special revelation, as we shall see later on.

That prophecy may not be a *habitus* properly so called matters little to our problem. It is sufficient for us to find in prophecy itself a perfect certitude.

We conclude: If the immediate assent which is accorded to revelations were an act of theological faith, the question of certitude would be regulated for the best; but if the assent is, as we believe it to be, the effect of prophetic illumination or some other supernatural influence, its certitude, without being absolute, is nevertheless real. The fact of this certitude is, moreover, emphasized by most authorized testimonies of those who have had such experience.

2. It is obviously not the same in the case of those who receive the revelations only through the visionaries. Is their assent truly certain? Certainly it is, but it does not attain the perfect certitude of which we have just spoken. Here it is not a question of an act of theological faith, whatever certain theologians have said of it. The prophetic light, on the other hand, is not necessarily excluded from it; it could manifest itself in the interpretation of a prophecy received by another, an interpretation which alone makes this prophecy perfect. This is the case in Joseph's interpretation of the dreams of Pharaoh. But here one can say that the true prophet is the interpreter.

Is not the assent in question to be attributed rather to Christian prudence? In any case, what St. Thomas says of this virtue is very much along the line of this position. Prudence is in the reason, and it is distinguished from the other intellectual virtues by its object, which is not necessary truth but contingent truth; it is applicable strictly speaking to those actions which a man should accomplish in himself (*Sum. Theol.*, II–II, 47, 5). Does not all this correspond to the assent to revelations which have reason for a subject and for object the contingent—action?

Despite that, it cannot be said that assent to revelations is the act or the effect of prudence. It is true that prudence governs the judgment relative to all human activity and thus it may counsel or impose assent of which the act proper (*elicitus*) is not prudence but the act commanded (*imperatus*) by prudence. The act proper is an act of faith.

The act proper does not mean an act of theological faith; but certain theologians like Soto and the Salmaticenses are thinking of a "particular faith" of which St. Paul speaks, a faith which is, according to Cajetan's commentary, a faith of action, *fides de agendis*. It might be a charismatic grace, or at the very least, a supernatural faith. This is possible. But it seems to us that here it is a matter rather of a faith-trust which forms part of the divine faith; it has for its object the primary truth which is a person—everything is possible to him who believes (Mark 9: 22).

Here, in our opinion, is the best solution to the problem. At the basis of the firm assent to revelations is an act of human faith, "commanded" (*imperatus*) by prudence and reinforced by the motives of the virtue of piety.

In our days everyone, it seems, is in agreement in confirming that there is human faith in this domain. Here is what the Salmaticenses wrote: "From all that we have just said, it emerges that all those who hear revelations, communicated to others and approved by the Church, accept them (*assentire*) at least by human faith, and that they are not bound by another faith; for they give assent only upon the testimony of persons who assert that they have received them from God. Now this testimony is fallible. How far the obligation to involve this faith goes, depends on many circumstances which it is difficult to measure exactly." [133]

The most authoritative decision on this matter is to be found in the encyclical *Pascendi* of St. Pius X who made his own the reply of the Holy Office to the question about the attitude of the Holy See in regard to the apparitions of La Salette and Lourdes, which had already been canonically approved by the ordinaries of the places concerned: "These apparitions or revelations," we read in the encyclical, "have neither been approved nor condemned by the Holy See, which has simply allowed them to be believed on purely human faith, on the traditions which they relate, corroborated by testimony and documents worthy of credence.

Anyone who follows this rule has no cause to fear" (cf. note 116a). Now the human faith with which revelations may be accepted comprises a true certitude. If the judgment has already reached certitude—more or less probable, it is true— with so much the greater reason, then, will it reach faith.

It is not necessary to determine whether there is a difference of degree or a specific difference between human faith and opinion. Those who see only a difference of degree between them insist upon texts like that of St. Thomas in his *De Veritate,* question 14, article 2, according to which faith is a very strong opinion (*vehementer opinari*). The others can rely upon a great many very clear texts for emphasizing the specific superiority of faith. But is this still a question of human faith? After comparing the texts of the works of St. Thomas's youth with those of his *Summa Theologica* we incline rather to the opinion that it is.[134]

However that may be, the fact is that faith, even human faith, was always simply considered by St. Thomas as superior to opinion, at a period in which he accentuated less the difference between the two (*supra opinionem*). And why? The great theologian repeated it everywhere: because faith comprises "assent" or "firm adherence" (*terminatur ad unum*). This is never admitted in the case of opinion which implies in its adherence the fear of the opposite. If there is assent it is only partial (*habet aliquid assensus*) or imperfect; at base, man, in so far as he relies upon opinion, does not give his assent—(*opinans non assentit*).

The point of departure is the same for faith as for opinion: reason does not succeed in making one *see* and as a result is incapable of leading the intelligence to assent. The faith succeeds in this by means of the will. The logical structure of human and divine faith is, in our opinion, the same. But in divine faith the certitude, under the influence of grace, surpasses the certitude of knowledge, of evidence; the certitude of human faith remains inferior to knowledge.[134a]

In short, even if human faith is only an opinion strengthened by proofs (*firmata rationibus*), as it is termed in the text quoted above, it is not, for all that, any kind of adherence, but a firm adherence. Certitude, according to St. Thomas, is simply the decision of the intelligence upon a thing without fear of the opposite, or again, the firm adherence of the intelligence to a true object.[135] It is the definition we gave above. It can be seen that three ideas are reunited in it: assent, certitude and human faith. The act of human faith comprises certitude.

We have now reached a final precision. The Holy See, according to the text already quoted (p. 199), allows pious belief in revelations (*pie credendas*). What does this mean? Does it imply a weakening of human faith? Certainly not. It is true that the expression *pie interpretatur* is often used in a pejorative sense: despite the absence of indications which are at least probable, or even in the presence of proofs tending somewhat toward negation, one allows an affirmation because of an authority which one respects.

This is not the present case since the foundation of the belief is shown—the faithful may believe in revelations "on the traditions which they relate, corroborated by testimony and documents worthy of credence" (cf. p. 205). It is indeed a question of intellectual motives for moral certitude.

But, as for all belief, there must be influence of a moral order in order to reach certitude. Piety exercises such an influence, that is, piety in the theological sense; this is a virtue of veneration accessory to the virtue of justice. Piety has for its objects the parents, father or mother. It is expressed by the respect one bears toward them—respect whose outward manifestation corresponds to an inner affection. In its proper meaning, the term piety is applicable in pre-eminent fashion to the heavenly Father and, by extension, to what belongs to our earthly fathers—thus one's country is also the object of piety.

But the Church is truly our Mother; we accept with piety what she allows. Thus we may arrive through our own investigation at belief in the apparition at Lourdes. However, we read in the encyclical *Fulgens Corona* a prolonged and emphatic reference to this event; the Pope speaks of it as of any other undisputed historical fact; therefore I believe "piously." And my faith is thereby more solid, surer. This is the respect I owe my Mother the Church, who increases the certitude of my faith; this faith remains, in regard to its structure a natural assent, but it is subject morally to supernatural influence.

That is all the more reason why we may consider piety in repect to revelations not only a moral virtue but also a gift of the Holy Spirit, the "principal act" of which "is to venerate God with filial affection" (*Sum. Theol.*, II–II, 122, 1, ad 3).

But this act of piety is, in the end, like every Christian act carried out under the influence of Christian prudence. Christian prudence is required in a particular way because of the subject; that is why it is often recommended in writings dealing with revelations. So the text quoted from the encyclical *Pascendi* begins thus: ". . . in this matter the Church uses the greatest prudence."

It is understandable that Ranwez, to quote only one among recent writers, wrote as follows about this matter: "Adherence of human faith. Assent, prudently based upon testimony which merits confidence and respect. An act of intellectual docility assuming good will, but a will calling for a perfect logic, a lofty wisdom, and thus eminently reasonable. For, if such a commitment binds the intelligence itself, it does so nonetheless without risk of dangerous error, since the door remains open to every possibility of retraction which the evidence might eventually demand, as also to all sworn statements which others might believe should be made to the authorities." [136]

No doctor has exerted so much influence upon the subject we have dealt with in this section as Benedict XIV; he visibly inspired the teaching which the Holy See has officially proclaimed. Having categorically declared that ecclesiastical approval does not indicate in this matter anything other than a permission to publish the revelation for the good of the faithful, he wrote the following which résumés everything we have just said: "While there must not and cannot be given an assent of Catholic faith, there may, however, be given (*debetur tamen*) an assent of human faith following the rules of prudence, and according to which these revelations are probable and piously credible." [137]

Benedict XIV, as did writers in general before him, used the term probable in the strict sense; here he opposes "probable" to the certitude of the faith but not to all certitude. He is of the same mind as the Fathers of the Council of Trent, for whom, as it appears from the discussions of this Council, probable certitude is what is sometimes called moral certitude (cf. notes 131a and 71).

These terms must be interpreted in the sense given to them by their authors and not in the sense which these terms may assume for readers of those authors at other periods of time.

PART THREE

THE MEANING OF REVELATIONS

WE HAVE reached the most important part of our work, the center "of a theology of particular revelations." This expression could be misleading if it were used to designate a theology built upon revelations as a foundation. It has that meaning only in so far as it aims at the elaboration of a systematic and theological body of knowledge about revelations, a knowledge drawn from the great Christian sources.

This is a knowledge *sub ratione Dei,* that is, due allowance being made, it sees what God sees in revelations. If there is a theology of revelations, it must be a knowledge of the design of God in them. And the same is true for the theology of any particular revelation.

It is understandable that, given the theological character of this study, the search for the meaning of revelations assumes capital importance. So the question, Why revelations? dominates all the others.

In the first chapter of Part Three we shall try to determine the meaning of revelations in themselves. We shall follow up this chapter with an inquiry into the fruit of revelations. The fruit signifies only the fulfillment of their meaning. In other words, the meaning is the intentional aim; the fruit is the realization of this aim. The last chapter presents some observations upon the use of revelations, aiming to show how their meaning may be realized in the widest possible way.

CHAPTER VIII

The Meaning of Revelations

1   THE "TRADITIONAL" PLACE OF
REVELATIONS IN THEOLOGY

IT IS A FACT that the meaning of revelations has never been carefully worked out in theological thought. In order to determine clearly the meaning of revelations, it would be good for us to review briefly what place revelations have rather commonly occupied in the theological thought of recent centuries. We are thinking especially of certain "traditional" views. By this term we do not mean the doctrines or views of the great Tradition, but only certain conceptions which were largely imposed in the Schools, conceptions which took into consideration other aspects than those emphasized by the Pastors of the Church. According to these conceptions, particular revelations would be only supererogatory resources in Christian life.

Furthermore, there is no dearth of theologians who find in revelations no more than an outgrowth of the popular taste for the miraculous; others see in them a sort of luxury enjoyed by the mystics, or a kind of spiritual fastidiousness.

It is a fact that a short time ago revelations formed no part of scholastic teaching. It required temerity to mention them, since revelations were considered as accessory and contingent things and theology was thought to concern itself only with the eternal verities.

The following are some of the reasons advanced to justify such views.

Why should dogmatic theology, for instance, interest itself in revelations when its object is the whole body of Christian mysteries explicitly proposed to the faithful by the Church and revealed, at least implicitly, before the death of the last Apostle?

Revelation being concluded, it has been said, what good purpose is served by these revelations? Do they bring us new doctrines—Yes or No? In the first case they must be rejected a priori: dogma does not admit new doctrines. In the second instance they can only repeat what has already been said: these revelations are therefore superfluous.

Thus in dogmatic theology they are most often defined in a negative way. These revelations are ones which do not commit Christians; it is normal therefore for them to be mentioned only in appendices as for instance, by Cardinal Franzelin,[138] although he is an author who recognizes positive values in revelations.

In "fundamental" theology they meet with scarcely any better treatment. If they are mentioned, they are not to be accepted as arguments upon which one could base the credibility of universal Revelation, which is the chief task of fundamental theology at least in its apologetical branch. Certainly miracles may serve as solid arguments for credibility, and appeal is sometimes made to revelations, especially when they are presented under the form of apparitions or "miracles"; but properly speaking revelations are not miracles. Taken in themselves they are not to serve as arguments since their authenticity cannot be sufficiently proved. To serve as a sign in so important an aim, this authenticity has to be very well established.

As far as exegesis is concerned, the fate of revelations is settled in advance. The Bible is the document of public Revelation. How, then, could there not be opposition between it and special revelations? Should not exegesis still defend—as in the first centuries—the purity of Revelation against the interference of revelations which weaken instead of enriching it? We should remember all those books on revelations which came near to being accepted by the Church but which were finally rejected as apocryphal, or permitted only as reading for the purpose of edification.

In moral theology one might expect revelations to be dealt with in two sections: in the treatise on the Faith—if this is not included in dogmatic theology, as it is by the majority of authors—and in the treatise upon prophecy. Now the great commentators of the sixteenth century on St. Thomas's *Summa Theologica* mention revelations, as we have already seen. But as the realization grew that assent to revelations was only of human faith, proportionately less was said about them in treating of the object of Faith.

It might have been expected that at least in the treatise on prophecy the question of revelations would be seriously posed. But it is a curious thing that in the treatises which have seen the light since the Council of Trent this has not been generally done. In treating of prophecy the writers think almost exclusively of biblical prophecies; the other prophecies, those which mark the history of the people of God until the second coming of the Lord, are practically put aside. These writers seem to forget what the theologians of the Middle Ages emphasized, namely, that prophecy is a permanent charism of the Church—there will always be prophecies in the Church, as there always have been.

It would surely seem that mystical theology at any rate should have given a place to revelations. God, in fact, does not communicate Himself in any special way to His enemies, but the closer a man is to God the more susceptible he would seem for the reception of revelations. There are writers who declare that the visions and revelations of souls who have not reached mystical marriage must be considered as illusions. There may be a question here of a general opinion based upon the teaching of St. Teresa of Avila and St. John of the Cross (cf. note 102).

If this is the case, revelations belong to mystical theology, and mystical theology should reply theologically to the questions posed to us by revelations. But does it? Is it not precisely among the mystics that we find the most definite reservations with respect to revelations? St. John of the Cross warns everyone against revelations and visions, and vigorously demonstrates that the mystics have no need of them, that the Bible and the teaching of the Church are perfectly sufficient for them, and, even more, that it would be a sin to desire them.

It is a general teaching that revelations, like charisms in general, are not essential elements of the mystical life. They are called, in fact, "epiphenomena of mysticism." Mysticism culminates in pure contemplation, in the ineffable. This mysticism without words or images is naturally prone to mistrust all prophetic activity, for the latter is normally expressed by words, and by that very fact is more liable to enter into conflict with the magisterium of the Church. Karl Rahner, who points this out, considers not without some slight exaggeration that the history of mystical theology is a history of devaluation of prophecy in favor of the approbation of infused contemplation, "pure" and non-prophetic.[139]

It is a fact that in their doctrinal expositions the mystics show themselves as a rule very reserved in regard to revelations, although these sometimes, or even frequently, play a very important role in their own lives.

That is not all. Canon law itself treats of revelations. A curious fact is that it is precisely in a treatise on canon law in the celebrated work of Benedict XIV that we find one of the best theological summaries which has been written upon revelations in past centuries; this work has had more influence upon the theologians than all the other writings upon the same subject. This was possible since in their treatises upon the canonization of saints canonists were concerned with the fruitfulness of the life of God and of the Church in souls. But the conclusions of the canonists are negative as are those of the other theological branches we have just mentioned—revelations, visions, apparitions do not by any means constitute a criterion in favor of the canonization of saints. This conclusion has been confirmed by the Sovereign Pontiffs in recent canonizations such as that of Gemma Galgani.

It is not surprising that the history of the Church, that "auxiliary" branch of theology, is concerned with revelations. This is so because revelations are actualities which are inserted into the human psyche and therefore their repercussions are fully reflected in history; it is normal that this should be so. However, this category of occurrences is so subject to illusions and to false representations of objective reality that the historian hesitates, in general, to recognize fully the historicity of revelations, despite the proofs which he might be able to advance in their favor.

Truly revelations are in a strange position in theology. This science speaks of them in all, or almost all, of its branches, but it is usually to reject them, to expel them from its particular domain; they are at home in no section of it, and everywhere they cut the figure of the poor relation. This situation is due to the fact that no one has considered studying revelations under all their aspects. Certain important dimensions of ecclesiology have been neglected as, for instance, the role of charisms in the Church. On the whole, if the place of revelations in theology has been reduced, this is chiefly because the question, What is the meaning of revelations? has not been asked. Once it is admitted that God, even after the death of the last Apostle, did not cease to communicate Himself through revelations, it must be admitted that God, by so doing, is fulfilling one of His designs. So, we are now going to see that to know this design is to know the theological meaning of revelations. We shall now ask, How is it that theology can exclude the designs of God from its object? If creatures considered in their relationship with God enter, as St. Thomas says they do, into the object of theology (*Sum. Theol.*, 1, 1, 7, ad 2), there is all the more reason for the designs of God to enter into it, designs which imply divine actions.

2   DETERMINATION OF
THE MEANING OF REVELATIONS

The meaning of a thing is its total significance: this is basically its aim, its final purpose. There is an essential connection between the aim and the nature of a reality; this aim implies this nature, and vice versa. That is why to explain the meaning of a reality is to specify its final purpose. This goes for everything which exists, but in particular for the reality which is action. The very nature of the action is directly specified by the end or final purpose (*actio specificatur ex fine*). The final cause, which is of itself an extrinsic reality, penetrates here, so to speak, into the nature of the action. So to indicate the end of revelations will thereby be the same thing as to indicate the meaning which specifies their character.

When we discussed the nature of revelations in the first chapter we noted two distinctive characteristics, their object and their proper destination. But these two characteristics are specified in the last analysis by the aim which is thus added as a new distinctive mark to the other two and which throws a new light upon revelations.

What, then, is the aim of revelations? It is the direction of human conduct in a particular situation, or in other words, a command given in a specified situation of life.

We may note, of course, that this definition is an abstract and general formula for something which is very concrete. Like all analytical procedure it considers only the aim in itself and makes no mention of the underlying reality.

Let us try to explain what this definition contains. The definition does not raise a question of doctrine but of practical direction. Certainly doctrine is not excluded from the aim of revelations. However, by comparison with their aim revelations are only a means of achieving an end.

The aim of revelations is, in a word, a "direction," and not the manifestation of a truth. It is not an affirmation but a command. The direction of human conduct which comes from heaven is always in accord with God's meaning. It is necessarily then, "an edification"; that is the most venerable and most traditional term by which to designate the aim of revelations. It is used in this sense in the Bible (1 Cor. 14: 3-4), as also in the writings of the Fathers, and it has remained in use right up to our own day.

This orientation toward edification is manifested as an order—most frequently expressed formally as a precept, but sometimes under the form of a counsel or of an invitation. It is always an impetus or a stimulus toward a more serious, more authentic spiritual life. The call to conversion, also, is the strongest expression of the aim of particular revelations.

We said that the aim of revelations was a direction of human conduct, and we added: "in a particular situation." If we were limiting ourselves strictly to revelations made in the post-apostolic period, we could omit that specification, for in that case we should be dealing entirely with particular revelations. However, although we have these latter in mind

—and especially those of our own times—we are here considering particular revelations in general; and we know that there were such revelations before the death of the last Apostle.

It is precisely this "particular situation" which especially characterizes the aim of a particular revelation, and this aim distinguishes it from public revelation. This applies to all particular revelation, whether it belongs to the Old or the New Testament, whether it was made before the Law of Moses or after, in the time of Christ or after Christ. We do not, therefore, have to ask ourselves whether there is "an essential, qualitative difference" between the "private revelations" after Christ and the others.[140] In order to maintain the necessity for such a difference, it is not enough in our opinion to take a stand based on a view of the content of the revelations. These revelations are inserted, it is true, into the situation of this or that period in the economy of salvation, that is to say, into a particular situation in the interior of a general situation proper to one of the great periods of this economy (cf. *Sum. Theol.*, II–II, 174, 6).

Is it a question of an intrinsic insertion? From the chronological point of view, undoubtedly it is, but from the point of view of content it would seem not to be. The particular revelation which St. Paul received after the shipwreck of Malta is related to a particular situation of the eschatological period which began after the death of Christ; but its content does not seem to belong exclusively to the period into which it was historically inserted: this content is the announcement of God's design to save Paul and all his traveling companions from the danger of death (Acts 27: 24). Announcements of the same nature were made also in the period of the Law.

But however an intrinsic insertion may be related to a revelation, the direction of human conduct in a particular situation specifies the aim of the revelation. The direction specifies the aim in such a way that no matter to what great period of the economy of salvation the revelation belongs, it is distinguished from public revelation which is valid for an enduring situation in at least one whole period.

3   JUSTIFICATION OF
THIS SPECIFICATION

The teaching of St. Thomas

It is easy to find support for these reflections in the different theological sources. Some idea of these sources is given in the first part of this book. To stay within the scope of our work, we must limit ourselves to a few theological citations in support of our thesis. We begin with St. Thomas and the doctrine he expounds in the *Summa Theologica,* II–II, 174, a. 6 which has been the source of a new orientation in our thinking on the problem of revelations. It has guided us as a beacon in our researches by showing us the issue from afar.

St. Thomas asks in this article whether prophecy has increased in the course of time. He replies by indicating the aim of prophecy. The reason for the existence of prophecy, he says, is the knowledge of divine truth. Prophecy has a twofold aim, because knowledge, the truth of which is not merely speculative, has a twofold aim. It not only enlightens us in the faith but also directs our conduct. This distinction divides the article into two parts and makes possible a precise and finely shaded reply. There are two categories of prophecy which correspond to the two ends he indicates.

The first part concentrates on prophecy that concerns the Faith, the second on prophecy directed toward action. Discussing prophecy which has for its aim divine Faith (*fidem Deitatis*), St. Thomas lays down three theses:

1. If one considers the three periods—that is to say, the period before the Law, the period under the Law, and the period of grace—it must be said that prophecy has developed. There has been a development in this sense, that the prophetic revelation of each later period is declared, according to the content, to be superior to that of the preceding period.

2. The following thesis gives a restrictive precision: At the interior of each of these periods the first prophetic revelation was each time superior to the following revelations.

3. This thesis marks the exceptional position of the Incarnation: the prophetic revelation of the mystery was richer when it was closer to Christ than it was before or after.

Here is the second part of the article concerning the second aim of prophetic vision:

"As regards the guidance of human acts, the prophetic revelation varied not according to the course of time, but according as circumstances required (*secundum conditionem negotiorum*); because as it is written (Proverbs xxix, 18), 'When prophecy shall fail, the people shall be scattered abroad.' Wherefore at all times men were divinely instructed about what they were to do, according as it was expedient for the spiritual welfare of the elect."

One perhaps may object that St. Thomas is not speaking of particular revelations but of prophecy which has for its aim either the Faith or morals, and which is always a matter of public revelation.

To think in this way is to misinterpret the text of St. Thomas. It is true that he treats directly only of prophecy. But whoever says "prophecy" says "revelation." Now prophecy, like revelation, may be particular or universal, that is, "public."

Among the examples which St. Thomas gives for the prophecies of Faith (*fides Deitatis*) there is not a single one which indicates what today we call "morality" as distinct from dogma. And in the text in question he means by *fides Deitatis* everything which has been revealed by God to be accepted by the people of God for the whole duration of the periods mentioned. Whether it was a matter of "truths to be believed" or of general laws which determined action does not matter; what we call, according to St. Thomas, the prophecy concerning the Faith is universally valid, at least for a period. If the moral law were not included in this kind of prophecy, it would be necessary to place it in the second kind mentioned, namely, "the prophecy of acts."

But that is inadmissible. For the last thesis clearly declares that in this second kind of prophecy there is no progress or variation according to the periods: this declaration is directly opposed to the interpretation of the objector. For if, in the domain of universal revelation there is a change in the course of periods, a variation—*revelatio diversificata est*, writes St. Thomas—it is precisely in the laws of morality.

Let us recall the change proclaimed by Our Lord in His Sermon on the Mount: ". . . it was said to them of old . . . but I say to you . . ." Such a change is not admissible in the prophecy of action: that variation is conditioned solely by the necessity of particular circumstances which change within each period. That is, it is determined by a particular situation which may occur in no matter which period.

The last thesis of the article is not a corollary; it touches, on the contrary, on the most sensitive point. It gives the definitive answer. The objections of the article seek to prove that there had been a change, a progress of prophecy in the course of the periods. The body of the article replies by admitting the value of the objections as applied to prophecy enjoined by faith in God, but it denies their conclusions as applied to prophecy which has for its aim the direction of human activity. Of this latter it is simply said that it bears different forms (*diversificata est*); but of the other that it has developed (*crevit*). In short, for the reason given there has not been progress in prophecy, but change according to the particular situation—a change which is not specified by general revelation.

The last paragraph of the article (II–II, 174, 6 ad 3) confirms our interpretation with all desirable clarity: "The prophets who foretold the coming of Christ could not continue further than John, who with his finger pointed to Christ actually present. Nevertheless, as Jerome says on this passage, 'This does not mean that there were no more prophets after John. For we read in the Acts of the apostles that Agabus and the four maidens, daughters of Philip, prophesied.' . . . And at all times there have not been lacking persons having the spirit of prophecy, not indeed for the declaration of any new doctrine of faith, but for the direction of human acts. Thus Augustine says that the emperor Theodosius sent to John who dwelt in the Egyptian desert, and whom he knew by his ever-increasing fame to be endowed with the prophetic spirit; and from him he received a message assuring him of victory."

The importance of this passage cannot be exaggerated. Anyone who would not see it should recall a message that John XXIII addressed "to all Christians" at the conclusion of the centenary of the apparitions at Lourdes: "They (the Roman Pontiffs) also have a duty to recommend to the attention of the faithful—when after mature examination they consider it opportune for the general good—the supernatural lights which it has pleased God to dispense freely to certain privileged souls, *not to propose new doctrines but to guide our conduct.*" The Holy Father made his own the essence of the doctrine of St. Thomas and cited the original text of the passage which we have just emphasized.[140a]

Thomas Aquinas, in his commentary upon St. Matthew, also makes an observation which illustrates very well what we have just said. It concerns the text: "For all the prophets and the law prophesied until John" (Matt. 11: 13). The commentator asks: Does it follow from this that after John there were no more prophets? Here is the reply: "The mission of prophecy is twofold: it is sent to establish the Faith and to correct morals; but (today) the Faith has already been founded, for the promises were fulfilled by Christ. But for that which is concerned with correcting morals, prophecy never has, never will be lacking." [141]

Let us note this carefully. Although St. Thomas does not explicitly pose the problem of particular revelations, as we are doing, this much can be seen from his teaching upon prophecy: the prophecy which is not the basis of the Faith or of the Law, but which is a stimulus or a recall to live according to the rules laid down by God, is not specified by the nature or the conditions of its recipient, but by its aim.

In the article to which we have just referred, the prophecies of the first period, i.e., before the Law, are ranked among the "prophecies of the Faith." But although they were made to found the Faith, they were designed only for certain persons or certain families such as that of Abraham. It is only in the second period, that of the Law, that prophetic revelation which has for its object divine Faith had to be addressed to all the people. "Under the law prophetic revelation of things pertinent to faith in the Godhead was made in a yet more excellent way than hitherto, because then not only certain special persons or families but the whole people had to be instructed in these matters" (*Sum. Theol.*, ii–ii, 174, 6).

Since on the one hand we must admit this theological statement to the effect that there have been "prophecies of Faith" not destined for all, and since on the other hand we may add that there are particular revelations which are addressed, if not in principle at least in fact, to all without restriction, we understand better that this type of revelation is not basically specified by its recipient but by its aim.

Historical reasons

One could peruse the whole history of the people of God from the time of Abraham to the present day and find facts everywhere in confirmation of our exposition. The prophets of the Old Testament revealed doctrines which were authoritative for the people of God; but their revelations were often simply an order recalling what had already been established and urging the people to fulfill the will of God which had been communicated earlier.

We often read exhortations to the prophets containing revelations of the nature of the one which Jeremias received from Yahweh: "Go, and say to the men of Juda and to the inhabitants of Jerusalem: Will you not receive instruction, to obey my words, saith the Lord? The words of Jonadab the son of Rechab, by which he commanded his sons not to drink wine, have prevailed: and they have drunk none to this day, because they have obeyed the commandment of their father: but I have spoken to you, rising early and speaking, and you have not obeyed me. And I have sent to you all my servants the prophets, rising early, and sending and saying: *Return ye every man from his wicked way and make your ways good,* and follow not strange gods nor worship them: and you shall dwell in the land which I gave you and your fathers" (Jeremias 35: 13–16).

This was a matter of directing human conduct in a particular situation. At the moment when Yahweh spoke, "the men of Juda and of Jerusalem" were in an attitude of disobedience. It was to them alone that He addressed Himself. The law of Yahweh was for all, but the attitude in respect to this Law depended upon particular individuals. It could change according to the circumstances and the people involved in those circumstances. This attitude might for a time be the attitude of a section of the people, or of all the people, or of practically all the people; but that could change. And the prophecy, if there was one, would have quite a different content. But it happened too that the revelation might contain a new order: Zachary received the order to give his son the name of John. To Ananias the Lord said: "Arise, and go into the street that is called the Strait, and seek in the House of Judas one named Saul of Tarsus. . . . I will show him how great things he must suffer for my name's sake" (Acts 9: 11, 16).

Here the action was directly controlled by the revelation and in a sense which was not specified by established laws. It was unexpected and was required of one man and not of another, in one set of circumstances and not in another. God revealed to Ananias that at a certain moment he was to go to a certain place; He willed for Paul to suffer greatly, something which He does not ask of just any man.

It has been the same with revelations in the history of the Church: most frequently there has been a direct command which has been often only a recall to the laws divinely established. The invitation to prayer and penance has been frequently expressed in particular revelations ever since the first centuries. These divine pressures have denoted something new in the sense that men in a particular situation have "forgotten" certain divine ideas. For them the matter has been new.

But also and very often there have been commands which have manifested divine initiative in a particular circumstance. The examples are innumerable. Here are a few: Despite the advice of the theologian Velasquez, despite the demand of the municipal council of Villanueva de la Jara, St. Teresa hesitated about founding a convent in this city. "Now," she wrote in the book of *Foundations* (chap. xxviii, note 15), "His Majesty said to me in a very severe tone: '*With what treasures have you built the convents up to these days? Do not hesitate any longer to accept this foundation. It will contribute greatly to My glory and to the advancement of souls.'* What power is there like that of the words of God! Not only do they have great impact upon the understand-ing, but they enlighten it so that it grasps the truth, and they dispose the will to accomplish what they require. This is what happened for me. I accepted the foundation joyfully at once."

On another occasion Mother Teresa had decided not to undertake a foundation, that of Burgos, when the Lord ad-dressed these words to her: "Do not be concerned with these chills; I am the true warmth. The devil is neglecting no means to prevent this foundation. Make all efforts on your side to achieve it. Do not weary of going there in person. It will become a great benefit." At these words she changed her opinion (*ibid.*, chap. xxxi).

At Lourdes it was a whole series of orders that Bernadette received: Pray to God for sinners. . . . Go and drink at the spring and wash in it. . . . Go and eat the grass that you will find there. . . . You will tell the priests to build a chapel here. And so on.

When revelations contain facts, accounts, information or when they draw the attention of the faithful to certain aspects of doctrine, they always have for their aim action, edification: they are striving to make the faithful grow in their love for God or to urge them on to apostolic under-takings. They are first of all given for the salvation of souls. And what St. Thomas says about prophetic revelations holds good for all revelations. Their aim is to promote the salva-tion of the elect (*expediens in salutem electorum: Sum. Theol.*, II–II, 174, 6).

It is understandable too that St. Thomas points out as their aim the well-being of the Church: ". . . prophecy is given for the good of the Church." [141a] It is true that he is thinking here of prophecy as a charism, which seeks the well-being of whomsoever the prophet addresses and not necessarily of the prophet himself.

But, it will be said, there are revelations which are strictly private. That is true in the sense that a revelation may be addressed directly to a single person for his own good. And it may happen that no one else knows anything about such a revelation. However, the conversion or the spiritual progress brought about in that person through the revelation has an influence in the Church, often through apostolic movements which may be set in motion by this person, and always at least through prayer and sacrifice. And so "a soul which rises lifts up the world," and more directly, such a soul lifts up the Church.

4   OBJECTION DRAWN FROM MORALITY

But what are we to say of the following reflection which, if it is just, removes the whole strength from our exposition regarding the aim of revelations: The aim of a thing belongs to it in its own right. Now this does not apply in this case. What is pointed out as the aim of revelations, that is, the direction of human conduct in a particular situation, applies just as well to Christian morality as to revelations. The laws, for all that they are general, specify particular actions, at least by means of deduction which works through reason and conscience. If the observation were made that it is a revelation which specifies that special direction, the reply might be that we are also acting in virtue of a revelation through the moral laws, for they are revealed.

This reflection is not convincing, for it neglects important aspects of the question. First of all, it is not true that the moral laws succeed in determining all the details. Sometimes they clash or cross one another in a particular situation to such an extent that it is impossible to determine the action desired by God. Certainly there are always pastors of the Church who show us the way to follow. But there is something else, and this is more important. Let us suppose that one has found, by means of the best deduction, the conduct which should be adopted in a particular situation. Does this conduct correspond with the will of God? Not necessarily.

God is the Lord of history. He did not establish merely its principles. He is the God of Abraham, of Isaac and of Jacob. He is present at each moment of history whose course He directs, sometimes visibly, on His own initiative. Private life as well as the history of human and Christian society is full of divine initiatives which change their direction, even when this direction has been taken in accord with Christian principles.

Thus we saw in the life of St. Teresa that, after deciding for the best reasons indicated by conscience, not to found such and such a convent, she changed her decision on the spot because she received an order from the Lord through revelation.

Thus too, powerful pious movements have been set in motion or nourished under the impulse of revelations. This was, moreover—and let us note it in passing—one of the reasons why particular revelations, before being recognized by the Church, encountered such stern resistance, above all in theological milieu. The revelations of St. Margaret Mary, for instance, and the great Marian apparitions, gave expression to the devotions to the Sacred Heart and to the Blessed Virgin which they would not have received, at least at that moment of history, if these extraordinary manifestations had not taken place.

The Lord revealed His clearly specified wishes to St. Margaret Mary. They applied to her own life as well as that of the Church: "I will be your strength," He said to her, "fear nothing; but be attentive to My voice and to what *I ask of you in order to dispose you for the accomplishment of My designs.* First of all you will receive Me in the Blessed Sacrament as often as obedience will permit. . . . You will receive Communion in addition on the First Friday of each month. . . . I ask you that the First Friday after the Octave of Corpus Christi be dedicated to a particular feast in honour of My Heart. . . ." [141b] At the end of her message the Apparition of La Salette gives this order: "See that this is passed on to all my people." [142]

The direction of human activity of which we spoke is directly revealed for the particular situation in which the individual or Christian society finds itself. It is not a matter of an order deduced from general Revelation.

5   GENERAL VIEW

Now that the conception of the meaning of particular revelations is established, it is necessary to define them so that they may be better understood. They are heavenly and verbal manifestations of the divine will made to man in an extraordinary way in order to direct human activity in a particular situation of the life of private persons or of humanity in general.

The "verbal manifestation" expresses in this definition *the act* of particular revelation. A purely visual manifestation is not a revelation. The word "heavenly" indicates the agent: agents may be saints or angels acting as God's intermediaries, or God Himself. "Divine will" designates the object of the revelations. The subject of the revelation is "man"— whether cleric or lay person, Christian or pagan does not matter. The revelation is made "in an extraordinary way":

this is only a characteristic of its reception in the subject. The significance of this mode of the revelation is quite restricted. The "extraordinary way" of the occurrence of the revelation so far as the subject is concerned is not to be compared with the direction which general Revelation exercises on human activity by means of the magisterium and the pastoral function of the Church; it depends on the situation of the subject who receives the revelation.

The divine laws, revealed once for everyone, are always imperative and apply in all cases; particular revelations are given only for a definite situation. But that God manifests Himself through them is a habitual form of the divine pastoral activity. This pastoral activity, it is true, manifests itself more or less sporadically; but these manifestations through which God acts directly and in a manner apparent to the senses upon men is an expression, normal although secondary, of His providence, always concerned for our eternal salvation.

The remainder of the definition has been explained at length in this chapter. We have deliberately chosen the vague term "humanity in general," since it may apply to a group, a class, a community, a society, a people, the Church, etc. It distinguishes social revelations from those which are strictly private. The point is that it is the destination of the revelations which is determined by their end and not vice versa. It is not the destination which basically characterizes the particular revelation, but the aim.

It is true that the destination is an element of distinction which is more visible; things are more commonly distinguished from one another by their characteristics which compel our attention than by the essential differences inherent in their nature. It is because revelations have for their aim the direction of human activity in a particular situation that they are not addressed, that they cannot be addressed officially and directly, to the Church. Not referring directly to the ages of the economy of salvation, they cannot commit the

Church or the divine and Catholic Faith which has for its object the unaltered mysteries, revealed once for all time. What St. Thomas often emphasized in respect to acts or virtues applies to our case. The specification is made by the object, but the object is specified by the end.

Since revelation is made for the direction of life in a particular situation, its object, the divine will, is equally particular—it is not a universal law or truth. God sees, for example, a great danger or an abuse in the life of a person or in a section of the Church; He decides to remedy it by an intervention; but this ceases when the danger or the abuse is removed; the divine will is no longer the same. This proposition has been verified in the post-apostolic period, but it was also so in Old Testament times when the people of God, or at least a section of them, neglected the Laws of Yahweh. Then Yahweh made them feel His anger, but as soon as He saw their repentance, He relented and forgave.

If the aim of revelations is, as we have just shown, a "direction" or orientation given in a specified situation, the means employed to give this direction are the signs. Revelations, in fact, are expressed according to their aim by signs which normally attract attention forcibly. "It is obviously within the perspectives of this providential economy of sacred signs," writes Father J.-H. Nicolas, "that we must set the different manifestations of the divine will which were produced and are produced in an extraordinary manner in the Church. More striking because of their marvelous character, they provoke among certain people, and sometimes in the whole Christian people, a salutary shock which the sacramental signs, neglected and familiar, do not always produce. That is their providential *raison d'être*." [143]

"Their marvelous character," "their providential *raison d'être*," are to be found in brilliant fashion in the Marian apparitions of our epoch. Every revelation involves a certain shock, at least for whoever receives it. Barth, Brunner and other Protestant theologians have dwelt upon this point when talking of the "occurrence" aspect (*das Ereignishafte*) in the act of revelation. In a particular revelation this aspect manifests itself precisely in the fact that the orientation of a life is changed in that particular situation. Such a change always assumes a shock of some kind.

Here is one final reflection before ending this chapter. The theological idea which we have just explained throws light upon the relationship of revelations and theology. One cannot resolve this question by saying that since revelations refer to particular situations of life they cannot form part of theology which, being a science, is concerned with the universal.

Particular facts are not the object of science. But according to St. Thomas, they do in fact form part of theology, not as a principal object, but as examples of life set forth in the moral sciences or as the corroboration of sacred writers (*Sum. Theol.*, I, 1, 2 ob. 1).

Certainly our knowledge of God cannot be elaborated outside the laws of our intellectual cognizance, which proceeds from the particular to the universal. The fact remains, however, that the object of theology is one single concrete being. It must not be forgotten, moreover, that all cognizance of God is analogical. Thus the knowledge of God is also analogical.

From this standpoint one other idea assures the integration of revelations into theology: Everything which comes from God, everything which concerns Him, enters into the object of theology (*Sum. Theol.*, I, 1, 7 ad 2; cf. I, 1, 2, ad 2). How could the direction of life, even in the most particular situations, not form part of theology, especially if this direction comes directly from God? Revelations belong to the divine pastoral activity which itself is an expression of Providence and of divine government. Providence is concerned with everything in an immediate way.

Even when Providence makes use of secondary causes its rule extends to everything, and, therefore, to all the situations in which man may find himself (*Sum. Theol.*, I, 22, 3; I, 103, 6).

The divine pastoral activity is exercised in and through the Church and thus particular revelations, although they have in view a particular situation, constitute a stable and divinely established function. That is to say, if God intervenes in such and such a particular situation, He does so according to a constant will. And even if these interventions are irregular, sporadic, they will not cease until the end of time. The irregular has a certain norm. In so far as it is a function established by God for the life of the Church, particular revelation justifies once more its place in theology.

And the function which may be called prophecy has, according to St. Thomas, exactly the aim of correcting the morals and directing human activity. Thus a theology of revelations is essentially linked with the meaning of revelations.

CHAPTER IX

Fruits of Revelations

THE FRUITS of revelations are simply the realization of their meaning. In treating of these fruits we shall not, therefore, go outside the subject of our last section—on the contrary we shall be able to complete it, or at least to confirm it, by means of ideas less abstract than those we have just expressed regarding the meaning of revelations. First we shall give a general survey of the fruits of revelations, and then we shall make a few reflections regarding the value of these fruits in so far as they are reaped in particular domains limited by the destination or the content of the revelations.

1 GENERAL CONSIDERATIONS

The grace of a particular revelation is not sanctifying grace which elevates the soul itself. Revelations stimulate the soul to live according to that grace or they predispose it, sometimes in an irresistible fashion, to receive it.

It is a matter of the awakening of a life or of the orientation of its activities. Revelations shake the soul; they turn its powers upside down, disturb its false peace, fill it with a holy fear in order to flood it with a delicious peace. We have already had occasion to mention this or that fruit of revelations. Now let us consider them in themselves and as a whole.

Spiritual writers often distinguish humility (which manifests itself among other fruits) as one of the marks of true revelations. St. Teresa dilates upon this subject in chapters three and eight of the Eighth Book of *Abodes:* "God," she says, "has another method of awakening the soul (*despertar al alma*) . . . this is by way of words which God addresses to the soul in many ways" (*Moradas*, vi, cap. 3, note 1). A few words such as, Do not be troubled, are enough to bring calm to a soul disturbed by trial and tribulation or plunged into darkness and dryness. A few words flood it with a divine light and remove all fear from it; a few words immediately give certitude on the outcome of an important matter with which it is concerned. Despite all the interior or exterior obstacles, the word of the Lord which promises success accomplishes it. And then "the soul apprehends from it so much joy and lightness that it wants to do nothing else but to praise His Majesty continuously" (*Moradas*, vi, cap. 3, note 8).

St. John of the Cross, as we know, urges the rejection of revelations. But in rejecting them, he writes "one does no injury to God" and one is not thereby deprived from receiving the effect and the fruit which God proposed to produce in the soul by their means (*Subida*, ii, 12, 11).

In speaking of "substantial words" he extols their fruits with more force than does St. Teresa. Here is what he has to say of them in the *Ascent of Mount Carmel:* ". . . every substantial word . . . impresses substantially (*imprime substancialmente*) on the soul that which it signifies. It is as if Our Lord were to say formally to the soul: 'Be thou good'; it would then substantially be good. Or as if He were to say to it: 'Love thou Me'; it would then have and feel within itself the substance of love for God. . . . And even so with Abraham, when He said to him: 'Walk in My presence and be perfect'; he was then perfect and walked ever in the fear of God. And this is the power of His word in the Gospel, wherewith He healed the sick, raised the dead, etc., by no more than a word. And after this manner He gives certain souls locutions which are substantial; and they are of such moment and price that they are life and virtue and incomparable good to the soul; for one of these words works greater good within the soul than all that the soul itself has done throughout its life" (*Subida*, II, cap. 31, note 1).

Can one expect richer fruits of revelations? What really happens is an immediate direction of the life toward its eternal destiny. These fruits of "substantial words" make one think of the conversions brought about through revelations or apparitions as, for example, that of Ratisbonne.

But, it may be said, these revelations are strictly private and they take place only very rarely. Their fruit is therefore extremely restricted. First of all, it must be plainly stated that for the person privileged this fruit is of capital importance. Revelations are probably less rare than one thinks. The spiritual masters, it is true, say that a quarter or a third of them are false, and this percentage is very likely still below the real proportion. But among the incalculable number of revelations known, most of the time to confessors and spiritual directors only, there remain very many which are true.

However, it is somewhat pointless to wish to apply quantitative criteria here. This is much more important—so far as the fruit is concerned, hardly any revelations are strictly private. It may happen that a revelation remains always the secret of one individual. The spiritual progress which it produces in that individual increases the sanctity of the Church. Every cell of the Mystical Body, by the very fact that it is itself expanding, augments the vigor of the whole Body.

The fruit of revelations, however, is not limited to this. The person who preserves the secret of his revelation inevitably communicates to others something of the fruit which he is receiving from God. But there are revelations which are directly intended for many people. These revelations, called "social," bear the most abundant fruits and their influence upon the life of the Church is immense. The number of extremely beneficial movements which such revelations have inspired in specific groups of the faithful is incalculable. The Church has received powerful impulses through them. For example, one should read the bull of canonization of St. Bridget, proclaimed by Pope Boniface XI, to realize to what extent this saint's revelations regenerated the members of the Church.

Particular revelations were at the source of the movements of reparation of these latter centuries. We know that the devotions in honor of the Sacred Heart and of the Eucharist are due to revelations. The value and the abundance of their fruits are confirmed by the fact that they lead the faithful to the great sources of the life of the Church of the Word Incarnate, that is, toward the Faith and the sacraments.

It is a fact that the manifestations of Christian faith in the places of the great Marian apparitions of our epoch find their completion in the greatest of the sacraments. In these places God acts upon souls, not only through the sacrament of penance, which is greatly sought in them, but He is loved and glorified there in the Sacrament of Sacraments. The life of the pilgrims in these places is marked by the celebration of the Eucharist, by the procession of the Blessed Sacrament. So revelations bear the most wonderful fruits by intensifying the Church's life in places where Jesus, Mary and the faithful are most intimately united and where human activity receives the highest and most discerning direction.

If we consider revelations such as the great Marian apparitions in their consequences, and if we look at these revelations from the point of view not only of their verbal expression, but also of other expressive forms (gestures, attitudes, circumstances) which allow us to elucidate their total significance, we can establish the continuance of the wonderful action of God upon His people. Through these revelations God continues to guide and exhort His people just as He did in the Old Testament and in the time of Christ. Through them, God communicates His designs to the world and to us.

Certain apparitions and the pilgrimages which they have occasioned have passed into the public domain. Not only has the Church, after mature reflection, recognized their supernatural origin, writes Abbé Lochet, not only has she approved the building of places of worship on the sites of these pilgrimages, but she takes part officially in them and she turns their message toward the whole Christian people. On many occasions bishops and popes, in their capacity of leaders of the Church, have themselves participated in the pilgrimage devotions. On many occasions the Pope, in documents addressed to the universal Church, has noted these facts and drawn from them lessons and commands which are addressed to all.

Finally and above all, the liturgy which Catholics follow throughout the year in celebrating the mysteries of God's people includes the most remarkable of these apparitions— those of Lourdes. It would be no exaggeration to say that in this and many other ways accepted by the universal devotion of the Christian people, these facts have passed into the life of the Church, or rather that the Church has recognized, through the prompting of the Spirit who guides her, that these facts are a part of her life. God's people recognize these events and celebrate them; these events belong to the people and to their history.[144]

It serves no purpose and is even unworthy of a theologian to ignore these fruits of revelations or to wish to fight against these expressions of the life of the Church on account of abuses which may accompany them. It is the abuses which should be fought—the trivialities, the sentimentality, the affectations of artistic expression, the satisfaction of an inner religious need—and there are abuses worse than these. But the parable of the wheat and the cockle should be remembered. Until the end of time the devil is going to attack the Church and above all in those places and in those forms wherein she is manifesting her life. Pascal's saying applies to the manifestations of which we speak: "There is enough clarity to enlighten the elect and enough obscurity to keep them humble." [144a]

The abundance of the fruits of these apparitions is not surprising if we think of the Incarnation. God wishes to accomplish His work of redemption through the Incarnation. And the apparitions, which by their nature make appeal to the senses, belong to the consequences of the Incarnation. Within this perspective we better understand why prophetic revelations have for their aim the good of the Church (*Sum. Theol.*, II–II, 172, 4).

2   REVELATIONS AND THE HIERARCHY

If revelations are given for the good of the Church then the hierarchy must also benefit from them. But is this so? Protestants like von Harnack believe it to be historically established that the hierarchy, in proportion to its evolution, succeeded finally in suppressing the prophetic function. And all those for whom "the history of the Roman Church is the history of a progressive, radical and perfect transformation of the Church into an institution and law" cannot think otherwise.

To think thus is to misunderstand the nature and the life

of the Church. That there should be oppositions and tensions, of greater or lesser degree, between the very different elements which comprise the Church, is absolutely normal. It would, however, be erroneous to state that one element could make another disappear. Thus it is not surprising that the relationship between the prophetic function and the official priesthood should occasionally provoke conflict. This relationship already preoccupied the Church during the first centuries; but from the beginning the Church also resolved this problem by her life and her teaching which, although sometimes misunderstood, "must remain immutable because it concerns the essential structure of the Church."

"That teaching," writes Father Labourdette, whom we have just quoted, "is essentially this: in the Church of Christ, according to the consummated economy which is that of the fullness of time, the Spirit is before all communicated through the hierarchy. The great *charism of truth is bestowed on the episcopal body.* The man of the Spirit, the 'pneumatologist,' the true prophet, the true 'gnostic,' is first and before all *the bishop.* . . . Once Revelation was consummated the Spirit did not withdraw; far otherwise, He has been given to the Church in a fullness and with a permanence never previously known. The episcopal body united to the Pope, and the Pope personally, have the assurance of this charism of truth. And the infallible proposition of the revealed teaching is but the principal form of this assistance which is extended under various forms to the whole exercise of the magisterium, of power of jurisdiction.

"But this fundamental doctrine must not make us overlook the fact that the spirit of prophecy, whose role is considerable in the Church, remains there also in a subordinate way. It is this spirit which animates the great strides forward, and the great renewals in the Church, sometimes in the most humble of souls. And under this form certainly the prophetic charism is in no way connected with the hierarchy, but is submitted to it. There is no period in the Church when this animation by the Spirit cannot be discerned. It is assuredly a charismatic movement which has extended devotion to the Sacred Heart throughout the whole Church, from the time of the revelations made to a little Visitandine . . . the Church is living; to live is to encounter new risks, it is to find oneself face to face with constantly changing circumstances, it is to feel the need to rise above the weight of all human aging. What is more, this life of the Church is not a 'human' life at the level of reason; it is a strictly supernatural life which God alone gives and which He alone can sustain; outside of the permanent institutions which substantially insure the maintenance and spread of the Church, He will always be there in His inspirations to revivify her, to guide her, whether in very humble circumstances which effectively concern a small number of souls, or, on the other hand, by starting a movement which will extend to the whole Church." [144b]

Here then is the solution in principle. If in fact there are conflicts between the prophetic function and the hierarchical power, this is due to a defective interpretation or application. Thus it was that the ecclesiastical tribunal presided over by the bishop of Beauvais, Pierre Cauchon, condemned Joan of Arc by rejecting the "voices" which she would not recognize as false. The highest hierarchical authority rehabilitated the martyr of Rouen.

In the lives of true visionaries, who were to be counted among the finest sons of the Church, there have been moments when—due allowance being made—they found themselves confronting her, their Mother, as Christ confronted His Father when He said to Him: Why hast Thou forsaken Me? In this way they have been able to suffer not only for the Church but also through the Church—an exceptional suffering, temporary and extremely fruitful.

But these unusual oppositions allowed by Providence emphasized the importance of revelations. Besides, if the hierarchy show themselves reserved or even sometimes hostile

with respect to revelations, this is really in order to protect
them. The hierarchy is not the enemy of divine revelations;
it is the enemy of men who falsify their transmission and the
enemy of the devil. The hierarchy believes in the positive
interventions of God in the world. But by vigorously elimi-
nating false revelations it gives more weight to the true.

The attitude of Curé Peyramale of Lourdes was providential. His was an attitude often adopted by representatives of
the hierarchy—rejection right up to the moment when enlightenment took place. But then this rejection was the holy
protection of divine action against all adversaries. Thus the
hierarchy has protected and defended revelations against
theologians. The hierarchy has not only a teaching function
but also a pastoral and sacerdotal responsibility. It judges,
not from one particular point of view, but by taking the
whole matter into consideration. In establishing the great
benefit which revelations bring to the faithful it does not
reject them a priori despite the dangers they involve.

However, we want to emphasize at this point that when
we speak of the faithful we are thinking of all the members
of the Church. It is not only the "Church taught" which is
the beneficiary of revelations, but also the hierarchy.

A superficial consideration of the facts has led many to
believe that revelations and the prophetic gifts belong rather
to the laity, and creates a certain balance between the laity
and the hierarchy. But it is not because of prophetic gifts
that certain non-clerical people, even women, enjoy among
the faithful, *de facto* at least, the authority proper to a doctor of the Church.

When St. Peter announced to the first gathering of Christians the realization of the prophecy of Joel: "I will pour out
my Spirit upon all flesh: and your sons and your daughters
shall prophesy . . ." he was applying this to the whole
Church—to men and women in all walks of life, old people
and young people. He certainly intended to say that in the

Messianic epoch the Spirit of God could manifest Itself in any member of the Church; no one was excluded in advance from the gift of prophecy or of visions, members of the hierarchy any more than anyone else.

In fact, the Apostles were also prophets. Members of the hierarchy may be both the subjects of revelations and the people for whom the revelations are intended. As we saw in the first part, St. Peter and St. Paul received heavenly revelations, as did St. Ignatius of Antioch and St. Polycarp. And there is nothing to prevent members of the hierarchy from receiving divine communications today.

That revelations were intended for members of the hierarchy is a fact. The tenth chapter of the Acts of the Apostles shows how God acted through revelations to St. Peter, either directly, or indirectly by means of the visions of Cornelius, in order to direct his action in a way not foreseen by men.

It has happened frequently in the history of the Church that teachings and especially public exhortations by bishops or popes have been occasioned or instigated by revelations.

The secrets which the shepherds of La Salette would not reveal to anyone except the Sovereign Pontiff had very probably a content destined for the man who bore the burden of responsibility for the Church. If in these circumstances the secrets did not reveal to the Pope something which should have been known by him alone so that he might take action in the Church in a specific way, it would be hard to know why they should have been communicated.

Let us note the most important facts. We shall take two examples from our own era, two consecrations of the human race. On May 25, 1899, Leo XIII in his encyclical *Annum Sacrum* announced to the Christian world a great plan from which he expected abundant and lasting fruits not only for Christians but for all humanity. This was the consecration of the human race to the Sacred Heart. Among the reasons explaining this move the Pope gave this: "There is finally one reason which urges Us to realize our aim; We do not

want to pass over it in silence. It is of a personal kind, but
it is fitting and important. God, the Author of all good, has
looked after Us, curing Us recently of a dangerous illness." [145]

The consecration was to be, as we read in the encyclical,
"the culmination of all the honors which have ever been
tendered to the Sacred Heart." And so he carried it out, after
a great *triduum* and with tremendous solemnity.

Nevertheless while the Catholic world took part in this
consecration which Leo XIII called "the greatest act" of his
pontificate, the facts which had most powerfully contributed
to its realization were known to hardly anyone. Who knew
that far from Rome a nun was then singing her *Nunc dimit-
tis* in the silence of her convent? At first vespers of the day
which was to be marked by this great act, Sister Marie of the
Divine Heart, superior of the convent of the Good Shepherd
at Oporto, was dying.

On June 10, 1898, this religious had addressed a letter to
Leo XIII, written, she said, on the order of Our Lord, who
wished His Vicar to consecrate the entire world to the divine
Heart. The Pope did nothing. That is very understandable.
But on January 6, 1899, she wrote another letter in which she
emphasized the order of the Lord and her confessor's approval of what she was doing. She stressed the order of Our
Lord who had spoken expressly to her of the consecration.
She suggested to the Pope that he exhort the clergy and the
faithful to intensify the devotion of the First Fridays of the
month and grant new indulgences. She said that she divined
in these measures the object of a burning desire of the Sacred
Heart.

And here is an extract: "When Your Holiness was suffering last summer from an indisposition which at your advanced age filled the hearts of your children with anxiety,
Our Lord gave me the sweet consolation that He would
prolong the days of Your Holiness in order to carry out the
consecration of the whole world to His divine Heart." [146]

The Pope was touched by this letter, and he decided to take action. He directed that inquiries should be made. The inquiries proved to be favorable to the nun. She was looked upon widely as a saint and it would not have been imprudent to believe in her communications. The result was such that Cardinal Mazzella, Prefect of the Sacred Congregation of Rites, who was now fully informed about all aspects, said to the Pope that the letter had indeed been dictated by Our Lord. Leo XIII directed the Cardinal to examine its content.

A difficulty arose which emanated directly from the essential element of the letter: how could one consecrate to the Sacred Heart infidels who acknowledged neither Christ nor the Church? The difficulty was resolved by the distinction pointed out by St. Thomas in the *Summa Theologica* (III, 59, 4, ad 2): If the infidels are not subject to Christ with respect to "the exercise of His power," they belong to Him nevertheless "in respect of the power which He received from the Father over all things." This was, in the main, the thought expressed by the nun.

A remarkable thing was that Mother Marie of the Divine Heart was favorably heard not only in regard to what she expressly requested on the part of Christ—and that with an astonishing rapidity when one considers the importance of the action and the prudent delay exercised by the Holy See in such circumstances—but also in respect of her second wish. A few weeks after the memorable day of the consecration, on July 21, the Prefect of the Sacred Congregation addressed to all the bishops in the name of the Sovereign Pontiff a pressing invitation to spread devotion to the Sacred Heart of Jesus, through confraternities, the month of the Sacred Heart, and the practice of making First Fridays.

As with the consecration to the Sacred Heart, the consecration to the Immaculate Heart of Mary also was accomplished under the influence of particular revelations. On December 8, 1942, twenty-five years after the events at

Fatima, Pius XII, in the Basilica of St. Peter, officially consecrated the human race to the Heart of Mary: "Finally, as the Church and the whole human race were consecrated to the Heart of your Jesus," proclaimed the Pope, terminating the consecration, "we also consecrate ourselves forever to you, O Immaculate Heart, O our Mother and Queen of the world" (A.A.S., 34 [1942] 346).

The Holy See, in publishing the office of the feast of the Immaculate Heart of Mary, returns to this subject in a declaration, *urbi et orbi*, also inserted into the *Acta Sedis Apostolicae*. And on July 7, 1952, the Holy Father addressed himself "to all the peoples of Russia."

Here is the most important passage of the apostolic letter: "As We consecrated the whole human race some years ago to the Immaculate Heart of the Virgin Mother of God, so We now consecrate to the same Immaculate Heart very particularly all the peoples of Russia" (A.A.S., 44 [1952] 511).

It is enough to have only a very minor knowledge of the occurrences of Fatima and the attitude of the supreme hierarchy in regard to them to discover their decisive influence upon the acts of Pius XII which we have mentioned. The Pope would not have acted in this way, or at least not at that time, if there had been no revelations at Fatima.

It is true that the consecrations of Leo XIII and Pius XII make no mention of revelations or apparitions. They avoid even mentioning the revelations as a reason for or an occasional cause of their actions. This was entirely to be expected. These actions must be justified by the great sources of Faith. But the fact that they were performed by the Church at a given moment in her history, in a particular situation of her life in order to direct her in a specific way, shows the decisive importance of revelations. Here is realized their meaning, namely, the design of God in the history of the Church or of man individually.

3   THE DOCTRINAL INFLUENCE
OF REVELATIONS

It goes without saying that revelations, in view of their meaning, produce their fruit in the domain of life.
But this life is inseparable from the teaching which guides and nourishes it. Thus it is also as a means of teaching that revelations realize their objective; by orientating doctrine they act upon the direction of life. That influence, however, does not make itself felt equally in the different forms of teaching. It is felt chiefly in exhortatory teaching which seeks directly to orient and direct action. This is confirmed to such an extent by the facts and the preaching of the prophets of all ages that it is unnecessary to dwell upon it. But in regard to the influence of revelations upon the hierarchical teaching of the Faith, or upon the theological teaching which scientifically considers the things of the Faith, certain questions may be posed.

Revelations and dogma

Only hierarchical teaching has for its object dogma, that is, the mysteries of Faith which the Church proposes to all the faithful. Now dogma is infallible and invariable. As a general and absolute rule of life it is concerned in all situations in which man may be placed and extends beyond them in some measure, for it does not belong to any one situation in particular. It is precisely the role of particular revelations to direct action within the meaning of the dogma or to specify it in one interpretation or another not determined by the dogma.

It is clear that particular revelations cannot enrich dogma and they never act to supplement it. This emerges so plainly from all that we have been saying in this treatise, and is emphasized to such an extent by all authors who are writing on this subject in our time, that it is pointless to dwell upon it.

Revelations cannot enrich dogma either from the point of view of the object or that of criterion. With regard to the object, there is no doctrine which is totally new. When the Church proposes a doctrine as a dogma, she does so because she knows that this doctrine is already contained in general Revelation, at least implicitly. All dogmatic progress is but an explanatory statement of what has already been revealed, once and for all time.

However, in the attempt at explanatory statement revelations may play a part. That part would be the role of implementing the explanatory statement and not of its doctrinal consequences.

This does not, however, exclude the following case. God may reveal a doctrine "privately" which is implicitly contained in the Bible. That doctrine might one day, after a long work of exposition, become a dogma. Would the revelation in this case enrich the dogma? Certainly not. Its content would have no dogmatic value. Before the Church proposes it as a dogma it would simply be a theological doctrine. This is for the dogma what the working hypothesis is for science; it powerfully stimulates research toward a result which is not necessarily that of the working hypothesis. In other words, it acts upon the plane of action rather than upon that of doctrine. Indeed the revelation in question might be rejected by certain people, or it might be widely considered as a "new doctrine." But with the progress of the theological work which organically considers the different aspects of revealed data, theological conclusions would be reached. Theologians have seriously asked whether, in cases where a theological conclusion appears to a believer as being obviously contained in general Revelation, this believer would be obliged to accept such a conclusion as a dogma, that is to say, to believe it with a divine and Catholic faith.[147] We shall not attempt to answer this question because it would not shed any light upon our problem. It is enough to note: if the believer in question is not obliged to believe (*fide divina et catholica*), the revelation would remain particular as previously, with the restricted value placed upon it by its definition; if he is obliged to believe it, then he would believe it not by virtue of post-apostolic revelation but because he is a believer in general Revelation. It is general Revelation which is the basis of his divine and Catholic faith. In short, when the Church defines a doctrine formally expressed through a particular revelation, she does not elevate this revelation to the dogmatic plane, but regards it as either a confirmation or an occasion which she has used to rediscover this same doctrine in the great sources of general Revelation.

Revelations exert their influence upon dogmatic progress especially as occasional causes: "The Church," writes Father Marin-Sola, "instead of using private revelations to judge the content of Revelation always proceeds in the opposite way. Private revelations are never, for the Church, a source for her definitions. They may, however, become for her an occasion to examine whether a doctrine, perhaps unsuspected by the theologians, does or does not figure in Revelation." [148]

The occasion or the occasional cause is a circumstance which facilitates or induces the production of an effect through a cause; it comprises a certain exteriority because of the link between cause and effect.

If this exteriority is very pronounced, it means an occasion in the broad sense—any fact, even an error, may be the occasion of dogmatic progress. If, however, it is a question of a very minor exteriority which precedes and summons the movement from the cause toward the effect, then we would have an occasion in the strict sense of the word.

Suppose that someone receives a violin from his uncle, a musician. This would be just an occasion in his career as a violinist, but it would not be just any kind of an occasion. The violin would facilitate and stimulate its new owner in a specific sense. It is in this way that revelations have most frequently been occasional causes of dogmatic progress. They are special decisive occasions which may be the conditions *sine qua non* of producing the effect in question, and not merely general occasions which set an action in motion as much in one direction as in another.

This is the case, for example, with the revelation of Helsin, the Abbot of Ramsey. Here, according to very early accounts (D.T.C., VII, 1001–1004) is what occurred. Around the year 1070, Abbot Helsin went to fulfill a mission for William the Conqueror at the court of the King of Denmark. On the return journey his life was threatened by a violent storm. He called upon Our Lady. A messenger, clothed in pontifical robes, appeared to him and said: If you wish to save your life, if you wish to return to your country and your house "promise the most holy Mother of Christ very faithfully to celebrate the feast of her Conception." [148a] The date was fixed by the apparition as December 8. The Abbot made his promise. And having returned home, safe and well, he established the feast of the Conception in his monastery and propagated it to the best of his ability.

De Bachelet, who examines this revelation and its influence upon the progress of the dogma of the Immaculate Conception, is of the opinion that nothing warrants its immediate rejection as impossible or even as unlikely. And he concludes: "One thing, in any event, is incontestable—namely, the great influence which the publication of the *Miraculum de conceptione* exercised upon the development not so much of belief in the glorious privilege as in the feast of the Conception. . . . This is a fact which cannot create any dogmatic difficulty if one takes the trouble to distinguish in this, as in other devotions, especially to that of the Sacred Heart, between the occasion or the decisive cause of a devotional movement and the object or real cause of the devotion." [149]

Exercising a more direct influence upon the development of the dogma of the Immaculate Conception were the revelations made to St. Catherine Labouré. By means of the Miraculous Medal, devotion to the Immaculate Conception was universally spread. Thus the pastors and the doctors of the Church were stimulated by that very fact to consider this belief more attentively.

Finally, one significant detail—on February 14, Cardinal de Cienfuegos, archbishop of Seville, addressed a letter to Mgr. Quélen urging him to solicit in Rome permission to insert into the Litanies of Loreto the invocation *Regina sine labe concepta.* He stated in the letter that the revelation of the rue du Bac was the origin of this pious appeal. He was so conscientious that he declared he did not wish (by his appeals) to pronounce upon this revelation. But the fact that his move was stimulated by it can be seen from the same letter in which he said that this move was "very much in conformity with the designs of Divine Providence in the manifestation of the miraculous medal, now so well known throughout the Christian world." [150] Devotion has always been one of the powerful stimuli in the development of dogmatic teaching.

Revelations and theological teaching

What holds true for dogma also holds true, in a certain sense, for dogmatic theology, whose principles make up the articles of faith. Revelations may furnish it with certain proofs to the extent to which they succeed in forming the *consensum fidelium*.

The "classic" apologetic which seeks to defend the Faith especially against rationalism cannot rely upon revelations. Since rationalism does not even admit Revelation as such, how could a particular revelation be used as an argument, considering that proof is so difficult? But since the Church at the First Vatican Council invoked prophecies and miracles as arguments for Revelation, it must be admitted that revelations have their probative value. In fact, many unbelievers have found or refound the faith because of revelations.

Even exegesis is subject to the influence of revelations. These revelations, by drawing attention to a doctrine which seems new, may draw the theologian into biblical research which justifies or condemns it. Revelations concerning the life of Christ may also stimulate biblical study by presenting details which serve at least as working hypotheses.

Since revelations have the aim of directing action, it goes without saying that they may be factors, more or less important, in the history of the Church. Countless foundations of convents, pilgrimages, and all sorts of institutions owe their origin to revelations. It is true that the authenticity of these accounts of apparitions or visions is often not very well established. Sometimes they bear plainly the character of a creation of the popular imagination; however, these accounts are such that one cannot reject them if one wishes to remain faithful to the principles of historical research applied to other facts accepted as authentic.

We do not wish to state that the discovery of the holy Cross or of the body of St. Stephen are facts which are historically well established (cf. p. 183), but the testimonies are such that it is difficult not to retain at least the substance of the facts.

The return of Pope Gregory XI from Avignon is an important fact in the history of the Church. It shows the influence of St. Catherine upon the Pope's decision, and the saint's influence was due to her reputation as a prophetess: "The presence of Catherine at Avignon at the crucial moment of the return of the papacy to Rome was decisive in this sense that she revealed to the Sovereign Pontiff the vow he had made on the day of his election." [151]

It is precisely through these non-hierarchical prophecies, we may say in conclusion, that revelations produce their best fruits. And revelations are normally all the more fertile in so far as they obtain the approval, fully consented to, of the hierarchy, since by this approval they more abundantly and more certainly influence the whole Church. "The non-hierarchical prophets," writes Mgr. Journet, "contribute to the orientation of the conduct of the faithful of the Mystical Body in innumerable ways. They may draw the attention of the jurisdictional power to this or that aspect of the Christian message and thus provoke speculative or practical decisions which will benefit the entire Church. . . ." And although they cannot add new data to the Catholic Faith, "they retain, nevertheless, an immense role in the work of the enlightenment of the Mystical Body." [152]

God corresponds on His part to the boundless variety of tasks which He asks of men by a boundless variety and wealth of gifts.[153] Among the most important of these is the prophetic gift which often expresses itself under the form of particular revelations.

These revelations are often characterized by the same doctrinal limpidity and penetrating unction which are to be found in the inspired books. Simple, good and intelligent persons, who are open-minded and entrenched neither in a hypercritical attitude nor in a taste for the miraculous, find in the reading of such revelations truly comforting and edifying food for the soul in the biblical sense of the term.

Who has spoken as glowingly as St. Gertrude of the delights hidden in the sacred Humanity of Christ? Who has written better of the action of God in the soul than St.

Teresa of Avila? St. Francis de Sales, after quoting St. Paul,
St. Thomas, Gerson, and the Carthusian, Denis, as the
authors who have worthily written upon this most important
of subjects, adds in the introduction to his *Treatise on the
Love of God:* "But in order to make known that this kind of
writing is more happily accomplished by the devotion of
lovers than by the doctrine of scholars, the Holy Ghost has
willed for certain women to achieve wonders in this field.
Who has better expressed the heavenly passions of sacred
love than St. Catherine of Genoa, St. Angela da Foligno,
St. Catherine of Siena, St. Mathilda?" [153a]

If these women wrote in this way and if they influenced,
and still powerfully influence, so many souls, it is above all
due to their gift of revelations.

CHAPTER X

The Use of Revelations

THE ABUNDANCE of the fruits which we have just described is in large measure conditioned by the use men make of revelations. Men may abuse them and then, instead of the fruits which they could bear, harm ensues. It is important, therefore, for us to pose the question: How should we use revelations fruitfully? In answer to this question we shall first of all set down a few reflections of a general nature. We shall then try to define the way in which pastors and preachers should direct Christians in the use which can be made of revelations. We shall then draw conclusions from our work as a whole.

1   GENERAL CONSIDERATIONS

The abuse of revelations

The more precious a good thing is, the more dangerous is its abuse. And revelations are very precious things for they help us to conform our lives to the plan which God has for us in a particular situation. They are equally precious because of the way in which they act upon men. They come as a surprise and engage man's feelings and his attention in such a way that they are effective in cases where other methods would not be.

It is chiefly here that abuses creep in. Normally speaking, man loves change (*varietas delectat*). He flees from the boredom that comes from the monotony of the actions of ordinary life. He feels the need for some new experience, some event, some sensation. In the spiritual life especially, in those periods of dryness when it becomes necessary to live by pure faith, the danger of abusing revelations is great. There are Christians who have an irresistible need to *feel*, to *see*, if possible, something staggering.

Léon Bloy wrote to Jeanne Fermier: ". . . the hour has not yet come, I do not see *signs*. God is not showing Himself in a sensible, indisputable way. . . . I am awaiting Signs and up to the present I do not see them. So long as the Supernatural does not appear manifestly, incontestibly, dreadfully, deliciously, there is *nothing* real." [154]

From such a state of mind emerges the danger of interpreting particular revelations in too universal a manner and applying them to things which have no connection with them. Certain apparitions have been tragically abused by being mixed up with the social, political and religious struggles of the time when they occurred. It is understandable that the ecclesiastical authorities have intervened.

Again, the need for startling happenings encourages abuses in the sense that authors seek to impress their readers by interpreting, from a standpoint of terrible apocalyptic catastrophes, messages which contain promises and warnings of chastisement.

"It is remarkable," writes Father J.-H. Nicolas, "that what interests the majority of people in these private revelations is the announcement of future events . . . the trials from which people are emerging or in the midst of which they are struggling do not occur at all. The apocalyptic events with which we are threatened are always imminent at any moment of the time when the prophet—or any one of his interpreters—speaks." [155]

Revelations are subject to another kind of abuse. It is considering them as the discovery of a method of self-sanctification at little cost. Then the spiritual life grows upon stony, thin soil which is not nourished by the great Christian mysteries.

A new devotion, for instance, may be presented as a spiritual panacea.

The right not to make use of revelations

In order to defend oneself against all the abuses to which revelations are exposed, there is one radical method to adopt —to ignore revelations completely. We have the Gospels and the Church, the Faith and the sacraments, and these are sufficient to raise Christian life to the sanctity desired by God.

At all events, provided that the Christian retains the respect due to the authority which has pronounced upon a revelation, he has, generally speaking, the right to refuse to accept it. Anyone who does this for good reasons and in a spirit of humility need not fear a refusal of grace. It is properly one of the essential characteristics of particular revelations that they are not addressed at once to all and to each of the faithful.

St. John of the Cross expressed himself categorically upon this point: "Nothing is to be believed in a supernatural way, save only that which is the teaching of Christ made man, as I say, and of His ministers, who are men." [156]

The usefulness of belief in revelations

Here is the content of a quotation from the Mystical Doctor: "And so we must now be guided in all things by the law of Christ made man, and by that of His Church, and of His ministers, in a human and visible manner, and by these means we must remedy our spiritual weaknesses and ignorances, since in these means we shall find abundant medicine for them all. If we leave this path, we are guilty not only of curiosity, but of great audacity."

Must we conclude from this that all those who believe in Lourdes, for example, are curious and audacious? No. The Doctor of Carmel would not allow such a conclusion. He is thinking of the personal revelations, not approved, of mystics. Here is a doctrine which we find in *The Ascent of Mount Carmel* (Book II, chap. XVII): God sanctifies man according to his nature. He begins with what is the least elevated and the most exterior—the senses. He perfects them by supernatural communications. By this means the senses are greatly confirmed in virtue and withdrawn from their inclination to evil. The supernatural visions which God is accustomed to give afterward to a soul which is well disposed, enlighten the senses, spiritualize them and produce great fruits in the spirit.[156a]

But if this is the case, the question arises: Should one, because of the danger of abuses, refuse means of such benefit for the Christian life? On the contrary. We are invited to profit by these fruits, for it is normal to use all means which favor our ascent toward God.

When the Church approves revelations, when she grants privileges and indulgences to the devotions connected with them, when delegates of the Sovereign Pontiff, cardinals and numerous bishops go in pilgrimage to the places of these apparitions, how could we not see in all this an invitation to make use of these revelations in order to receive the fruits of which we spoke earlier?

But there may be certain cases where there is an obligation to believe in revelations. The saints testify to us that there are revelations which present themselves with so much clarity that it would be impossible not to believe in them.

Theologians admit, moreover, that in particular circumstances, for example, when revelations present the visionaries with clear evidence of their effects, the visionaries are obliged to believe in them. Some theologians even think that an act of theological faith is involved (cf. pp. 202–205).

But apart from these particular cases, the following must be considered as a guiding principle. The recipients of revelations may be called upon—even obliged—to believe according to the tenor of the revelation. That others may have the right, even the duty, to reject them may be so, but for the recipients it is another matter. Otherwise why would God make revelations? Was not Zachary punished because he hesitated to accept what the angel said to him? The Lord reproached the Apostles for not having believed the testimonies of the women who recounted their vision of His resurrection (Mark 16: 14).

These reproaches, punishments and insistences often reappear in the history of revelations. We recall the threats made to St. Joan of Arc because she hesitated to obey her voices.[157]

One could apply to all apparitions or visions what Bishop Ginoulhiac of Grenoble said in his pastoral of November, 1854: "La Salette is not a new doctrine, it is a new grace; it is not a new teaching . . . it is an additional admonition."

Now an admonition is given in order that it may be believed and obeyed. The only question is to know to whom it is addressed. No one can oblige us to accept a new doctrine to be added to the teaching of the Church. But I, in my particular situation, may be obliged to accept a grace which is presented under pain of losing the friendship of God.

We are at this point entering into the mystery of vocation. Within the domains of the Faith and of the Law different vocations are to be found. Every Christian should live his vocation in his own way. Should a particular Christian refuse to follow the path laid down for him—which from the general point of view is a detail—he may be endangering his eternal life. Speaking of these personal matters, St. Paul says: "For if I preach the gospel, it is no glory to me, for a necessity lieth upon me: for woe is unto me if I preach not the gospel" (1 Cor. 9: 16).

In somewhat the same way Bernadette Soubirous could have said: "Woe to me if I keep silent as to what I have seen and heard"! The visions of Bernadette were for her a grace, a grace which determined her life. Who would dare to say that she was not obliged to accept this grace and to live according to it? When Bernadette Soubirous went to find her pastor an hour after the apparition of March 2, 1858, she spoke to him of the procession which the Lady of the apparition had asked, but did not have the opportunity to remind him of the matter of the chapel. She was again badly received by the Curé who dismissed her from the presbytery together with her Aunt Basile. Through fear of the priest she had not dared to go to see him the second time without having someone with her. And now she must go back! Bernadette said: "The Lady wishes me to go." And actually she did have the courage to return to the presbytery the same day. She saw in this a strict obligation. Again we see confirmed the importance of the aim of revelations. The obligation does not depend upon a general law, but upon the particular situation in which an action is to be directed.

2   THE FRUITFUL USE OF REVELATIONS

According to the testimonies of the saints, the visionary may not only be aware of the obligation of which we have been speaking, but he also may feel irresistibly urged to carry out at once what the revelation demands.

While it is useless to lay down rules of usage or lines of conduct for cases which appear similar, nevertheless an exception must be made: the first reaction in regard to revelations is examination; the fruitful use assumes first of all the effort for discernment.

Here again we must distinguish between revelations of a strictly private kind and others. When we speak of the latter we are thinking only of those approved by the Church. When dealing with the former the problem of use—which will be dealt with further on—arises for the visionary alone and sometimes also for the spiritual director.

The first thing to do with regard to revelations of every kind is to submit them to the Church and to await her decision. This is not always possible. For the revelations may require the visionary to take instantaneous action. When the Lady of the Grotto at Massabielle said to Bernadette: "Now, my child, go and drink and wash yourself in the spring," the visionary had not the time to reflect. She thought only of obeying at all costs, even to the extent of performing strange actions which endangered her good name. "As there was no spring at Massabielle," Bernadette told M. Estrade, "I went off toward the Gave: the Lady called me back and gave me a sign with her finger *repeating her order* that I had to go in under the grotto. Seeing no water, I scratched the earth; a little came out of it and I drank." [158]

But every time that it is possible, the first thought should be to inform fully a representative of the Church. Actually the history of revelations teaches us that visionaries of every type and their associates have understood that they were obliged to tell everything to the priests.

It goes without saying that one must in such cases follow the directives of the representatives of the Church. Even if these are opposed to the strongest convictions of the visionary, they must be obeyed. God will always arrange things for the best, and, if necessary, change the feelings of His representatives. We recall the case of St. Teresa—through obedience she was made to deride the visions of the Lord, and He told her that she had been perfectly right to act obediently.[159] The Lord blesses all obedient people.

As a general procedure one must display prudence and reserve, at least as long as one is not fully enlightened either by personal experience or by the approval of the Church.

St. Teresa of Avila writes in the *Interior Castle* (VI, 3, note 3): "It is always necessary to distrust these things (the words which God addresses to the soul) until one understands their spirit. So I say that, at the beginning, the best thing to do is to fight them unceasingly. If they come from God this resistance will be a means of achieving further notable progress; the more one tests out these favors the more they increase; yes, that is truly the way with them."

To be detached in the matter of these graces—even of the best of them—is the first condition of enjoying them without peril. That is one of the reasons why St. John of the Cross declares that it is a sin to desire divine communications.

Father J.-G. Arintero states that there is in this position "a certain exaggeration, or a dangerous confusion": it is not illicit, he says, to desire them, if one does so solely as a means of getting to know God better and to love Him more and to increase in ourselves a horror of the spirit of the world.[160]

The visionaries use their privileges well if they are and remain humble. Humility, more than any other virtue, draws down God's graces; and here in particular it helps to avoid the dangers of illusion and of abuse. "If we are humble the vision, should it be the work of the devil, will not do us any harm; if, on the other hand, we are not humble, the vision, should it have God for its Author, will not produce any good fruit in us. Our Lord in His mercy wishes to manifest Himself to a soul so that it may know Him and love Him more. He discloses to it some of His secrets or He accords it some graces or special favors. But if the soul, I repeat this, considering that which should make it wholly abashed and aware, in its lowliness, of how unworthy it is to receive such a favor, thinks itself immediately a saint, if it seems to it that this grace is the reward of some service it has rendered, it is evident that the great benefit which it should derive from the vision will be converted to evil" (*Foundations*, viii, 3–4).

Those whose only knowledge of the revelations is through the visionary will derive all the profit from the revelations by using them prudently. It is not good to want to know about as many revelations as possible and to restrict one's spiritual reading to books on revelations received through apparitions or visions. It is very much to be recommended, upon two conditions, that those who are leading a sluggish Christian life should make use of one or other particular revelation. The conditions are that they approach their content by the light of the great Christian sources and that they refer to the evangelical law when there is a question of giving status to acts demanded by a revelation.

It is through the realization of these conditions that the use of revelations is proved to be fruitful. In other words, the criterion of the abuse or the fruitful use of revelations is to be found in the docility with which one accepts the directives of the Church.

If someone, for example, goes to Lourdes solely to satisfy some vague interior religious sentiment, he will end up with those "crowds of the faithful" referred to in such strong terms in the article "Siate Cristiani" in the *Osservatore Romano* of February 4, 1951. This article speaks of those crowds of the faithful who betake themselves to places of presumed visions and miracles and at the same time abandon the Church, its sacraments and its preaching!

It is quite different with a person who makes this pilgrimage with the intention of finding God in a place where He has strikingly manifested Himself in a manner less ordinary than in the pilgrim's own parish. In this place the pilgrim goes to confession, or makes a better confession; because he is the witness of an immense movement of faith, he is better able to grasp the meaning and reality of the Eucharist and the mystery of the Cross. The apparition of the Blessed Virgin, and still more the personality of the visionary, Bernadette, pass into the background of his consciousness. It is indeed a particular revelation of Mary which draws him hither; but once drawn, he discovers, through her, the Church and in the Church, God, the infinitely Merciful. This is the best use of revelations which could possibly be desired.

3 THE PASTORAL MINISTRY AND THE USE OF REVELATIONS

The private influence of the pastoral ministry

Not only can revelations assist persons in discovering the Church; the Church herself exercises a capital influence on their use. It is she who guarantees that this use can be fruitful. The influence of the Church may make itself felt in a public or a private way. Normally it is the pastors of souls who first of all speak privately in the name of the Church; most frequently it is parish priests or spiritual directors who are involved, as for instance Father Peyramale in the case of Bernadette Soubirous and Father Aladel in the case of Catherine Labouré. Father Peyramale, who was not the confessor but the pastor of the visionary's parish, examined her privately, gave her orders and, so to speak, influenced the apparition itself. Humanly speaking, it was at the urging of M. Peyramale that the Blessed Virgin revealed her name. Father Aladel guided his penitent in complete secrecy, indicating to her the attitude to adopt in regard to the revelation she received.

It is impossible to exaggerate the responsibility which falls upon such representatives of the Church. That is why it would be very useful for them to study the best procedures of discernment. They should apply carefully the rules which tradition and experience have laid down for them. Here are the chief ones:

1. No special interest, much less admiration, should be shown, either in the visionary or in his revelations. St. John of the Cross writes: "Let us speak of the confessor who, whether or not he be inclined toward these things, has not the prudence that he ought to have in disencumbering the soul of his disciple and detaching his desire from them, but begins to speak to him about these visions and devotes the greater part of his spiritual conversation to them, as we have said, giving him signs by which he may distinguish good visions from evil. Now, although it is well to know this, there is no reason for him to involve the soul in such labor, anxiety and peril. By paying no heed to visions, and refusing to receive them, all this is prevented, and the soul acts as it should. Nor is this all, for such confessors, when they see that their penitents are receiving visions from God, beg them to entreat God to reveal them to themselves also, or to say

such and such things to them, with respect to themselves or to others. . . .

"And, if it come to pass that God answers their petition and reveals it, they become more confident, thinking that, because God answers them, it is His will and pleasure to do so; whereas, in reality, it is neither God's will nor His pleasure" (*Ascent*, II, 18, note 7–8). From this situation to allowing oneself to be guided by the visionary is but a step.

2. That, however, is not to say that pastors of souls should act toward visionaries with harshness and severity; on the contrary, they should treat them with kindness. "It is not well," says the same saint, "that spiritual fathers should show displeasure in regard to them, or should seek to avoid speaking of them or despise them, or make their penitents reserved and afraid to mention them, for it would be the means of causing them many inconveniences if the door were closed upon their relating them. For, since they are a means and manner whereby God guides such souls, there is no reason for thinking ill of them or for being alarmed or scandalized by them; but rather there is a reason for proceeding very quietly and kindly, for encouraging these souls" (*Ascent*, II, 22, note 19).

3. There should be no rush to pass judgment. The visionary, often a saint, in any case normally a simple soul, would like a clear opinion as to his conduct: "Tell me, Father: is it the devil, or is it God? Or am I psychasthenic?" The answer should be handled by dwelling upon the difficulties of pronouncing with certitude in this matter. One should observe all and precipitate nothing.

4. Prayer. It is necessary to pray and to get others to pray, and to add sacrifices to the prayers. Through the divine light one knows best what is of God.

These counsels are equally applicable in the pastoral ministry when the faithful ask for guidance regarding a particular revelation; but in this case one may and always should advise awaiting the canonical judgment of the Church. Disobedience in this matter should be met by energetic measures.

Revelations and preaching

What we have just said applies also to the public measures of the pastoral ministry. These, like every action of the public ministry, must be in conformity with the requirements of the Church. The Church may approve or condemn such and such a revelation. Sometimes she imposes silence in regard to it in order to avoid injurious effects or the better to assure its fruits. However, the judgment which she pronounces upon a revelation is a decisive act and one which is made once and for all. Once this decision has been taken, the Church does not lose interest even though she has established the facts; nevertheless, her attitude will be expressed thenceforth at a different level—at the level of the pastoral ministry, of preaching.

This attitude may be quite different among pastors of souls. We shall not enter upon this subject for it is not necessary from the standpoint of our study. We shall reply only to a question which does demand enlightenment. May one preach upon revelations? Is it permissible, for instance, to give a sermon upon a revelation which is approved by the Ordinary of the place where it has occurred?

Although preaching is a hierarchical and public function, it does not commit so rigorously as a signed and published document. Thus, for example, a priest does not have to ask approval for a sermon he is going to give; but if he wants to publish it he must have an *imprimatur*. That does not arise from the fact that the sermon is not something of a public nature. Every form of preaching is by definition addressed to the public. It is precisely because of the greater liberty which the minister enjoys in the matter of the spoken word

by comparison with written publications that one is sometimes asked whether it is permissible to preach upon revelations which are approved only by the Ordinary of the place.

To answer this question, we must recall the object of
preaching, and determine what revelation is in question.
Preaching is the enunciation of Christian truths by someone
who has been given the mission to do so.

The Christian truths, that is, truths about the Person of
Christ and His work, as well as their practical consequences
for living, are the object of preaching. It was Christ Himself
who specified this object when He ordered His Apostles to
bring "the Good News to every creature" (Mark 16: 15). "Going therefore, teach ye all nations: baptizing them in the
name of the Father, and of the Son, and of the Holy Ghost.
Teaching them to observe all things whatsoever I have commanded you" (Matt. 28: 19–20).

Pope Pius IX warned against abuses of preaching: "It is
Christ whom we preach, the holy dogmas of our religion,
the precepts according to the teaching of the Catholic
Church and of the Fathers." [161] That is what must be
preached, that is the true object of preaching, as the scholastics would say. Undoubtedly other matters slip into
preaching, matters even of a profane kind such as historical
facts, human experiences, scientific conclusions, human wisdom. But these matters are only means of illustrating the
object.

One may apply to preaching about revelations the teaching of St. Thomas upon the object of theology. He sets out
this objection: "Whatever conclusions are reached in any
science must be comprehended under the object of the science. But in Holy Writ we reach conclusions not only concerning God, but concerning many other things, such as
creatures and human morality. Therefore God is not the object of this science." St. Thomas replies: "Whatever other
conclusions are reached in this sacred science are comprehended under God, not as parts or species of accidents, but

as in some way related to Him" (*Sum. Theol.*, i, 1, 7 ad 2).

This is the case with revelations in relation to preaching. They do not enter into its formal or principal object but they have the value of facts solidly established which illustrate and emphasize that object, and especially help people to live according to the demands of the object, as we explained earlier.

Thus there is nothing to prevent the use of revelations in the ministry of the spoken word. One may, for example, "preach on Lourdes." Tradition, moreover, widely confirms this point of view. Let us recall the facts mentioned in Part One, Chapter Two. St. Paul, who wanted to preach Christ only, spoke sometimes of his personal revelations, but this was always for the cause of Christ.

We have also noted that the Fathers allowed particular revelations to enter into their preaching. In the sermon of St. Augustine upon "the destruction of the City," the revelation made to the soldier plays an important part. The Bishop of Hippo there expounded the fact of the revelation in order to draw from it lessons regarding the Christian life (cf. p. 70).

It is to be noted, however, that there has been also a strong current of opposition. Visions, apparitions and dreams, which are most often the modes by which revelations are communicated to men, have always been more or less subjects for caution.

In order to safeguard the infinitely precious revealed Truth, the Church has shown herself reserved right from the start. Thus she excluded the pseudo-gospels and the apocrypha from her preaching. And she saw very early the necessity to determine what beside the essential sources of the Christian life could be read in the churches and received by Christian people.[162]

But there came a time when true revelations were accepted sometimes upon the same footing as the Gospel and false ones were being spread to the detriment of Christian life. The Lateran Council then solemnly established exact standards, as may be judged by the decree of September 19, 1516: "We desire that henceforth when divine communications are reported and before they are published or preached to the people (*aut populo praedicentur*), that they be generally and legally reserved to the examination of the Holy See."[163] Permission to publish or to preach these communications depends in principle upon the Holy See. But in the cases indicated by the decree we have just mentioned, it depends upon the Ordinary of the place (cf. note 111).

These decisions were strictly applied to the first of the great Marian apparitions of modern times—the apparition of the Blessed Virgin at La Salette. The bishop of Grenoble, Msgr. de Bruillard, after declaring that the faithful had good grounds for believing the appearance of Our Lady at La Salette to be indubitable and certain, adds in his pastoral of September 19, 1851: "We authorize the cult of Our Lady of La Salette. We permit for it to be preached so that the practical and moral consequences of this great event may be reaped." As we know, this document had been submitted to the Holy See before its publication.[164]

According to the legislation of the Church, one can preach upon revelations only if the episcopal authority or the Holy See itself gives permission to do so. This permission is normally granted after a canonical examination. Private revelations which are known only to the inner conscience may not be preached. Preachers may make use of only those revelations approved by the Church. It is easy to see to what extent the good use and wide fruitfulness of revelations depend upon the Church. Once more we note the remarkable link between two realities—revelations and the Church.

Conclusion

THE LINK between revelations and the Church seemed to us as a new light which became more and more illuminating as we progressed in this study. At times we had the impression that we detected opposition to particular revelations on the part of the Church—an opposition which might impress an observer who looked at the matter only in a general way. But as we came to examine the details, we quickly noted certain facts which helped us to understand the unity of all aspects of the problem.

First of all we have noted that the best proofs for the existence of revelations reside in the supreme authority of the Church herself, which has provided them through the popes and the Council of Trent.

Then, in the very difficult quest for discernment, we have taken into account that, in the last analysis, the certitude and authenticity of revelations depend upon the Church because miracles, which are generally considered to be the decisive criteria for the discernment of revelations, assume their value as a proof only after they are recognized by the Church. Certainly the miracle may be sufficient in itself for one who has experienced it personally or who is the eyewitness of it, or who can study it at leisure. But there is still the whole body of the faithful for whom it will always remain problematical. Miracles are difficult to discern because of the hidden forces of nature, because of the always possible intervention of the devil, and because of the considerable attraction which appearances may exercise upon the human mind.

Finally, it is in the life of the Church that revelations find their meaning. They show that the Lord remains always with the Church to direct her not only in an invisible way, but also through sensible manifestations of His presence in the affairs of a community or of an individual. Revelations are, moreover, very frequently occasions of a remarkable expansion of the life of the Church, for in places of apparitions one sees men of every race and language coming together in a unity of faith, prayer, sacramental penance, and Eucharistic communion.

Again, the fruitful use of revelations depends in a very intimate way upon the Church. This is demonstrated especially when social revelations are involved, but private revelations do not escape her vigilance. Through confessors and spiritual directors, who are normally aware of these revelations, it is still the voice of the Church which is making itself heard.

Thus, throughout the course of the three stages of this work, we have been able to note that revelations receive their strongest supports from the Church. It is in the Church, indeed, that they find the best guarantee for their existence, the surest criteria of their discernment, and it is in her that they realize their meaning and fruit.

All this does not surprise us when we consider the link which exists between the Church and revelations. They are inscribed in her history and they belong to her as subsidiary signs by which God manifests invisible realities to men. That is why, if one does not recognize in the Church a close and mysterious union between the visible facts and the invisible realities, one can understand neither the existence nor the meaning of charismatic revelations.

If the Reformers rejected revelations in principle it was not solely because of abuses which they found. More profound reasons—among others, lack of understanding of the

Church as the "Body of Christ" (Col. 1: 18)—induced them to reject revelations. Thus an eminent representative of our separated brethren, Emile Brunner, could write: "What is the Church? That question is the unresolved problem of Protestantism." [165] If one does not see in the Church the Body of Christ, that is, a mysterious continuation of the Incarnation of the Word, one cannot understand why God intervenes in the history of the Church and touches her through the medium of the senses.

Now God willed to realize the Incarnation through the Blessed Virgin. Within that perspective we can understand why theologians, following the example of many of the Fathers, call the Blessed Virgin Mary "the prototype of the Church." They refer to her thus chiefly because Mary is Mother, Mother *before* the Church, *for* the Church and *in* the Church. Since this is so, it should not surprise us to witness today devotion to the Church and to the Blessed Virgin Mary progressing simultaneously in the consciousness and the life of Christian people. Neither should it surprise us that theological thought dwells with special interest on both the Church and Mary. It is not by chance that Pius XII, at the end of his encyclical upon the Church, *Mystici Corporis,* gives a whole doctrinal synthesis upon her who is the "Mother of all the members of Christ" (Epilogue).

But a mother is naturally solicitous for her children who are in danger. Thus Pius XII said, at the end of the Marian Year of 1954, that Mary "has not ceased to pour out upon poor humanity all the treasures of her affection and of her sweet attentions *(dolce premure).*" [166]

Did she not display these sweet attentions in striking fashion in such places as Lourdes, La Salette, Fatima? Is it not permissible to think that it is because she is a Mother, solicitous for her children that she, more than any other heavenly personage, has had recourse to such extraordinary means as apparitions? Thus she seeks to reconcile a great number of her wayward and disobedient children with God.

Because of the great Marian apparitions and in order to understand them better theologians are seriously seeking the proper meaning of revelations and to construct a theology of them. It may be affirmed that this meaning will be found only in the mystery of the Church, "the Body of Christ" of which Mary is not only the most illustrious member but also the Mother.

Notes

1 Thus Karl Barth and Emile Brunner themselves described their theology, at least prior to 1933. The name "dialectical theology" which they also gave to it was chosen to indicate not the object and basis of the theology, but its method.

2 See below, pp. 42–43 and n. 27.

3 L. Bloy, *Belluaires et Porchers* (Paris, 1923), p. 206.

4 St. John of the Cross, "Llama de amor viva," especially Canto II: "oh mano blanda," with commentary, no. 16 ff. Cf. "Noche oscura," II, 11. In *Obras*, ed. P. Silverio de S. Teresa (Burgos, 1931).

5 Here are some sources treating of the terms revelation, vision and apparition:
Cardinal Bona thus defines revelation: "Revelatio quae a Deo, vel eo jubente a bonis spiritibus fit, nihil aliud est quam manifestatio divinorum mysteriorum et secretorum, supra totius naturae vires ad communem Ecclesiae, vel privatam personarum particularium utilitatem." *Lapis Lydius vitae spiritualis, sive Tractatus de discretione Spirituum* (Paris, 1847), chap. xx, 1, p. 287. Thinking of particular revelations, St. John of the Cross writes: "revelación no es otra cosa que discubrimiento de alguna verdad oculta, o manifestación de algun secreto e misterio." *Subida del M.C.*, II, 25, 1. Cf. Benedict XIV, *De Servorum Dei Beat.*, III, 53, 15.
How do visions and apparitions compare with revelations? Here are some texts from St. Thomas on the subject: ". . . differentia est inter visionem et revelationem. Nam revelatio includit visionem et non e converso. Nam aliquando videntur aliqua quorum intellectus et significatio est occulta videnti, et tunc est visio solum, sicut fuit visio Pharaonis et Nabuchodonosor, Dan. 2, et Genes. 41. Sed quando cum visione habetur significatio intellectus eorum quae videntur, tunc est revelatio." *Expos. super II Cor.*, chap. 12, lect. 1, ed. Marietti (1929). Nomen visionis "primo impositum est ad significandum actum sensus visus; sed propter dignitatem et certitudinem huius sensus, extensum est hoc nomen, secundum usum loquentium, ad omnem cognitionem aliorum sensuum." *Sum.Theol.*, I, 67, 1.
While with the vision the emphasis is in the person perceiving it, with

the apparition the emphasis is on the object seen: "Apparitio dicit re-
lationem visibilis ad videntem." *Expositio in Esaiam,* cap. I (initium), in
(Venetiis, 1593), Tomus XIII.

Father Staehlin defines it: "Aparición es la manifestación sensible de un
ser cuya presencia real y sensible en ese punto del tiempo y del espacio es
naturalmente inexplicable." "Apariciones," *Razón y Fe,* 139 (1949), 445.

Writers, especially modern writers, do not explain the terms with which
we are concerned here in the same way. Some see no difference between
"vision" and "apparition." Others identify vision with apparition. There are
some for whom an apparition necessarily implies an extraordinary mode of
presentation to the senses, which is not the case in a vision. For others there
is no revelation if nothing new is transmitted to us. According to yet another
group, revelation refers rather to the person who receives the revelation.
Others explain the terms in question in yet different ways.

We shall hold to this distinction: While the vision may be intellectual,
the apparition remains in the domain of the senses: it does not go beyond
the imaginative representation; it makes visible an object which is invisible
in itself, or at least in the given circumstances. While revelation does not
necessarily imply either a vision or an apparition (although it can include
one or the other), these two realities have their *raison d'être* in the revelation.
Cardinal Bona writes: "Omnes visiones et apparitiones eo potissimum ten-
dunt, ut aliquid occultum hominibus reveletur." (*Loc. cit.,* p. 287).

Undoubtedly there are visions whose meaning is not understood by the
visionary but by someone else: nevertheless, they are revelations in the
sense that they reveal at least the presence of a divine action. We need
only think of the vision of Baltasar (Dan. 5: 5 et seq.). However, we are
considering visions and apparitions as forms through which revelations are
expressed.

[6] *Sum. Theol.,* II–II, 171, 1, ad 4; cf. *Contra Gent.,* III, 154. Cf. also
Sum. Theol., II–II, 174, ad 3 and art. 3.

[7] *Conc. Trid.,* sess. VI, chap. 12. As examples of the discussion which
preceded that expression of Christian doctrine see the opinions of Richard
Cenomanus and Andreas Navarra, cf. *Conc. Tridentinum,* Editio Societatis
Goerresianae (Friburgi Br., 1911), vol. v., pp. 537, 561, 569.

[8] John of Saint Thomas: *Cursus theol.* (Quebecci, 1948), in II–II de fide,
art. 3, vol. x, n. 220–222, pp. 61–62: "Revelationes privatas in presenti
distinguimus contra eas quae nobis revelantur et proponuntur per Ecclesiam;
inde possunt dupliciter dici revelationes privatae. *Uno modo,* solum quia
non proponuntur per Ecclesiam, sed modo particulari fiunt ex parte materiae
revelatae versantur circa aliquod contentum in Sacra Scriptura vel tradi-
tionibus Ecclesiae ut si Deus declararet mihi mysterium contentum in Sacra
Scriptura quod nondum Ecclesia declaravit. Et tales revelationes dicuntur
privatae ex parte modi proponendi, non ex parte materiae; *alio modo* dicuntur
revelatio privata quando et jam ex parte materiae non pertinet ad fidem
communem . . . ut si Deus revelaret mihi quot stellae sunt in coelo, vel
quot arenae in mare aut alia similia sive naturalia sive supernaturalia."

We must be careful to distinguish this theological concept, with its re-stricted use of the term private, from the other commonly in use in order to understand that the degree of truth in the following statement should be expressed with finer shades of meaning: "Anyhow it (the word *private*) seems to us in no way an adequate term, and it makes us disinclined to call a *revelation private*, a revelation like, for instance, that of the Heart of Jesus to Margaret Mary Alacoque, or like the Marian revelation of Fatima, both of which are, obviously, destined for the whole of Christianity. In these cases it is very much a matter of charismatic revelations which are destined for the very greatest publicity." R. Ernst, *Y a-t-il encore des révélations?* (Brussels, 1958), pp. 20–21.

9 J. M. Staehlin, *Apariciones, Ensayo critico* (Madrid, 1954), p. 22. Cf. "Apariciones," in *Razón y Fe,* 139 (1949), 446.

10 Cf. Journet, *L'Église du Verbe Incarné* (Paris, 1951), II, pp. 47, 303.

11 Encyclical *Divinum illud munus* of May 9, 1897, in *Leo XIII, P. M. Acta* (Rome, 1898), vol. 17, p. 135. Cf. P.L. 38, 1231.

12 *Theologische Traktate* (München, 1951), pp. 417, 419.

13 E. Jacquier, *Les Actes des Apôtres* (Paris, 1926), p. 59. Cf. also G. Ricciotti, *Gli Atti degli Apostoli, Tradotti e Commentati* (Roma, 1951), p. 83.

14 *La Bible de Jérusalem*, note on Joël, 3, 1, p. 85.

15 *Lapis Lydius* (cf. n. 5), chap. 20, 1, p. 288.

16 D. Deden, "Le mystère Paulinien," in *Ephem. Lovanienses*, 13 (1936), 416.

17 Cf. G. Ricciotti, *Le lettere di S. Paolo* (Roma, 1949), p. 200.

18 *Les Epîtres de saint Paul aux Philippiens* (Paris, 1949), p. 89, n. f.

19 Cf. H. D. Wendland, *Das Neue Testament,* Deutsch. 7. *Die Briefe an die Korinther* (Göttingen, 1948), p. 87.

20 *La Communauté apostolique* (Paris, 1943), p. 86.

21 *L'evangile de Paul* (Paris, 1948), p. 262.

22 H. Lietzmann, *Geschichte der alten Kirche,* Bd. 1 (Berlin, 1932), p. 145.

23 According to G. Estius, who relies here on Cajetan, the Apostle distinguishes two methods of prophesying: "alterum velut ordinarie prophetan-tium, id est eorum qui ad conventum venirent instructi ex previa Dei inspiratione: de quibus praecipit apostolus ut *duo aut tres dicant:* alterum eorum qui in ipso conventu nova revelatione ad prophetandum movebantur. Ac de tali nunc loquitur, de priori genere recte acceperis illud quod ante dixit: *apocalypsum habet." In omnes Divi Pauli Apostoli epistulas Commentarium tomus prior.* (Ad 1 Cor. 14: 30), col. 464 (Duaci 1614).

24 A. Lemonnier, "Charismes" in *Dict. de la Bible:* Suppl. I, c. 1236 and 1241.

25 A. von Harnack, *Texte und Untersuchungen*, II: *Lehre der Zwölf Apostel* (Leipzig, 1893), p. 129. Cf. p. 119.

26 H. Hemmer, *Les Pères Apostoliques* (Paris, 1907), I–II, p. LV.

27 Th. Camelot, *Ignace d'Antioche, Polycarpe de Smyrne, Lettres* (Paris, 1951), p. 147; cf. *ibid.*, note 2: "If the martyr was not allowing himself to be deceived, this is not a simple calculation of human prudence, but because indeed the Spirit which was in him urged him to speak 'in God's voice'"; cf. also p. 44, n. 3.

28 *Martyre de Polycarpe*, v, 2; XII, 3, XVI, 2. In H. Hemmer, *Les Pères Apostoliques* (Paris, 1910), III, pp. 135, 145, 151.

29 C. de Otto, *Justini Philosophi et Martyris Opera* (Ienae, 1876), I, 1, p. 286 (*Dial. cum Tryphone*, n. 82). And in regard to the prophecy of Joël on the future prophetic gifts of the servants of God, Justin is quoted (*Dial.*, n. 88 p. 319).

30 Translation by A. Lelong in: H. Hemmer, *Les Pères Apostoliques* (Paris, 1912), IV, "Le pasteur d'Hermas," pp. 59–67.

31 A. Lelong, *loc. cit.*, p. VIII, cf. n. 30.

32 Ake v. Ström, *Der Hirte Hermas, Allegorie oder Wirklichkeit* (Uppsala, 1936), p. 15, defends the authenticity of the majority of the revelations. He finds in it, as criteria of real revelations, ineffableness, importance, new knowledge and the fear of the visionary.

33 *Enchiridion Biblicum* (Romae, 1954), n. 7.

34 In the Harvey edition, II, p. 213, in which is transcribed the Greek text which is found in the *Histoire Ecclésiastique* of Eusebius of Caesarea, v, 8. Cf. *Sources chrétiennes*, vol. 41, p. 36: "Here is what Irenaeus reports regarding the Apocalypse. . . . Not only does he know but he even accepts the writing of the *Shepherd*, saying, 'Scripture therefore says fittingly: First of all believe that there is one God who has created and governed all. . . .'" The translator, G. Bardy, notes, regarding the "he accepts": "That is to say, he counts it among the inspired Scriptures." Cf. Th. Zahn, *Geschichte des neutestamentlichen Kanons* (Erlangen, 1888), I–1 p. 335.

35 *Stromata* I, c. 17; P.G. 8/800; cf., *ibid.*, II; P.G., 8, 992–993.

36 Translated by G. Bardy, "Hist. Eccl.," III, 3, n. 6, in *Sources chrétiennes*, vol. 31, p. 99.

36a *Sophía Solomõntos*, P.G., 26, 1437.

37 Th. Zahn, *Geschichte d. Neut. Kanons* (Leipzig, 1888), I–1, pp. 333, 335.

38 O. Bardenhewer, *Geschichte der altkirchlichen Literatur* I (Freiburg i. B., 1913), p. 471.

39 Saint Jerome, *Comment. in Hab.*, L. 1, cap. 1, P.L., 25, 1286; *de viris illustribus*, cap. 10, P.L. 23, 625.

[40] P.G., 2, 842.

[41] Eusebius of Caesarea, "Hist. Eccl.," v, 16, in: *Sources chrétiennes,* vol. 41, pp. 47–48, n. 7–8.

[42] *Die Mission und Ausbreitung des Christentums in den ersten drei Jahrhunderten* (Leipzig, 1906), II, p. 264.

[43] P. de Labriolle, *La crise Montaniste* (Paris, 1913), p. 38. Cf. *De Trinitate,* III, 16, 1.

[44] P. de Labriolle, *loc. cit.,* p. 135.

[45] This is often emphasized by the representatives of the Church who were fighting Montanism. One example is given by St. Jerome writing in the prologue to his commentary on the prophet Habacuc. P.L., 25, 1274.

[46] Cf. A. Hilgenfeld, *Die Ketzergeschichte des Urchristentums urkundlich dargestellt* (Leipzig, 1884), p. 596.

[47] *Panárion,* XLVIII, P.G., 41, 855. Text and translation by Labriolle in: *Les sources de l'histoire du Montanisme* (Paris, 1913), pp. 115–116.

[48] P. de Labriolle, *La crise Montaniste* (Paris, 1913), p. 195.

[49] Cf. for these quotations, Eusebius of Caesarea, *Hist. Eccl.,* v, 1, 9–10.

[50] "Contra Haer.," III, 11, 9, *Sources chrétiennes,* vol. 34, p. 202.

[51] *Contra Haer.* (Catabrigiae, 1857), II, 49, 3; ed. Harvey, I, p. 375, a passage of which the Greek text is to be found in Eusebius (*Hist. Eccl.,* v, 7, 5) which prolongs the quotation (n. 5–6): "It is not possible to say how many charisms the Church, throughout the whole world, receives from God." And in another place the same (Irenaeus) writes: "As we have heard it said, many brethren in the Church have prophetic charisms and speak by the Spirit in all kinds of languages; they make manifest the secrets of man, if that is useful, and they explain the mysteries of God" (*Adv. Haer.,* v, 6, 1; Harvey, II, p. 334).

[51a] *Corpus Christ. Series Lat.,* II, 1159–1160.

[52] C. van Beek, *Passio Sanctarum Perpetuae et Felicitatis* (Noviomagi, 1936), vol. I, p. 6. Cf. also p. 52.

[53] *Les passions des Martyrs et les genres littéraires* (Bruxelles, 1921), p. 67.

[54] R. Aigrain, *L'Hagiographie, ses Sources, ses Méthodes, son Histoire* (Paris, 1935), p. 136, says of the Passion of Perpetua that it is a work of literary form, a book, but one which should not be criticized for literary exaggeration, in the unfavorable sense of the word.

[55] Aion, *Untersuchungen zur Symbolgeschichte mit einem Beitrag von Dr. phil. Marie Louise von Franz: die Passio Perpetuae, Versuch einer psychologischen Deutung* (Zürich, 1951), pp. 287–496.

M. L. von Franz states explicitly that the change of sex during the dream and the fact that Perpetua remembers the name of Dinocrates in the midst of prayer are things which Christians do not expect of a martyr: this could not be invented. And the author adds: "Zudem geht aber eine einheitliche *innere* Linie durch alle vier Visionem hindurch, die nicht in äussern Motiven, sondern nur durch die moderne psychologische Deutung sinnfällig wird, also durch einen Menschen jener Zeit gar nicht erfunden werden konnte." *Ibid.*, p. 411.

⁵⁶ *Sitzungsberichte* (Berlin: 1910), p. 116. Cf. also p. 119.

⁵⁷ As principal sources for the last observations, cf. *De Anima et ejus origine*, IV, cap. 18, P.L., 44, 539–541, and *Sermo 280: In natali martyrum Perpetuae et Felicitatis*, P.L., 38, 1281; cf. 1282–1284.

⁵⁸ S. *Thasci Caecili Cypriani opera omnia*, Edited with a critical commentary by Hartel (Vindebonae, 1871), in C.S.E.L., III–2, p. 520. (For St. Cyprian I shall continue to use this abbreviation for the Hartel edition.)

⁵⁸ᵃ Ep. 2: 3–4, C.S.E.L., III, 497–498.

⁵⁸ᵇ Ep. 63: 1 and 17, C.S.E.L., III, 702 and 715.

⁵⁸ᶜ Ep. 66: 10, C.S.E.L., III, 734.

⁵⁸ᵈ Ep. 78: 2, C.S.E.L., III, 837.

⁵⁸ᵉ Cf. Ep. 43: 5, C.S.E.L., III, 594.

⁵⁸ᶠ Cf. *De Genesi ad lit.*, L. XII, c. 13. C.S.E.L., XXVIII, 398.

⁵⁸ᵍ *Sermo 309*, c. 2, P.L., 38, 1411.

⁵⁸ʰ *Sermo 318*, n. 1, P.L., 38, 1438. Cf. P.L., 41, 807.

⁵⁸ⁱ Ep. 159, P.L., 33, 700. Cf. Ep. 162, P.L., 33, 706.

⁵⁸ʲ M. V. O'Reilly, *Sancti Augustini de excidio Urbis Romae sermo*, text and translation with introduction and commentary (Washington, 1955), cap. 6, n. 7, page 68.

⁵⁹ H. Denifle, "Das Evangelium aeternum" in: *Archive für Literatur und Kirchengeschichte des Mittelalters* (1885) I, p. 54.

⁶⁰ Cf. Denifle, *loc. cit.* (n. 59), p. 52, 104, 107.

⁶⁰ᵃ *Paradiso*, 12, 139–142.

⁶¹ David ab Augusta, *De exterioris et interioris hominis compositione secundum triplicem statum incipientium, proficientium et perfectorum*, (Quaracchi, 1899), L. III, cp. 67, pp. 240, 261.

⁶¹ᵃ *Loc. cit.*, pp. 355–356.

⁶² *Revelationes S. Brigittae, olim a card. Turrecremata recognitae nunc a Consalvo Duranto a Sancto Angelo . . . notis illustratae* (Romae, 1606), L. I, cp. 1, 1–4, pp. 1–2, also Prologue (no pagination).

⁶³ *Joannis Gersonii Doctoris Theologi et Cancellarii Parisiensis Opera Omnia* (Antwerpiae, 1706), Tomus I, *Tractatus de probatione spirituum, editus propter aliqua de canonizatione Brigittae in praefato Concilio ageban-*

tur. Col. 43; cf. col. 37. *Tractatus de distinctione verarum visionum a falsis,* col. 44.

[64] *Ibid.,* col. 42; cf. col. 16 and 38.

[65] In the prologue to the *Revelations of St. Bridget, loc. cit.,* cf. n. 62.

[65a] J. Fontanino, *Codex Constitutionum quas Summi Pontifices ediderunt in solemni Canonizatione sanctorum* (Romae, 1729), p. 156.

[66] *De servorum Dei beatificatione,* L. III, cp. ult., n. 15.

[67] Cf. *D. Martin Luthers Werke,* Kritische Gesamtausgabe Weimar (= W.A.), 27, 298.

[67a] For the vision of the Sister in the cell, cf. W.A., 47, 300.

[68] W.A., 46, 65 (cf. n. 67).

[69] Cf. for this paragraph, W.A., 46, 60–63, p. 61.

[70] "Sixteenth Sermon on the Book of Job"; *J. Calvini opera,* in Corpus Ref. 61, 203.

[71] Cf. n. 6 and *Concilium Tridentinum,* ed. Societas Goerresiana, vol. 12, pp. 693–694. Résumé of the discussions made by the Servite, Laurentius Mazocchius.

[72] F. Suarez, *Opera omnia* (Paris, 1858), vol. 12, "Tr. de fide," disp. III, sect. 10, n. 1, 5, p. 90.

[73] Cf. *Cani M. Opera, de locis theologicis* (Vassairi, 1746), 1, XII, c. 3, concl. 3, p. 350.

[74] *Obras de San Juan de la Cruz,* ed. Silverio de S. Teresa (Burgos, 1931). *Ascent of Mount Carmel,* L. II, cp. 22, n. 3–4: cf. cp. 22, n. 6.

[75] P. Silverio de Santa Teresa, *Obras de Santa Teresa de Jesus* (Burgos, 1919), VI, p. 67.

[76] *Ibid.,* L. II, chap. 22, n. 19.

[77] *Collectio Bullarum et Constitutionum, ac diplomatum, quas Summi Pontifices ediderunt in solemni canonisazione sanctorum accurante Justo Fontanino* (Romae, 1752), p. 306.

[78] Having summed up, in his own way, the exposition of the Bishop of Luçon, the journalist then took his stand: "In this instance we see something more than an extravagant or erroneous system of doctrine, a deliberate attempt to obtain money of the people under the grossest and falsest pretences. The Virgin wants money, and so she causes her statue to wink its eyes . . . and reveals herself to two little boys(!)."

[79] Brief of April 25, 1911: *Arch. Brev. Ap. Pius X* (1911), Div. L. IX, p. 1, f. 337.

[79a] Letter from Firmilian included in the collection of the letters of St. Cyprian, Ep. 75, C.S.E.L. 3, 816–817.

80 R. Laurentin, *Lourdes, Dossier des documents authentiques* (Paris, 1957), I, p. 282.

81 Des Brulais, *L'écho de la Sainte Montagne* (Nantes, 1853), p. 138.

82 *Sum. Theol.*, III, 76, 8.

83 J. Fröbes, *Lehrbuch der experimentellen Psychologie* (Freiburg i. B., 1923), p. 230.

84 H. Thurn, in *Geist und Leben*, 21 (1940), 170.

85 P. Quercy, *L'hallucination* (Paris, 1930), pp. 136–137.

86 P. Lhermitte, *Mystiques et faux mystiques* (Paris, 1952), pp. 61–62.

87 *Études sur la psychologie des mystiques* I, (Bruges, 1924), p. 211.

87a *Les hallucinations* (Paris, 1951), pp. 30–31, 179, 183.

88 L. Volken, *Der Glaube bei Emil Brunner* (Freiburg, 1947), pp. 15–17.

89 *Träume eines Geistersehers erläutert durch Träume der Metaphysik*, Text der Ausgabe, 1766; K. Kehrbach, Reclam (Leipzig, Anhang), pp. 69–70.

90 Cf. Foreword in F. Moser, *Spuk, Irrglaube oder Wahrglaube? Eine Frage der Menschheit* (Baden bei Zürich, 1950), p. 11

91 *La pensée catholique* (1953), p. 94, n. 23.

92 *The Third Revolution* (New York and London, 1955), pp. 207–208.

92a St. Thomas, *Sum. Theol.*, I, 110, 1.

92b *De Malo*, 16, 9 ad 1.

93 *De Malo*, q. 16, a. 11.

94 *Daemoniaci, hoc est: de obsessis a spiritibus daemoniorum hominibus, liber unus, auctore Petro Thyrraeo* (Lugdunii, 1603), cap. 23, p. 98.

95 This was during the second apparition on February 14, 1858. R. Laurentin, *Dossier des documents auth.* (Paris, 1957), I, p. 153.

96 *Dict. apologétique de la Foi cath.* (d'Alès) (Paris, 1922), IV, 76–77.

97 E. Amort, *De revelationibus et apparitionibus privatis regulae tutae ex Scriptura, Conciliis, ss. Patribus aliis optimis Authoribus collectae, explicatae et exemplis illustratae* (Augustae Vindelicorum, 1744), pp. 161–162.

97a *Ibid.*, p. 46.

98 At Beauraing Albert Voisin was the only male visionary among four female visionaries who played a more important part than he in the series of apparitions. At Fatima Lucia's testimony was the important one; at La Salette the female visionary prevailed over the male. Here is a pointer from the last mentioned. It was only with great difficulty that the visionaries of La Salette were convinced that they must make known their secrets to the Holy Father. The children set them down in writing. After reading Maximin's, Pius IX said: "There is in this the candor and the simplicity of a

child." But of Mélanie's secret the Pope made this observation: "I must read this letter again with some reflection." During the reading of this second letter a witness, M. Rousselot, noted that the Pope's countenance betrayed a certain amount of emotion. His lips tightened and his cheeks puffed out. When he had finished reading, the Holy Father said to us: "These are calamities with which France is threatened. She is not the only guilty one. Germany, Italy, all Europe are guilty too and deserve chastisements. I have less to fear from Proudhon than from religious indifference and human respect." L. Bassette, *Le fait de La Salette* (Paris, 1955), p. 227.

[99] *Collectio Bullarum . . . accurante Justo Fontanino* (Romae, 1752), p. 304.

[99a] *Sum. Theol.*, II–II, 172, 2, ad 2.

[100] *De servorum Dei beat.*, L. III, chap. 51, n. 1: "Recte ait: non sunt apparitiones et visiones improbandae ex quo mulieribus accidant."

[100a] *Obras de Santa Teresa de Jesus, Vida* (Burgos, 1949), chap. 29, notes 5–6, pp. 184–185.

[101] L. Cros, *Histoire de N.-D. de Lourdes* (Paris, 1925), I, p. 310.

[102] Cf. K. Hock, Johannes vom Kreuz und die Nebenerscheinungen der Mystik, in *Theol. und prakt*, Quartalschrift 78 (1925), p. 703.

[103] St. Thomas, *Comment. in Ev. Joan.*, chap. 9, lect. 3, n. 8. Cf. *Quodlibet*, II, q. 4, a. 6, ad 4.

[104] Sermon of St. Bernardine of April 28, 1424. C. Cannarozzi, *S. Bernardino, Le prediche volgari* (Ristoria, 1934), II, p. 413. Cf. also P. Misciatelli, *Le più belle pagine di S. Bernardino da S.* (Milano, 1924), p. 242.

[105] A. Monin, *Notre-Dame de Beauraing* (Bruges, 1952), pp. 227–228.

[106] *Enchiridion biblicum*, n. 6: "Apocalypses etiam Johannis et Petri tantum recipimus, quam quidam ex nostris legi in Ecclesia nolunt."

[107] See note 33.

[108] E. v. Dobschütz, *Das Decretum Gelasianum, de libris recipiendis et non recipiendis . . .* (Leipzig, 1912), p. 286.

[109] *Ibid.* (Gelasianum, cap. IV), pp. 5, 8–10.

[110] *Ibid.*, IV, 4, p. 9, 10. Cf. Delehay, *Synaxarium Ecclesiae Constantinopolotianae . . .* , col. 485. Cf. P.L. 67, 419–413.

[111] J. D. Mansi, *Amplissima Collectio . . .* , vol. 32, col. 947.

[112] *Bullarium diplomatum et privilegiorum sanctorum Romanorum Pontificum . . .* (Augustae Taurinorum, 1868), vol. 13, p. 309.

[113] H. L. Maréchal, *Mémorial des Apparitions de la Vierge dans l'Église* (Paris, 1957), p. 66.

[114] J. Giray, *Les miracles de La Salette*, p. 353.

115 L. Bassette, *op. cit.*, p. 241.

116 F. Trochu, *Sainte Bernadette Soubirous* (Lyon, 1958), pp. 324–5.

116a *Actes de Pie X* (Paris, 1938), t. III, p. 175.

117 *De servorum Dei beatif* . . . , L. II, chap. 32, n. 12.

118 *Leonis XIII P. M. Acta* (Romae, 1900), p. 72.

118a Second nocturn of the Office.

119 *Actes de Pie X* (Paris, 1936), t. I, p. 140.

119a "Di fronte a queste rivelazioni private non sempre omogeneo è stato l'attegiamento dell' autorità ecclesiastica." C. Balic, "Apparizioni Mariane dei sec. XIX–XX," in *Enciclopedia Mariana* "Theotocos" (Genova, 1954), p. 263.

120 Cf. for this paragraph: I. Congar, "La Crédibilité des révélations privées," in *Supplément de la Vie Spir.*, 53 (1937), 44 and 46.

121 St. Thomas, *In III Sent.*, dist. 26, q. 2, a. 4.

122 Cf. *Sum. Theol.*, I, 12, 12, 7; *In Boet. de Trinit.*, III, 1.

122a *Sum. Theol.*, II–II, 49, 6.

122b Ch. Pesch, *Praelectiones dogmat.* (Friburgi i. B. 1899), III, n. 694.

123 This teaching of St. Albert is contained in his *Liber I Topicorum*, tract I, the whole of chapter 2, "De syllogismo dialectico." *B. Albert. magni* . . . *opera* II (Paris, 1890). An especially significant passage appears on p. 241.

124 *Grammar of Assent* (London, 1870), pp. 187, 219, 225, 247.

125 A. Gardeil, "La certitude probable," in *Revue des Sciences phil. et théol.*, 5 (1911), 262, 265.

126 J. Bona, *De discret. Spirit.* (Paris, 1847), XX, 1, p. 289.

127 Benedict XIV, *De servorum Dei beat.* . . . (Romae, 1747), L. II, chap. 32, n. 11, p. 402.

128 L. Bassette, *op. cit.* (n. 115), p. 128.

129 F. Trochu, *Sainte Bernadette Soubirous* (Lyon, 1953), p. 325.

130 L. Fischer, *Fátima à Luz de Auctoritade Eclesiastica* (Lisboa, 1932), p. 105.

131 *Collegii Salmaticensis* . . . *Cursus theologicus* (Paris, 1879), XI, tract. 17, "de fide," disp. I, dub. 4, n. 103, p. 48. Cf. also *ibid.*, n. 134, p. 62, for the opinion which the Salmaticenses opposed.

131a *Concilium Tridentinum*, ed. Societas Goerresiana, vol. 12, p. 693, n. 71.

132 *Sum. Theol.*, II–II, q. 171 a. 5.

133 *Collegii Salmat., Cursus theol.,* xi, tr. 17, "De fide," disp. i, dub. 4, n. 115, p. 54.

134 Cf., for instance, *In Boet. de Trinit.,* 3, 1 ad 4; *De verit.,* 14, 1; i–ii, 55, 4; i–ii, 17, 6; ii–ii, 1, 4 et 4, 5.

134a St. Thomas, *In* iii *Sent.,* q. 2, a. 2, sol. 3.

135 D. Bañez, *De fide, spe et caritate,* In ii–ii S.T.S. Thomae, q. 4, a. 8 (Lugduni, 1588), p. 382.

136 "Révélations privées" in *Revue diocésaine de Namur,* 5 (1950), 170.

137 See note 127.

138 *De divina Traditione et Scriptura* (Romae, 1870), p. 234.

139 K. Rahner, *Visionen und Prophezeiungen* (Innsbruck, 1958), p. 21.

140 K. Rahner, *op. cit.,* p. 26. For a discussion of this position, as well as many others which Rahner puts forward in the book quoted, cf. L. Volken, "Um die theologische Bedeutung der Privatoffenbarungen, zu einem Buch von Karl Rahner": *Freiburger Zeitschrift für Philosophie und Theologie,* 6 (1959), 431–439.

140a A.A.S. 51 (1959), 144, 147.

141 *Divi Thomae Aquinatis Expositio in . . . Matthaeum,* chap. xi, 13. (Neapoli, 1858), p. 102.

141a *Sum. Theol.,* ii–ii, 172, 4.

141b *La renaissance du livre, Sainte Marguerite-Marie* (Paris, 1947), pp. 47, 80.

142 P. Andrieux, "Les notes Lagier" in *Notre-Dame de la Salette, Études d'histoire religieuse et de théologie* (Tournai, 1935), iii, p. 117.

143 J.-H. Nicolas, "La foi et les signes" in *Supplément de la Vie Spirituelle,* 25 (1953), 139.

144 L. Lochet, "Apparitions" in *Nouvelle Revue Théol.,* 76 (1954), 960.

144a J. Chevalier, *Pascal, Oeuvres Complètes* (Paris, 1954), n. 582, p. 1273.

144b "Thèologie morale" in *Revue thomiste,* 50 (1150), 406–407.

145 End of the encyclical, *Annum Sacrum,* of May 25, 1899, *Leonis XIII P.M. Acta* (Romae, 1900), vol. 19, p. 71.

146 L. Chasle, *Schwester Maria vom göttlichem Herzen Droste zu Vischerring . . . ,* trans. by L. Sattler (Freiburg i. B., 1929), p. 367. This book contains the original French text of the letter in the appendix; for the communication of the Sister with Leo XIII on the matter of the Sacred Heart, *ibid.,* pp. 283–313; cf. "Coeur Sacré," *D.T.C.,* 341–343.

147 Cf., for instance, the Salmaticenses above, n. 131.

148 *L'Évolution homogène du dogme catholique* (Fribourg, 1924), i, n. 220², pp. 376–377.

[148a] P.L., 159, 324.

[149] "Immaculée Conception" in D.T.C., VII, 1004.

[150] Ibid., D.T.C., VII, 1191.

[151] Art. "Caterina," Enciclopedia Cattolica, III, 1153.

[152] Charles Journet, l'Église du Verbe Incarné (Paris, 1951), II p. 243.

[153] Einführung in die christliche Mystik (Paderborn, 1922), p. 591.

[153a] Oeuvres complètes de saint François de Sales (Paris, 1857), t. I, p. 303.

[154] Léon Bloy to Jeanne Fermier, September 10, 1814, in H. Beguin, Léon Bloy (Paris, 1946), p. 251.

[155] "La foi et les signes," in Supplément de la Vie Spirituelle, 25 (1953), 152–153, n. 23.

[156] Ascent of Mount Carmel, II, 22, n. 7.

[156a] Ascent . . . , II, 17, n. 4.

[157] J. Calmette, Jeanne d'Arc (Paris, 1946), p. 45.

[158] L. Cros, op. cit. (n. 101), p. 28.

[159] "Vida," cap. 29, nn. 5–6, in Obras de S. Teresa de Jesus, ed. P. Silverio d. S. T. (Burgos, 1949), pp. 184–185.

[160] La Evolución mística en el desenvolviemento y vitalidad de la Iglesia (Madrid, 1952), p. 612.

[161] "Qui pluribus," Pii IX P.M. Acta (Romae, 1854), I, p. 19.

[162] Cf. notes 33 and 110, as well as: G. Vasquez, In III Partem, Sum. Theol., s. Thomae, t. II, disp. 117, cp. 6, nn. 77–78.

[163] See reference, n. 111.

[164] L. Bassette, op. cit. (n. 98), pp. 243 and 233.

[165] E. Brunner, Das Missverständnis der Kirche (Zürich, 1951), p. 7.

[166] Allocution of Pius XII on the day of the proclamation of the feast of the Queenship of Mary, in Osservatore Romano, November 2–3, 1954. Cf. for this subject our study "Marie au Ciel souffre-t-elle . . . ?" in Marianum, 17 (1955), 421–472, in particular 467–72.

Index